THE CAUSES OF
ENGLISH

THE CAUSES OF THE ENGLISH CIVIL WAR

The Ford Lectures
Delivered in the University of Oxford
1987–1988

CONRAD RUSSELL

CLARENDON PRESS · OXFORD

OXFORD
UNIVERSITY PRESS

Great Clarendon Street, Oxford OX2 6DP

Oxford University Press is a department of the University of Oxford.
It furthers the University's objective of excellence in research, scholarship,
and education by publishing worldwide in

Oxford New York

Auckland Cape Town Dar es Salaam Hong Kong Karachi Kuala Lumpur
Madrid Melbourne Mexico City Nairobi New Delhi Shanghai Taipei Toronto

With offices in

Argentina Austria Brazil Chile Czech Republic France Greece
Guatemala Hungary Italy Japan South Korea Poland Portugal
Singapore Switzerland Thailand Turkey Ukraine Vietnam

Oxford is a registered trade mark of Oxford University Press
in the UK and in certain other countries

Published in the United States
by Oxford University Press Inc., New York

Database right Oxford University Press (maker)

First published 1990

British Library Cataloguing in Publication Data
Data available

Library of Congress Cataloging in Publication Data
Russell, Conrad.
The causes of the English Civil War: the Ford lectures
delivered in the University of Oxford, 1987-1988 / Conrad Russell.
p. cm.
1. Great Britain–History–Civil War, 1642-1649–Causes.
I. Title. II. Series: Ford lectures; 1987-1988.
DA415.R78 1990   941.06'2–dc20   90-3054.3
ISBN 0-19-822141-X; 978-0-19-822141-8

Printed in Great Britain by
Biddles Ltd., King's Lynn, Norfolk

TO THE WARDEN
AND FELLOWS OF MERTON

Preface

THIS work came to exist in its present form because of an invitation to serve as Ford's Lecturer in the University of Oxford for 1987–8. My first thanks are therefore due to the Reverend James Ford, Fellow of Trinity College, Oxford and Vicar of Navestock in Essex, the 'onlie begetter' of these lectures. My thanks are due to the University of Oxford, for inviting me to give the lectures, and for providing a large and thoughtful audience whose comments and suggestions have much enriched the resulting work. I was told by previous Ford's Lecturers that I would find the University's hospitality one of the nicest rewards of giving the lectures, and experience amply confirmed the truth of what they said. For this too, I owe much thanks.

Within the University, my thanks are especially due to the Warden and Fellows of Merton. One of the most pleasant experiences of delivering the lectures was that of having all three of my tutors, Ralph Davis, Roger Highfield, and John Roberts, in the audience, so that the experience was assimilated to the familiar one of reading my weekly essay. They collectively made me a historian, with assistance from my fellow-Mertonians Henry Mayr-Harting, John Fletcher, Michael Clanchy, Bob Moore, and Anthony Fletcher, among others. It is in appreciation that I dedicate this book to the Warden and Fellows of Merton.

All historical research, however much it may be organized on a cottage industry basis, is nevertheless a co-operative enterprise, and in doing the work which has been incorporated in these lectures, I have benefited beyond measure from the community of scholars, national and international, at the Institute of Historical Research. More especially, I owe thanks to the Tudor and Stuart seminar, to which parts of Chapters 3 and 4 were delivered on an experimental basis. The experience, as usual, saved me from errors and gave me fresh insights. The task of acknowledging all my debts to members of that seminar is one for which a preface does not allow space, and in any case, they are probably more numerous and more manifold than even I am aware of. Nevertheless, I would like to acknowledge some particular debts. I owe thanks to the late Joel Hurstfield, both for being my good lord, and for insights which have contributed substantially to Chapter 7. I owe thanks to those responsible for the major realignment of English religious history which has been taking place over the past twenty years, notably to Nicholas Tyacke, Peter Lake, and Kenneth Fincham. Much of this realignment has been hammered out in the Tudor and Stuart seminar, and without it, this book could not have been written. I owe thanks to Pauline Croft, who has picked up the torch so sadly left by Joel Hurstfield, and to Christopher Coleman and David Dean for sharing their knowledge of the Elizabethan Exchequer and Parliaments. I owe thanks to all those who have so generously shared their archival discoveries, and especially to John Adamson, the Prince of Serendip, to Richard Cust for a fourteen-year dialogue which continues, to Jenny Wormald and Peter Donald for sharing many discussions of Scotland, and to Michael Perceval Maxwell for doing the same for Ireland. I owe thanks to Peter Lake, Pauline Croft, Peter Donald, Anthony Milton, Richard Cust, and Johann Sommerville, who have kindly read chapters of this book and made many helpful comments. I am particularly grateful to Johann Sommerville for the care and courtesy he devoted to the task of identifying the real issues between us: the debate will continue. I owe thanks to David Starkey for being able, as an early Tudorist, to bring detachment to these debates, and for his ability to turn a subject inside out in one sentence. If I could have answered his question, why the main religious and cultural trends of Elizabethan England were so different, this would have been a much better book than it is. Chapter 8 is the Friends' Lecture at the Institute of Historical Research for 1988. I would like to thank the committee of the Friends of the Institute of Historical Research for inviting me to give the lecture, and the audience for comments, some of which have been incorporated in the text.

I owe thanks to my former colleagues and pupils at Yale, notably to Louis Martz and Bob Stacey, for providing a literary and a medieval perspective, and to Jim Wilson, David Venderbush, and Martin Flaherty, for helping to point me in a British direction. I owe thanks to those who have allowed me to read their family papers, notably to His Grace the Duke of Northumberland, the Marquess of Anglesey, the trustees of the Bedford Settled Estates, the Earl of Crawford and Balcarres, and Viscount De L'Isle, VC,

KG. I owe thanks to all those archivists who have helped in the hunt for papers, notably to Mr Colin Shrimpton, archivist at Alnwick Castle, Mr T. I. Rae of the National Library of Scotland and Mr Stephen Parkes of the Osborn Collection at Yale, and to the librarians of Corpus Christi College, Oxford and of the House of Lords.

Historical research, especially across the Atlantic, grows increasingly expensive, and the work which went into this book could not have been done without assistance from grant-awarding bodies, including the A. Whitney Griswold Fund of Yale University, the Concilium on International and Area Studies of Yale University, the American Philosophical Society, the American Council of Learned Societies, the Central Research Fund of the University of London, the Small Grants Fund of the British Academy, and the Dean's Fund of University College, London. To all of them I owe thanks.

I would also like to thank them for not imposing 'relevance' on my researches. Relevance chosen before the work is done is a straitjacket on the resulting findings, and this work has been done with a resolute determination to eschew all arguments of relevance, and to follow where the sources lead. The result was that they led me, somewhat unwilling, to Edinburgh, and plunged me into a study of the relations of England with the supra-national British monarchy which, I think, is quite as relevant to the concerns of 1988 as anything it may replace.

These financial acknowledgements relate to a larger corpus of work, to which what is published here should be seen as an extended conclusion. My order of researching, and of writing, has been to compose a three-kingdom narrative of events, *The Fall of the British Monarchies 1637–1642* (OUP, forthcoming), and only then, when I had decided what I needed to explain, to consider *The Causes of the English Civil War*. My publishers, to whose kindness and patience I am deeply grateful, have persuaded me to publish the books in reverse order. For the first few months, then, I will have to ask my readers to take on temporary trust some points which are fully substantiated in the bigger book. In the end, however, I hope the two books will be taken as a single corpus of work, and judged as a whole.

Finally, I would like to thank my wife, whose resolute determination to test my findings has sometimes led me to wonder

whether these should have been called the Father William Lectures.
It does appear to be true that every little historian born into this
world alive is either a little Calvinist or a little Arminian, and I am
one and she is the other. It is, in large measure, our debates which
led me to the key perception that it was people's religious inclination
in 1641–2 which determined their perception of what had
happened. The need to make these lectures acceptable to both these
perspectives has been, perhaps, the biggest intellectual challenge I
have ever faced. I do not know whether I have met it, but I am
certain these lectures have been immeasurably enriched in the
attempt. The fact that three quotations used here first became known
to me through her undergraduate essay on Laud is very far from
being a coincidence. Without being equipped with her spectacles, I
would not have spotted the importance of such figures as Francis
Alford and James Dalton. It is a coincidence, though an entirely
appropriate one, that Chapter 4, the lecture which was most
crucially a debate between us, was delivered on the twenty-sixth
anniversary of our engagement. I would like the resulting product
to be regarded, among much else, as a silver wedding present.

Conrad Russell

University College, London
December 1988

Contents

Note

THE English pound was made up of 20 shillings, and of 240 pennies. One shilling was made up of 12 pennies. The sign '*d.*' indicates an old penny.

Dates are given in Old Style, save that the year is taken to begin on 1 January, as the Scottish year already did. In Anglo–Scottish correspondence, dates for beginning the New Year are inconsistent, and it is hard to be finally certain which style is being used unless it is clear from the context.

Place of publication for all references is London unless otherwise stated.

Abbreviations

APS	*Acts of the Parliaments of Scotland*, ed. T. Thomson and C. Innes (Edinburgh, 1814–75).
Baillie	*Letters and Journals of Robert Baillie*, 2 vols. ed. David Laing (Bannatyne Club, Edinburgh, 1841–2).
BIHR	*Bulletin of the Institute of Historical Research*.
BL	British Library.
BL Add. MSS	British Library, Additional Manuscripts.
BL E.	British Library, Thomason Tracts.
BL Harl. MSS	British Library, Harleian MSS.
Bodl.	Bodleian Library, Oxford.
Bowyer	*The Parliamentary Diary of Robert Bowyer 1606–1607*, ed. David Harris Willson (repr. New York, 1971).
Calderwood	David Calderwood, *The True History of the Church of Scotland*, 7 vols. (Wodrow Society, Edinburgh, 1842–9).
CJ	*Commons' Journals*. All references are to England unless otherwise specified.
Clar. SP	*Clarendon State Papers*.
Collinson, *EPM*	Patrick Collinson, *The Elizabethan Puritan Movement* (1967).
Collinson, *RP*	Patrick Collinson, *The Religion of Protestants* (Oxford, 1982).
Cope	*Proceedings of the Short Parliament of 1640*, ed. Esther S. Cope and Willson H. Coates, Camden Society, Fourth Series 19 (1977).
Cosin	*The Works of John Cosin*, ed. J. Sansom, 5 vols. (Oxford 1843–55).
CSPD	*Calendar of State Papers, Domestic*.
CSP Ire.	*Calendar of State Papers, Ireland*.
CSP Ven.	*Calendar of State Papers, Venetian*.
CUL	Cambridge University Library.
D'Ewes (N.)	*The Journal of Sir Symonds D'Ewes*, ed. Wallace Notestein (New Haven, Conn., 1923).
D'Ewes (C.)	*The Journal of Sir Symonds D'Ewes*, ed. Willson H. Coates (New Haven, Conn., 1942).

ECR	*An Exact Collection of Remonstrances* (Edward Husbands, 1643).
EHR	*English Historical Review.*
Fincham and Lake	Kenneth Fincham and Peter Lake, 'The Ecclesiastical Policy of James I', *Journal of British Studies*, 24 (1985).
Hamilton MSS	Scottish Record Office, GD 406/1, Hamilton MSS.
Hartley	*Proceedings of the Parliaments of Elizabeth I, 1559–1581*, ed. T. E. Hartley (Leicester, 1981).
HJ	*Historical Journal.*
HMC	*Historical Manuscripts Commission.*
JBS	*Journal of British Studies.*
JEH	*Journal of Ecclesiastical History.*
JRL	John Rylands Library, Manchester.
KAO	Kent Archive Office.
Knowler	W. Knowler, *The Earl of Strafforde's Letters and Despatches*, 2 vols. (1739).
Lake, *A. & P.?*	Peter Lake, *Anglicans and Puritans? Presbyterianism and English Conformist Thought from Whitgift to Hooker* (1988).
Lake, *MP*	Peter Lake, *Moderate Puritans and the Elizabethan Church* (Cambridge, 1982).
Laud, *Wks.*	*The Works of William Laud*, ed. W. Scott and J. Bliss, 7 vols. (Oxford, 1847–60).
LJ	*Lords' Journals* (England unless otherwise specified).
NHI	*New History of Ireland*, ed. T. W. Moody, F. X. Martin, and F. J. Byrne, iii (Oxford, 1976).
NLS	National Library of Scotland.
Peterkin	*The Booke of the Universall Kirk of Scotland*, ed. A. Peterkin (Edinburgh, 1839).
PJ	*The Private Journals of the Long Parliament*, 3 vols., ed. Willson H. Coates, Anne Steele Young, and Vernon F. Snow (New Haven, Conn., 1982–).
PRO	Public Record Office.
PRO SP	Public Record Office, State Papers.
PRO WO	Public Record Office, War Office.
RO	Record Office.
Rothes	John Leslie Earl of Rothes, *A Relation of Proceedings concerning the Affairs of the Kirk of Scotland from August 1637 to July 1638*, ed. James Nairne (Bannatyne Club, Edinburgh, 1830).
RPCS	*Register of the Privy Council of Scotland.*
Rushworth	J. Rushworth, *Historical Collections*. This is a serial

	publication beginning in 1659. I have used a version of volume iii, part 1 published in 1692; this volume is listed as 'iv' in some other editions.
Russell, *FBM*	Conrad Russell, *The Fall of the British Monarchies 1637–1642* (Oxford University Press, forthcoming).
Russell, *PEP*	Conrad Russell, *Parliaments and English Politics, 1621–1629* (Oxford, 1979).
1628 Debates	*Proceedings in Parliament 1628*, ed. Robert C. Johnson, Mary Frear Keeler, Maija J. Cole, and William B. Bidwell, 6 vols. (New Haven, Conn., 1977–83).
Sommerville	J. P. Sommerville, *Politics and Ideology in England, 1603–1640* (1986).
ST	*State Trials*, ed. W. Cobbett and T. B. Howell, 33 vols. (1809–26).
TRHS	*Transactions of the Royal Historical Society.*
Tyacke	Nicholas Tyacke, *Anti-Calvinists: The Rise of English Arminianism c. 1590–1640* (Oxford, 1987).
ZL	*Zurich Letters*, ed. H. Robinson (Parker Society, 1842–5).

I

The *Corpus Delicti* 1637–1642

'THESE are times for historians to write who seek to avoid all calm narrations as a dead water, to fill their volumes with cruell wars and seditions. I desire not employment at these times'.[1] So wrote Sir Henry Slingsby at the beginning of the Bishops' Wars. As James Bond put the point in the inimitably different idiom of the late twentieth century, 'it reads better than it lives'. Interesting times are often more interesting to those who do not suffer the misfortune of living in them. In these days of social history, it is no longer clear that historians, as a profession, deserve Sir Henry Slingsby's reproaches, but we have certainly spilt enough ink on the causes of the English Civil War. Contemplating the umpteenth assault on this subject, I feel bound to echo Eric Shipton on Mount Everest: 'for God's sake let's climb the bloody thing, and then get back to real mountaineering'. The hunt for the causes of the Civil War has not, on the whole, had a beneficial effect on seventeenth-century historiography: not all the most important developments in the early seventeenth century can be assumed to be causes of the English Civil War. There is a risk that important themes may be either ignored, or strait-jacketed in order to turn them into causes of the Civil War when they are not. To take a couple of examples, the fact that England reached the top of the demographic curve sometime around 1640 is clearly of the highest long-term importance. The coincidence of dates makes it tempting to see whether this can be turned into a cause of the Civil War, but though it is possible to make a connection by way of resistance to taxation, such a connection is highly tangential, and it is hard to make it of the first importance. In the long term, the slow growth of cultural diversity is also of the highest importance. This at first sight looks a little more promising, but in fact it turns out that only those manifestations of diversity which can be directly related to religion, such as maypoles or the sabbath, will fit at all accurately into the jigsaw.

---

[1] *Diary of Sir Henry Slingsby of Scriven*, ed. Daniel Parsons (1836), 14.

Yet even if the search for the causes of the Civil War has a distorting effect on historiography, the fact remains that the Civil War, like Mount Everest, is there, even though Professor Elton may occasionally be moved to doubt it.[2] If we want to get back to real mountaineering, we must climb it first. The war casts a long shadow, and we will never have a clear view of the things which were not causes of the Civil War until we can identify the things which were. In investigating causes, the first necessity is to match them with effects, and it therefore seems a logical priority to begin by trying to establish the effects for which causes must be found. If the effects are wrongly postulated, the causes will be wrong also. If we discuss causes without any investigation of effects, we are simply indulging in unverifiable speculation. The title of this chapter is derived from Perry Mason, and while it does not pretend to offer results as sensational as tend to follow Perry Mason's exclamation, 'your Honour, I object: the prosecution must first prove the *corpus delicti*', I think the logical principle involved in Mason's favourite rule of law is a very sound one. That is why this chapter is devoted to effects and not to causes. It is an attempt to summarize some of the findings of a very large book, completed but not yet sent to press. In this sort of summary, it is not always possible to outline the proofs as fully as would be desirable, but for any point which is not fully proved here, proof will be forthcoming at great length in the not too distant future. In due course I hope this book will stand as one of a pair with my forthcoming *The Fall of the British Monarchies 1637–1642*, and that the corpus of work will be judged as a whole.

The first point to emerge is that some of the supposed 'effects' for which we have tried to find causes were imaginary: we deduced the effects from the supposed causes. For a historian, this is back to front. For example, it has become painfully clear that it is impossible to interpret the Civil War as the clash of two clearly differentiated social groups or classes: the fullest possible knowledge of men's social and economic background, if it leaves out the preaching available in their home parishes, tells us nothing about their likely allegiance in the Civil War. We may take two minor gentlemen clients of Parliamentarian peers beginning the long struggle to make fame and fortune at the bar, and find the people we

---

[2] G. R. Elton, 'English National Selfconsciousness and the Parliament in the Sixteenth Century', in *Nationalismus in Vorindustrieller Zeit*, Herausgegeben von Otto Dann (Munich, 1986), 79.

have chosen are Oliver St John and Edward Hyde: the similarity of background does not show up in any similarity of behaviour. If we look at the sons of a Colchester baker, a London merchant, a Westminster tallow-chandler, and a Reading draper, we are drawing from the 'industrious sort of people', but we do not find we have drawn four Puritans out of the hat: we have drawn Samuel Harsnett, Lancelot Andrewes, Richard Neile, and William Laud: the cream of the English Arminians. No group was unanimous, and no area was unanimous either. Even in London, the drinkers in the Guildhall buttery at the beginning of 1642 were claiming that there were a thousand who would stand for the Lord Mayor and the Cross—the City equivalent of church and King. It is well known that in January 1642, after the attempt on the Five Members, the King was greeted at the Guildhall with shouts of 'privilege of Parliament', but it is not so well known that these shouts had to compete 'which was the loudest' with other shouts of 'God bless the King'.[3] On Candlemas Day, when the crowds gathered around Cheapside Cross, there were apprentices ready to riot for it as well as against it, and the Lord Mayor, emancipating himself from the control of Pennington's Committee of Safety, put a double watch on it and preserved it.[4] It is worth remembering that some City parishes presented petitions in favour of bishops, and that there were disturbances in favour of altar rails, as well as against them. It is equally worth remembering that according to Saye, the reason for engaging Prince Rupert at Turnham Green in 1642 was the fear that if he advanced further, he would pick up too many allies in the City. We should not forget the qualification in the report in the Wharton–Willingham newsletters in September 1642 that 'the whole City were now real or constrained Roundheads'.[5] Nor does the Long Parliament's record suggest that they were mainly concerned with social issues, on which they spent remarkably little time: the enclosure bill offered in November 1640, for example, in two years never progressed beyond a first reading.[6] Where we can find a genuine social issue, like forest clearance or fen drainage, it normally turns out to be one on which the leaders of the two sides

[3] PRO SP 16/488/29. On the general point, see M. Ingram, *The Church Courts, Sex and Marriage in England 1570–1640* (Cambridge, 1987), 93–124.
[4] *LJ* v. 239, 247, 256–7; *HMC Twelfth Report*, ii. 304.
[5] PRO 31/3/72, p. 419; House of Lords Main Papers 10 June 1641; D'Ewes (C.) 17; PRO SP 16/492/21; William Fiennes, Viscount Saye and Sele, *Vindiciae Veritatis* (1654), BL E. 811 (2), p. 68. [6] *CJ* ii. 21.

were in full agreement. The most explosive social discontents appear to be those resulting from forest clearance and fen drainage, in each case involving loss of rights of common. In the Fens, it is common knowledge that the King and Bedford were acting in partnership. In Blackmore and Pewsham forest, whose clearance led to some of the worst disturbances, the Crown's local agent happened to be Pym. Professor Buchanan Sharp has stressed that in the issues arising from forest clearance, consecutive regimes, those of the King, the Lords, and the Protector, all followed broadly similar policies. He has described the attitudes of the forest rioters as ones of 'positive political indifference, rather than passive neutrality, a statement that the issues raised by the conflict between King and Parliament were of little or no concern to many local people when weighed in the balance against pressing local issues such as disafforestation and enclosure.'[7]

We are not trying to find causes for a conflict of classes. Nor are we trying to find causes for a conflict between a court and a country, or a government and an opposition. Professor Zagorin, at the end of his lengthy investigation of the theme of the court and the country, said that it did not correspond to the divisions of the Civil War, and this finding is entirely correct.[8] One shrewd observer, looking at those who attended the King at Windsor in January 1642, reported that there were not many 'old courtiers' among them.[9] This comment should be set beside Clarendon's rather catty comment on Sir John Culpepper, that 'sure no man less appeared a courtier', 'having never sacrificed to the muses, or conversed in any polite company'.[10] One might correctly deduce from this comment that it was Culpepper and not Hyde who was Charles's most prominent ally in the House of Commons, but Hyde's own claims to be a courtier were not much stronger. He had, no doubt, conversed in polite company, but it does not seem to have been at court. On the other side of the fence, it is impossible to find a more archetypally court figure than the Groom of the Stool, and in 1642, for the only

---

[7] Alnwick Castle MSS Y III (2), box 4, envelope 6. I am grateful to His Grace the Duke of Northumberland for permission to examine these MSS, and to Mr Colin Shrimpton, Archivist at Alnwick Castle, for his kind assistance. PRO E. 178/4577; R. Buchanan Sharp, *In Contempt of All Authority: Rural Artisans and Riot in the West of England* (Berkeley, 1980), 8.

[8] P. Zagorin, *The Court and the Country* (1969), 305.

[9] PRO SP 16/488/56.

[10] Edward, Earl of Clarendon, *Life*, i (Oxford, 1857), 87.

time in the history of the office, the Groom of the Stool went into rebellion. He was not out of place among his Parliamentary friends: He was one of the key figures in the Parliamentary leadership of 1642, and Conway went so far as to describe him as the invisible head of the Puritan party.[11] Holland was not a unique case: John Crew, chairman of the Long Parliament's Grand Committee on Religion, was also a Gentleman Extraordinary of the Privy Chamber.[12] The evidence does not justify us in talking of a court Parliamentarian party and a country Royalist party, but it is possible that the picture might be no more inaccurate that way round than the other.

Nor is it easy to take the Civil War as a struggle between a 'government' and an 'opposition'. Just because it was a struggle involving major issues of principle, it divided those who might be classified as members of a 'government' along much the same lines as everyone else. In the 1620s it had been impossible to tell the difference between Laurence Whitaker Clerk of the Council and William Whitaker Pym's lawyer from the subject-matter of their speeches. In 1642, as it happens, both of them were still sitting, and it is sometimes just possible to tell them apart by their opinions—because Laurence Whitaker Clerk of the Council was the more bitterly opposed to the King of the two.[13] If we look at those who were members of the Privy Council in October 1640, and still alive and at liberty in August 1642, they divide as six Parliamentarians, nine Royalists, six neutrals, and three for whom it is hard to decide whether to classify their position in 1642 as Royalist or neutral. This at least shows a Royalist majority, but the numbers mask very different degrees of commitment. With the brief exception of Salisbury, the Parliamentarians Manchester, Holland, Pembroke, Northumberland, and Vane were always firmly and belligerently committed to their side, while among the Royalists, Berkshire,

[11] *CSPD 1640*, vol. cccclvi, no. 43. Holland's draft will of February 1642, which includes a passionate protest at the Parliamentary decision to deprive him of his monopolies, suggests that he did not side with them for his material interest. Llanfairpwllgwyngyllgogerychwyrndrobwllllantysiliogogogoch, Plas Newydd MSS, box XII. I am grateful to the Marquess of Anglesey for permission to examine his family papers. I am grateful to Dr David Starkey for confirming that no previous Groom of the Stool had ever been a rebel.
[12] PRO LC 5/134, p. 265. Gentlemen Extraordinary of the Privy Chamber had become too numerous to enjoy great significance, but they still will not pass for a 'country' embattled against a 'court'.
[13] Russell, *PEP*, pp. 230 and n., 381: *CJ* ii. 545.

Bankes, Littleton, and even Dorset were extremely and visibly reluctant warriors, leaving Lennox, Lindsey, and Newcastle as the King's only wholehearted allies on his own Privy Council.

Lord Keeper Littleton most visibly dissented from the King, perhaps because his office forced choices upon him which other Councillors were able to avoid. He set his hand to the ordinance of August 1641 against recusants, voted in favour of correspondence with the Commons over their order of 8 September 1641, refused to seal the Proclamation against the Five Members, refused to command Essex and Holland to give up their offices, accepted office as a Lord Lieutenant under the Militia Ordinance, and appears to have upheld its legality.[14] These are more than isolated incidents. Like the date of Littleton's preferment, they align him firmly with those Privy Councillors, such as Vane and Hamilton, who wanted a compromise settlement. Bankes, who admired Lancelot Andrewes, held beliefs which may in some ways have been closer to the King's, but his desire for office under the Militia Ordinance, and his resolute refusal, even to the King's face, to declare it illegal, mark him, at the least, as a supporter of the Royalist peace party.[15] Dorset in August 1642 told Salisbury that there would be an arbitrary government whichever side won. He said he was leaving York when Charles announced his intention to raise his standard, though he does not actually appear to have done so. In the winter of 1642–3, he was in trouble for pressing for an accommodation, and for calling the Civil War a 'shambles of men's flesh'.[16]

In the spring of 1642, when the Lords had to vote on a Commons' proposal to require the resignation of all the pre-1640 Privy Council, it was not the Councillors who opposed it. Of seven pre-1640 Councillors whose votes can be tentatively identified, six seem to have voted in favour of the proposal, and only one against it. That vote illustrates the case for arguing that the Civil War was not a struggle between government and opposition: it was nearer to being a struggle between Charles and his own government. At the

---

[14] BL Harl. MS 164, f. 887ª; Bodl. MS Clarendon, vol. 21, no. 1603; PRO SP 16/488/54; *HMC Montagu of Beaulieu*, p. 149; *LJ* v. 116; BL Loan MSS 29/46/12 (including dorse).

[15] Dorset RO Bankes of Kingston Lacey MSS, vol. M and Gospel Commentaries; G. Bankes, *Corfe Castle* (1853), 134–6; *PJ* i. 356.

[16] *HMC Salis.* XXII. 318–19; Alan Everitt, *The Community of Kent and the Great Rebellion* (Leicester, 1966), 59, 77. I am grateful to Dr David Smith for saving me from error about Dorset's movements in 1642.

same time, the vote illustrates why it was useless to attempt, as the Parliament hoped to do, to control Charles by giving him an 'advised Council'. He had one already, and by voting for their own dismissal, these Councillors were confessing their failure in that role.[17] When Charles finally gathered support for the Royalist cause in the Civil War, a very large proportion of it came from outside the ranks of his own government. One might legitimately parody Falkland on the bishops, and say the Privy Councillors who hated Charles hated him worse than the devil, and they that loved him loved him not so well as their dinner.

If we accept the argument that the Civil War did not produce a division between the members of an established order and its opponents, but divided people on almost entirely non-institutional lines, one of the major historiographical consequences which must follow is that the Royalists come to stand in need of as much explanation as the Parliamentarians. They did, it is true, claim to be defenders of an established order, but so, equally loudly, did the Parliamentarians, and we will beg every interesting question if we assume a priori that one of these claims is more valid than the other. We can no longer afford to treat Royalists as being like the memorable Professor in the *ancien régime* in the University of London, who once replied to a request to submit reasons: 'reasons? I cannot see that we need to submit reasons: we are defending established practice'. Dr Tyacke, in his important work on the rise of Arminianism, has shown that, in religion, Charles's claims to be defending established practice were distinctly questionable. It follows that if we are to explain Charles's success in gathering support, something more than respect for the established order must be invoked.[18] The Royalists stand just as much in need of reasons as the Parliamentarians do, and so, though a revolution-centred historiography has left less previous work to draw on than is available for the Parliamentarians, we must do our best to supply them.

This point underlines the fact that what we are dealing with in 1642 is a civil war and not a revolution: we need to explain the making of a positive commitment to the King by large numbers of people with no particular interest in maintaining the existing order.

[17] *LJ* iv. 700; Bodl. MS Clarendon, vol. 21, no. 1603. I am grateful to Professor R. C. Stacey for the point about an advised Council.

[18] Tyacke, *passim.*

Indeed, it is worth asking whether the idea of 'revolution' is one of those universals invented for the purpose of demonstrating the merits of nominalism. Does the attempt to impose a common label of 'revolution' on many disparate events result in a typology which makes us misunderstand those events by treating them as more generic, and less individual, than they really were?

In this context, it must be said that this book is only attempting to explain the events of 1642, not those of 1647–9, 1653, or even 1660. For events happening after 1642, it is never possible to eliminate the logical possibility that their causes lie in the course of the Civil War itself, and therefore arise after 1642. Before this possibility can be effectively checked, we need many more studies, like Professor Aylmer's article on 'Gentlemen Levellers?' or Dr Gentles's article on the Chidleys, which trace radicals of the 1640s back into the obscurity of the 1630s.[19] So far, we have very little evidence to suggest that the extremer radical ideas originated before the crisis of 1637–42, rather than as a response to it. In at least one case, we have evidence that the ideas *were* generated as a response to the crisis: Christopher Feake the Fifth Monarchist later said he was first provoked to study the prophecies of Daniel and Revelation by the excitement generated by the Prayer Book riots in Edinburgh.[20] In 1637 an Edmund Chillenden, possibly identical with the later Fifth Monarchist, was helping to distribute copies of *News from Ipswich*, a work with nothing in common with the sort of radicalism he was to show later.[21] A cursory study of those seditious words which were recorded in the *Calendar of State Papers* shows little sign of the seeds of those ideas which were to be characteristic of the years after 1645. There are occasional hints: for example, an anonymous libel found at Paul's Cross in 1629 claimed that the King was no king because he had violated the 'relation' between him and his subjects, a phrase which shows signs of contractual thinking. The invocation of idolatry as the reason for believing this, in the context of the rest of the document, suggests the double covenant of the *Vindiciae* rather than any more secular notion of contract.[22] The

[19] G. E. Aylmer, 'Gentlemen Levellers?', *Past and Present*, 49 (1970), 120–5; Ian Gentles, 'London Levellers in the English Revolution: The Chidleys and their Circle', *JEH* 29 (1978), 281–309, esp. pp. 282–5. I am grateful to Dr Gentles for further help and advice on this question.
[20] J. T. Cliffe, *Puritan Gentry* (1984), 207.
[21] *CSPD 1636–7*, vol. cccxlix, no. 52.
[22] *CSPD 1628–9*, vol. cxlii, nos. 92, 93.

dominant theme in the seditious words is not any secular radicalism with proto-Leveller overtones, but a straightforward fear of the growth of 'popery' associated with Laud,[23] with the Queen,[24] and alarmingly, with the King.[25] These remarks are based only on a reading of the *Calendar of State Papers*, and it would be interesting to see whether a fuller investigation of seditious words would confirm this picture.

Moreover, we should not exaggerate the extent of revolutionary upheaval even in 1647–9: the evidence for it is strongest in the published ideas, yet such works as *Jonah's Cry out of the Whale's Belly* proclaim, by their very titles, that they were not written from positions of power. There seems to have been less change in the social composition of the group with political power than is sometimes suggested. For example, Dr Adamson, in his recent article on 'The English Nobility and the Projected Settlement of 1647', has given us convincing reasons for believing that the programme which became known as 'The Heads of the Proposals' originated, not with the Army, but with the group of Parliamentary peers organized by Saye, Northumberland, Salisbury, and Wharton. A Percy and a Cecil will hardly serve for symbols of social revolution.[26] Also, if there were an inherent, as distinct from a contingent, revolutionary potential in the ideas developing before 1637, one would expect it to be much more visible than it appears to be in the very controlled experiment of New England. One final negative point before coming to the positive ones: it appears to be beside the point to try to explain an intention to create civil war, because it seems that right up to the last moment, little or no such intention existed. The best evidence for this is in the records of the Ordnance Office, which show the Parliamentarians, throughout the first half of 1642, vigorously sending off all the arms they could lay hands on to suppress the rebels in Ireland.[27] Where I have in the

---

[23] Ibid., vol. cxl, no. 55, vol. cxli, no. 27; *CSPD 1639*, vol. ccccxxix, no. 30; *CSPD 1635–6*, vol. cccxviii, no. 55.

[24] *CSPD 1628–9*, vol. cxl, no. 44, vol. cxlv, no. 55; *CSPD 1629–31*, vol. cxcvii, no. 73; *CSPD 1634–5*, p. 318; *CSPD 1640*, vol. clv. no. 42.

[25] *CSPD 1628–9*, vol. cxl., no. 44; *CSPD 1633–4*, vol. clxii, no. 16; *CSPD 1638–9*, vol. ccciv, no. 64; ibid., vol. ccccvi, no. 82; *CSPD 1640*, vol. ccccliv, no. 42.

[26] J. S. A. Adamson, 'The English Nobility and the Projected Settlement of 1647', *HJ* 30/3 (1987), 567–602.

[27] PRO WO 49/72 fos. 74–9, 82–9, 94–6, and other refs.; ibid. 49/77, fo. 61[r] and other refs.

past been wrong was in taking this lack of intention to fight as evidence of moderation. The lack of intention to fight is in fact not a moderate desire for compromise, but hope of a walkover resulting from the fatal weakness of politicians for over-estimating their own support, so that, as the Houses put it in May 1642, 'it is hoped they [the Yorkshire Parliamentarians] will so over-awe the other party as to keep them quiet'.[28] Nevertheless, the point remains that any attempt to explain an intention to cause civil war is an attempt to explain a non-event: for both sides, civil war represented a political failure, and that failure is one of the things which require explanation.

A large part of the logical confusion on this subject results from taking the coming of the English Civil War as a single event, whereas in fact it was a somewhat unpredictable sequence of events and non-events. Since the war was the result, not merely of these events and non-events, but of the fact that they came in the order they did, it is hard to build up an orderly sequence of long-term causes for the King's raising his standard at Nottingham. However, if we think of explaining a sequence of events, we make the welcome discovery that different events in this sequence may be the results of different causes. It thus becomes possibly to match cause to effect with a precision impossible in tackling such a diffuse happening as the outbreak of the Civil War. Moreover, even if we say that the precise sequence of events was, in Professor Koenigsberger's phrase, 'unpredictable even if we were to use game theory or a computer',[29] the possibility still remains that many of the individual events may be the results of long-term causes of some standing. It thus becomes possible to accept that England was not on the edge of civil war in 1637, without being therefore forced to confine our explanation of the Civil War to events after 1637. The English Civil War was not an isolated event. Charles ruled over three kingdoms, and within three years he faced armed resistance in all three of them, Scotland in 1639, Ireland in 1641, and England in 1642. Even if we were to accept the improbable, but not a priori impossible, hypothesis that these three upheavals were initially unconnected, the close coincidence of dates inevitably makes the other two part of the events which led to the English Civil War, and

[28] *LJ* v. 72.
[29] H. G. Koenigsberger, Dominium Regale *or* Dominium Politicum et Regale: *Monarchies and Parliaments in Early Modern Europe* (London, 1975), 25.

therefore takes any study of the causes outside England. In fact, the study of resistance in the three kingdoms overwhelmingly suggests the possibility that all three were connected, and therefore that we should be looking for causes in the things all three had in common: that they were members of a union of multiple kingdoms, and that they were all ruled by Charles I. It may be that the main reason why the causes of the English Civil War have created so much difficulty is our insular error in looking for them only in the study of English history: we have been trying to discover the whole of the solution by studying a part of the problem.[30] If we look at England in a British context, it shows two peculiarities: it was the last of Charles's kingdoms to resist him, and the one in which Charles gathered the largest party. What we should be explaining, then, is not why revolutionary propensities in England were so strong, but why they were so weak.

The first of the individual questions for which we need answers is why the Bishops' Wars broke out in 1639, since there is no doubt that they started the immediate sequence of events which led to the English Civil War. In order to give this primacy to the Bishops' Wars, it is not necessary to engage with the question whether the English Civil War might have happened without them: the fact is that it did not, and that without them, it could not have happened in the way it did. Since we are bound to explain what did happen, rather than what did not, we may safely say that the first thing we need to explain is why there were Bishops' Wars, and the acceptance of this point will immediately take our causal framework outside the borders of England. We cannot afford to treat the Bishops' Wars as some sort of irrelevant outside factor needing no more explanation than a storm of bad weather. Both sides were capable of foreseeing what sort of trouble they might be creating by fighting each other, since Hamilton had warned them both. He told the King in 1638 that if he tried to use England to suppress the Covenanters by force, he would risk provoking rebellion in England, and could not do it without hazarding his three crowns. He told the Covenanter Earl of Rothes that if the Covenanters fought Charles, they would never see peace again during their lifetimes, a prophecy which was barely

[30] Conrad Russell, 'The British Problem and the English Civil War', *History*, 72/276 (1987), 395–415: inaugural lecture delivered at University College, London on 6 March 1985. This lecture is in many ways a sequel to Professor Koenigsberger's inaugural lecture cited above, n. 29.

exaggerated.[31] The determination of both sides to ignore these warnings is evidence of a profound conflict which could not long continue on England's borders without becoming a polarizing force in English politics, and which must therefore be included among the things for which causes must be found. Moreover, the apparent predominance of the Covenanters in Scotland and of the King in England masks the very large extent to which the Bishops' Wars were, as the Covenanters constantly reiterated, not a national quarrel. They were a struggle between two Anglo–Scottish factions, and therefore a force in polarizing both kingdoms.

The next question we need to answer is why the Scots won the Bishops' Wars. The Scottish victory at Newburn was their first major success against England since Bannockburn, and so was unusual enough to cry out for scapegoats then, and for explanations now. The difficulty in explaining England's defeat in the Bishops' Wars is not that there are too few explanations, but that there are too many, and all of them may easily be made to look perfectly convincing.[32] Any of these explanations take us well back in English history. The shortage of money, the weakness of the English military system, and the growing polarization of English opinion between pro- and anti-Scots all open up causes whose roots lie well back. So does the fact that the First Bishops' War in 1639 was (with the token exception of the Scottish campaign of 1400) the first war to be fought without a Parliament since 1323. In 1639 it seems that the political explanation may be paramount: the King's army was still in pay when the Pacification of Berwick was signed. The Earl of Holland had, it is true, reported that it was unfit to fight, but the fact that Holland had for some time been employed as mediator by the Covenanters means that we should hesitate before taking his word for it.[33] Many people were aware that, as the Countess of Westmorland put it, 'they know our divisions, and— they have a party amongst us, and . . . we have none among them'.[34] The English party at Berwick had no need to scour the country to find the alarmingly divisive effect of what they were doing: it was perfectly visible in their own camp. The Earl of

[31] Hamilton MSS 327.1; Rothes, p. 137.

[32] I hope to discuss this question fully in Russell, *FBM*, ch. 3 *passim*.

[33] Crawford MSS 14/3/35 formerly in JRL, now in NLS. I am grateful to the Earl of Crawford and Balcarres for permission to consult these MSS.

[34] PRO SP 16/420/70.

Stamford, during the negotiations, described Alexander Henderson and the Scottish ministers as 'holy and blessed men, of admirable, transcendent and seraphical learning, and say grace longer and better than our campestrial chaplains, that ride before our regiments taking tobacco'. Secretary Coke shared the admiration for Alexander Henderson: 'in all his speeches you may find as much devotion, wisdom, humility and obedience as can be wished for in an honest man and a good subject'.[35] These are the voices of a Parliamentarian and a man whose angle of neutrality was distinctly Parliamentarian. For the Royalist voice, we turn to Thomas Windebank the Secretary's son, writing on conclusion of peace:

We have had a most cold, wet and long time of living in the field, but kept ourselves warm with the hope of rubbing, fubbing and scrubbing those scurvy, filthy, dirty, nasty, lousy, itchy, scabby, shitten, stinking, slovenly, snotty-nosed, logger-headed, foolish, insolent, proud, beggarly, impertinent, absurd, grout-headed, villainous, barbarous, beastial, false, lying, roguish, devilish, long-eared, short-haired, damnable, atheistical, puritanical crew of the Scottish Covenant. But now there is peace in Israel.[36]

In the Second Bishops' War, by contrast, it seems to be more important that English logistics broke down, and something between a third and a quarter of the army reached Yorkshire without any arms.[37] In explaining that failure, money, rather than politics, is likely to have been paramount, while the result of the battle itself reflects superior Scottish generalship.

The English defeat at Newburn led inevitably to a Parliament, and that Parliament to the first of the non-events for which we need to find an explanation: the failure to conclude a political settlement. A new political settlement, with scapegoats and an afforced Council, was a normal result of such political crises, and the belief that one was in the offing accounts for much of the belief that November 1640 was the beginning of a 'golden age'.[38] It was notoriously difficult to make such settlements stick, as the cases of 1216, 1261, and 1397 showed very clearly, but tne failure in 1641 to conclude

[35] *CSPD 1639*, vol. ccccxxiv, no. 28.   [36] Ibid., no. 50.
[37] Hamilton MSS 1229; *CSPD 1639–40*, vol. ccclxiv nos. 26, 44. For William Legge's dispatch notes for the artillery train, see Staffs. RO D. 1778/I/i/ 5. This confirms that many of the great guns left London dangerously late. I am grateful to the Earl of Dartmouth for permission to examine his family papers.
[38] Bodl. MS Clarendon, vol. 20, no. 1503; Cliffe, *The Puritan Gentry*, p. 223; *Diary of Sir Henry Slingsby*, ed. Parsons, p. 64; *LJ* iv. 575.

one at all was highly unusual, and cries out for explanation. It is a failure which underlines the fact that the English Civil War was not the result of an outburst of anger in the localities, but of a failure of the political process at the centre. It is hard to find much sign of impending war in the counties before May or June 1642, but at Westminster an acceptable settlement, meaning one which would have left both Charles and Pym's junto confident that they would be alive and at liberty in twelve months' time, had become remote by March 1641, and became a total impossibility between 3 and 12 May 1641.[39] This did not mean that civil war became inevitable at that date: dissolution or prorogation, or a division leaving one side with such overwhelming force that the other could not fight, remained practical possibilities for some time. Yet from the Army Plot and the death of Strafford onwards, what existed at Westminster was something Hobbes would have had no difficulty in recognizing as a state of war: a time wherein the will to contend by force if need be was sufficiently known.

Charles's share in this failure of the political process is well known, but the share of the group Edward Nicholas called Pym's junto is not as widely known as it ought to be. During the Bishops' Wars, some of the group responsible for the Petition of the Twelve Peers had colluded with the Scots to a point well the wrong side of treason. This fact was known to Charles, who chillingly assured Windebank in September 1640 that 'it shall not be forgotten',[40] and in January 1642 he remembered it. Those who commit treason, as Sir John Harrington could have reminded them, cannot afford to fail, and indeed, cannot afford partial success. The junto knew too much about the fate of the Lords Appellant to need reminding of this.

This bound them the more closely to those for whom they had committed treason, and who alone could protect them from its consequences: the Scottish army. It was only if the English settlement was part of the British settlement demanded by the Scottish peace treaty, and therefore protected by Scottish guarantees, that they could have any confidence in its durability. This meant that for the first six months of the Long Parliament, they were bound hand and foot to their Scottish allies. They could not risk taking the

---

[39] I hope to explain the reasons for this judgement fully in Russell, *FBM*, chs. 6, 7.
[40] *Clar. SP*, ii. 120.

only available route to a settlement with the King, which lay in ditching the Scots. They knew too well that they owed all the gains they had made since September 1640 to the presence of the Scottish army, and that the departure of that army could, at a stroke, destroy them all. In April 1641, when the Scots' departure might be regarded as imminent, Alderman Penington said that 'hee feareth as soone as the Scotch are gone those men yt desireth to be called prestes (which indeed are Balls prestes) will doe more mischeefe then they have before'. Henry Marten offered the truly revolutionary proposal 'for the Scotch armie to stay heare, and rather to disband our owen armie'. George Digby immediately offered a counter-proposal to disband the Scottish army but not the English. The failure of Digby's further proposal to call Marten to the bar is a sign of a House which had already developed a remarkable tolerance of the use of the threat of force to coerce the King.[41] Pym's junto were therefore unable to escape the two key Scottish negotiating demands, which were for British unity in a common Presbyterianism, and for the death of Strafford. The unacceptability of these demands to Charles would alone have been enough to make settlement impossible, but the Scots' religious demands aroused so much resistance that it would have been difficult for Charles to accept them if he had wanted to.[42] Bancroft and his allies, in denouncing 'Scotticizing discipline', had done their work well, and the Scots encountered resistance, not only to unacceptable proposals, but to the reopening of a closed argument. Those who emerged as anti-Scots in the first four months of the Long Parliament were Sir John Holland, Sir William Widdrington, Sir William Pennyman, Sir John Strangeways, Charles Price, Dr Turner, John Selden, Edward Hyde, Sir Ralph Hopton, Arthur Capel, and George Digby. Save for Selden and Sir John Holland, this list is almost a roll-call of the inner ring of the Royalist party in the Commons and it merely confirms the point that the list of anti-Scots soon clearly included Falkland, Culpepper, Kirton, and Waller. The Royalist party was an anti-Scottish party before it was a Royalist party, and its spiritual father was Richard Bancroft. This is not only true in the Commons: in the Lords, under the leadership of Bristol, this

---

[41] BL Add. MS 64, 807, fos. 7ʳ–9ʳ (diary of Thomas Standish). I am grateful to Dr Maija Jansson, who discovered this diary, for generously bringing it to my attention.
[42] This case is developed in Russell, *FBM*, chs. 5–9 *passim*.

pattern is even clearer, and Sir Thomas Knyvett, the nearest thing
our sources afford to the gentleman in the street, suggests that it may
be true elsewhere. In a letter to his wife at Christmas 1640, which
probably enclosed a copy of the highly-pro-Scottish ballad 'Gramercy,
Good Scot', he wrote: 'God a marcy good Scott! But mustris mark
the winding up. Scott is not gone yet. Behould I doubt we must be
acquainted with Mr. Knocks aswell Buchanan and Mas. Henderson
before we be ridd of them. Some heads may perhapps satisfye both
kingdomes, but thay must have better brains to do it without loss
then any I believe are amongst them.'[43] For Knyvett, as for the Earl
of Stamford and Sir John Coke, his attitude to Alexander
Henderson is an exact predictor of his ultimate allegiance. In
preventing a settlement, the Scots' contribution was as central as it
was in creating the opportunity to negotiate for one. It then becomes
vital to explain why they committed themselves, at such high
political risk, to what Dr Levack calls the 'Scottish imperial' vision
of British unity, in which England would fall into line with
Scotland.[44] The explanations of this lie far back in Scottish history
and in Anglo–Scottish relations, but they do not lie in the domestic
history of England.

Our next question is why there was no prorogation or dissolution.
In any contest between a King and a Parliament, dissolution or
prorogation, leaving the King in somewhat battered possession of
the field, was always the likeliest outcome, and a dissolution or
prorogation is perhaps the most important of the dogs in the night-
time of 1641. A dissolution or prorogation would have left the
King, even if badly shaken, still in possession of the field, and
would therefore have left a very different power structure from the
one which ultimately resulted. John Barry, an army officer and
future Irish rebel, was making a perfectly sensible calculation when
he said on 5 April 1641 that the Irish committee in London should
aim not to fly as high as other people, 'for it is not safe to shewe a
will, wheare there is no powre, and thoughe ye lyons clawes be
pared close, yet in tyme they will growe out agen, and it is then

---

[43] *Knyvett Letters*, ed. Bertram Schofield (Norfolk Record Society, 20,
Norwich, 1949, 97. For a version of the poem Knyvett may have been quoting, see
Diary of John Rous, ed. Mary Ann Everett Green (Camden Society, 66, 1856),
110–11. The 'winding up' in effect says that thanks to the Scots should be deferred
till the millennium.

[44] Brian Levack, *Formation of the British State* (Oxford, 1987), 108–11, 128–
9, and other refs.

better trusting to what is love and favor will obldge him too, then to what his necessities may inforce him to promise nowe'.[45] This eminently sensible calculation proved wrong, and the reasons why it proved wrong are one of the things we need to discover. The statute against dissolution or prorogation, which was part of the price Charles paid for the Army Plot, is of course part of the explanation, but it is not the whole answer. Members' letters to their wives, admittedly an *ex parte* source, but no more so than public pronouncements, give the impression that around August and September 1641 there would have been a serious possibility of a prorogation with the consent of the Houses. The General Pardon marking the end of the session had been prepared and laid before the Lords.[46] On 7 September 1641 Essex told Hamilton that it was necessary to adjourn the Parliament because it had sat so long, and everyone was so desirous to see their 'homs'. He said the plague increased much, and most at Westminster, and that he wanted to 'tak a little fresh aire in the countre'.[47] At this stage, a proposal for a six-month prorogation might well have been carried, and the cooling-off period might have had all the effects envisaged by the Taft–Hartley Act. This did not happen, partly because Charles failed to make it top priority, preferring instead to embark on the intrigue to end Covenanter control of Scotland which culminated in the Incident. Edward Nicholas's conviction that this was a mistaken strategy persistently bursts through the correct phraseology of the letters he sent to the King in Scotland.

There was another, and perhaps more important, reason: during 1641 the House of Commons deprived Charles of control of some 60% of his ordinary revenues. The most important part of this was Tonnage and Poundage. After reversing the judgment in Bate's Case, the Houses were voting this to Charles by temporary bills to last a few weeks at a time, and according to the figures submitted to Charles by Sir Robert Pye in August 1641, the sums covered by these temporary bills amounted to £482,305 a year.[48] This was not the sort of sum Charles could lightly dispense with, and he was under very heavy pressure to continue the Parliament in the hope of

[45] BL Add. MS 46, 925, pt. A, fo. 1ᵛ. I am grateful to Dr J. S. A. Adamson for drawing my attention to these MSS, which are the originals of the material calendared in *HMC Egmont*, 1.
[46] House of Lords Main Papers, LP 180/1.
[47] Hamilton MSS 1424.
[48] Bodl. MS Clarendon, vol. 20, no. 1539.

getting a permanent grant. By August 1641 Strode, 'whose boldness of speech had made many think him wise',[49] was saying in public that such a grant would be deferred until the King agreed to abolish bishops, and by October the junto were saying it would be deferred until Charles agreed to Parliamentary choice of the great officers, as he had just done in Scotland.[50] What needs explaining is not why the junto used this opportunity for a pursuit of power which was increasingly becoming a matter of life and death. We need rather to explain why members like Hyde, Strangeways, and Kirton, who had no sympathy with the junto's objectives, made no recorded attempt to stop them getting away with it. Here, the financial irresponsibility characteristic of the Commons since 1593 and longer was vital. Charles, in his speech of 16 February 1641, compared them to people who had taken a watch to pieces, and mildly expressed the hope that they were going to succeed in putting it together again.[51] They were not: taking it apart had been much more exciting. We need, then, to explain why Royalist members, who were not in any sense revolutionaries, had a view of their function which did not include officiously striving to make the King solvent.

The last time Edward Nicholas looked forward to the end of the Parliament was on the morning of 1 November 1641. By the afternoon of that day, the news of the Irish Rebellion had reached London, and Charles could no longer dissolve the Parliament without sacrificing one of his three kingdoms, or without branding himself for ever as the ally of the papists. The Irish Rebellion, as it were, caged the King and the Parliament together, and so eliminated the possibility that they could avoid fighting by separation. It then becomes necessary, in order to explain the English Civil War, to explain the Irish Rebellion, and it seems that the explanations of the Irish Rebellion, as much as those of the Bishops' Wars, reach deep into the history of the other kingdoms. With kingdoms, as with people, two is company and three a crowd, and any move to closer relations between two makes a gooseberry of the third. When the Petition of the Twelve Peers asked for 'the better uniting of *both* your realms' against the enemies of the

    [49] BL Add. MS 31, 954, fol. 182ᵛ.
    [50] BL Harl. MS 5047, fo. 57ʳ; *Diary and Correspondence of John Evelyn*, ed. H. B. Wheatley, iv. 115–16; D'Ewes (C.), pp. 44–7, 47 n.
    [51] *CSPD 1640–1*, vol. cccclxxvii, no. 29.

reformed religion, the ominous 'both' was not lost on the Irish rebels, who picked it up in their propaganda.[52] There were three points where the Irish were especially sensitive to the results of Anglo–Scottish *rapprochement*. One was whether the British Isles would remain safe for papists. John Barry, a future rebel leader, reported in some indignation that the Parliament had cashiered all the Popish officers in the King's army, 'and among the rest myself'.[53] The second, closely related, point was that they were deeply worried by the tendency, encouraged by the trial of Strafford, for the English Parliament to claim authority over Ireland. This was a trend in which the Scots, to whom Charles had given good reason to fear Irish papists, were full and willing participants. It caused great anxiety to Roger Moore the rebel leader, and particularly to such vital Old English recruits to the rebels as Viscount Gormanston.[54] The third issue, brought to the fore by renewed Irish demands to confirm the Graces, was the future of the policy of plantation, another matter of joint Anglo–Scottish interest. When the English House of Lords in August 1641 asked Charles to withold the Graces until Ireland's subordination to the English Parliament had been duly asserted, they added the coping-stone to the rebels' fears. The Irish Rebellion, like the Scottish National Covenant and the English Civil War, cannot be explained in terms of the history of a single kingdom.

Our next question is how, being unable to achieve a settlement or a dissolution, the Parliament, and then the political nation, split into two approximately equal parties. It is important to say that explaining the division into parties is not the same thing as explaining the Civil War, and indeed is not even necessarily the biggest part of explaining the Civil War. The parties of 1642 had been divided on many of the issues on which they then disagreed for a very long time, during which they never fought each other, nor ever seemed likely to do so. No amount of expounding the division will tell us why in 1642 that division was unexpectedly pushed to the point of war. The explanations of that are in the failure of the political process, not in the internal structure of the parties called

---

[52] PRO SP 16/465/16; *Discourse between Two Councillors of State, the One of England, the Other of Ireland*, ed. Aidan Clarke (Analecta Hibernica, 26, Dublin, 1970), 171.

[53] *HMC Egmont*, I. 122.

[54] Conrad Russell, 'British Background to the Irish Rebellion of 1641', *Historical Research*, 61/145 (1988), 180–1.

into action by that failure. Nevertheless, the division of the parties is one of the things for which we must find causes, even though it does not deserve the sort of primacy it has sometimes seemed to enjoy.

The division of parties worked along very different lines in the two Houses. In the Lords, only Brooke, and, as far as his intense Erastianism permitted, Saye and perhaps Warwick truly qualify as godly peers. The Paliamentarians in the Lords were very largely a court-based group, many of whom seem to have decided that politics was too important to be left to kings. For Northumberland, one of the best documented of this group, it seems to have been the King's decision to persist with the Second Bishops' War, without money and in the teeth of Parliamentary opposition, which convinced him that Charles needed to be forced to listen to advice. It is likely that this was a very common attitude among the King's opponents in the Lords. In the Commons, it was a different story: there, the Parliamentarians, with a few exceptions, were those in favour of further reformation, or, as Edmund Calamy put it, of a 'second Reformation' of religion.[55] The diagnostic sign of a Parliamentarian is D'Ewes's belief that Queen Elizabeth 'rather setled a beginning of a Reformation than a Reformation'.[56] Some 85% of Parliamentarians in the Commons would have agreed with that statement, but I am aware only of a single Royalist there who would have done so. I have listed 127 members of the Commons who seem to have been in agreement with this outlook, among whom William Coryton is the solitary Royalist, and in his case, it is not impossible that his Royalism was influenced by the Commons' hostility to his election to the House. The archetypal Parliamentarian members, the people whose steadiness held the cause together through the nervous first nine months of 1642, seem to have been men such as Barrington, Masham, Irby, Harley, Sir Robert Cooke, Francis Rous, Isaac Penington, and Oliver Cromwell, and all of these were people whose commitment to Calvinist theology and to further reformation had been clear for a very long time.

On the other side, members did not quite so freely wear their creeds on their sleeves, but I have identified 90 members who were clearly against further reformation, of whom ten were Parliamentarian. Among these ten exceptions, the most important are John Selden, Henry Marten, and Sir Neville Poole. They are

[55] Edmund Calamy, *Gods Free Mercy* (1642), 7.
[56] BL Harl. MS 164, fo. 1018ᵇ. D'Ewes was speaking for Root and Branch.

enough to prevent the picture from being too tidy to be credible, but
not enough to cast doubt on the proposition that in the Commons
religion was the main thing that divided the two sides.[57] This, of
course, is not the same thing as saying that they were fighting for
religion. No doubt a number were, but since Romans 13 forbade
them to do so, they tended to deny it. It is perhaps equally important
that religion was an explanatory tool for imposing order on an
otherwise unintelligible mass of material. For many people, of
whom Smith and Wiseman the newsletter writers will serve for
good examples, religion determined what they believed to have
happened. This perhaps did as much to make it a determinant of
allegiance as any desire to fight for it.

In the country, it is very hard to make much of any simple count
of allegiance, since many chose reluctantly, and for reasons which
may have been very largely contingent. Adam Martindale is one of
many who 'would have been quiet, and meddled on no side', but he
could not clear himself of suspicion for his brother's enlisting with
the Parliament, and so decided to do likewise. For poor Martindale,
it remained the most important fact about the Civil War that it
prevented him from taking up a place at Oxford. He left his
schoolmaster, 'being allowed by him as readie for the University.
But the worst was, the University was not so readie for me'.[58]
Rather than imposing an artificial pattern on such contingent
decisions, it is perhaps better to look at those who contributed to the
driving force which helped to make the war: those who volunteered
before the raising of the standard. Many of these volunteers were
collected by county, and therefore come from a region too large and
diverse to be clearly classified, but it is instructive to list the twenty-
two cases in which Parliamentarian volunteers were collected by
town or parish. The communities involved are Nottingham,
Basingstoke, Watford, Ashford (Kent), Gloucester, Cambridge,
Dorchester (Dorset), Shrewsbury, Boston (Lincs.), Poole, Bury St
Edmunds, King's Lynn, St Albans, Canterbury, Colnbrook and
the Chiltern Hundreds, Taunton, Rayleigh (Essex), Cranbrook,

[57] For these lists see Appendix. Some of the inclusions and exclusions are
inevitably tentative, but in no case has a mere anticlerical sentiment such as
support for Bishops' Exclusion, nor an Abbot-style dislike of Arminianism,
been used as sufficient evidence to classify a man as a supporter of 'further
reformation'.
[58] *The Life of Adam Martindale*, ed. Richard Parkinson (Chetham Society,
Manchester, 1845), 28, 35.

Coventry, Bristol, Southwark, and Bridport. At least twenty of these twenty-two communities had been centres of godly preaching for a very long time, and in a number of cases centres of heresy even before the Reformation. There is surely no doubt what is the common factor between them.

On the other side of the fence, there is little doubt of the motives of the crowd that rallied to defend Norwich cathedral at Shrovetide 1642. Faced with a threat to the rails and the organs, they let the rails go, but resolved to defend the organs. The singing men rallied, ready to 'blow the rebels away with their profound sounding, roaring voices'. So did the choristers, one of whom said that 'if I do but go into church and say my prayers, and hear the organs go, they make the water run downe my cheeks, they are so sweet and so good a music.' To guard them, there was a force of 500 men, with muskets, swords, and pistols. A hostile pamphleteer commented: 'oh, how loath they are to part with their Dianas'.[59] His image was not inaccurate: what they were defending was, at one and the same time, a religion, a way of life, and a corporate identity. This incident, and what it symbolizes, are somewhere near the epitome of Royalism.

Some questions remain to be asked, including why there was so little attempt at genuine negotiation during the spring and summer of 1642. The answer to this question seems once again to be Scottish, since both sides were concentrating on trying to win support in Scotland which might have made their opponents afraid to fight, Charles working through the Scottish Privy Council, and Pym, whose eyes were already fixed on the Solemn League and Covenant of 1643, through the General Assembly, and especially through its Clerk Archibald Johnston of Wariston. Charles risked reviving Pym's Scottish alliance by his attempt to impeach the Five Members, since the article impeaching them for treasonable correspondence with the Scots infringed the Act of Oblivion, and so threatened the Scots with whom they had corresponded. Will Murray in September 1642 warned Hamilton of the dangers of such an alliance, and warned him that if the King did not satisfy the Scots, 'the two kingdoms will shatt upon him in despight of what his best servants can doe'.[60] Once again the British dimension gave the

[59] R. W. Ketton Cremer, *Norfolk in the Civil War* (1969), 142–3.

[60] Hamilton MSS 1781. This story is further developed in Russell, *FBM*, ch. 13.

English factions a fatal alternative to deciding they had to live with each other.

We have to explain one more general phenomenon, which provides a constant thread running through these events, which is best described as the problem of diminished majesty: the King's orders, when they appeared, won neither respect nor even enough fear to secure compliance, so that, as Lord Brooke put it, even some of his closest servants had 'had the courage almost to despit him to his face'.[61] It was this which enabled Lord Brooke himself to make the mistake of believing it was possible to use coercion on Charles to 'reduce him to a necessity of granting'. This error was fundamental to the junto's thinking, and only Charles's death ever served to convince them that no such pressure existed. The problem of diminished majesty showed up in many other incidents, often in themselves not of the highest importance, but indicating a state of mind which is an important part of the coming of the Civil War. For example, in January 1642 the Lords commanded the Lieutenant of the Tower to attend them, and the King commanded him not to. When the Lieutenant of the Tower (unlike his predecessor) chose to obey the King, the Lords resolved that 'the Lieutenant of the Tower had committed a high contempt to the orders of this House, in not coming, notwithstanding the King's warrant, because the King's command is always supposed to be in an order of this House'.[62]

These words are an example, not only of the necessary special pleading, but also of a fascinating impersonalization of the notion of royal authority, developed out of the long-standing notion of the King's 'Two Bodies'. This, together with the claim that the King had begun the war, and therefore that what they were doing was no more than self-defence, were the two things which enabled the Parliamentarians, with almost complete success, to avoid the necessity to formulate any theory of resistance. My favourite example of this impersonalization of royal authority is the occasion when the Houses accused the King and his forces around Hull of being guilty of a breach of the public (*sic*) peace.[63] In their Declaration of 19 May the Houses said:

---

[61] *Two Speeches* (1642), BL E. 84 (35), p. 6. I am grateful to Dr J. S. A. Adamson for drawing my attention to this source.

[62] *LJ* iv. 508.

[63] Ibid. v. 70.

we hope that his Majesty will not make his own understanding or reason the rule of his government, but will suffer himself to be assisted with a wise and prudent counsel, that may deal faithfully between him and his people: and that he will remember that his resolutions do concern kingdoms, and therefore ought not to be moulded by his own.[64]

It was this impersonalization of royal authority which made Charles ask whether he was now the only person in England against whom treason could not be committed. This impersonalization is in part a reaction to the man Charles Stuart, illustrated in Pym's remark that diseases of the brain were most dangerous,[65] but it also tells us something about the structure of authority in England in the generation before the Civil War. When we find the Royalists being described as rebels, we find an idea which, by its very apparent absurdity, should tell us something important about power and legitimacy in the country in which we find it.[66] This too is something in which Scotland anticipated England, and produced the same reaction from Charles. In reply to a Covenanter document which referred to the costs of fighting him as 'the publict burthens', Charles wrote that 'I thinke that the Kings ar part of the publicke'. This was the heart of the Royalist case.[67]

These, then, are our effects: the Bishops' Wars, England's defeat in the Bishops' Wars, the failure to reach a settlement, the failure to dissolve or prorogue the Parliament, the choice of sides, the failure to negotiate, and the problem of the King's diminished majesty. It is surely clear that nothing except perhaps Charles I can be likely to have been a cause of all seven of these. It seems to follow that we are not easily able to collect things which are, in an absolute and immediate sense, causes of the Civil War. The removal of any one of these seven things could have prevented the Civil War as we know it. We are therefore driven to investigate a more contingent sort of causation, in which we look, not directly for 'causes of the Civil War', but for causes of the events which led to the Civil War. If they are tackled individually, and not collectively, it is possible that each of these events may have causes which may be long-term and deep-rooted. In the hope of matching cause with effect, we must

[64] Rushworth, III. i. 702.   [65] *LJ* iv. 431, 532.
[66] *CJ* ii. 470; *CSPD 1641–3*, vol. ccccxcii, no. 2; Peter Lake, 'Collection of Ship Money in Cheshire', *Northern History*, 17 (1981), 65. I am grateful to Dr Richard Stewart for drawing my attention to the second of these references.
[67] Tollemache MSS, Buckminster Park, nr. Grantham, nos. 4109, 4110. I am grateful to Dr J. S. A. Adamson for these references.

attempt, in every cause we discuss in later chapters, to say which of these effects we are invoking it to explain.

It is necessary to say in what sense such an attempt will be designed to explain the causes of the English Civil War. The immediate answer to the question 'what caused the Civil War?' is the conjunction of these seven events and non-events, but to give that answer and stop there would be a piece of question-begging worthy of a barrack-room lawyer of the first water. We must take the explanation a stage further back, and explain the conjunction. Here, as in explaining the recent conjunction between the earth and Halley's Comet, we need to plot the separate movements of the individual bodies concerned, yet the study of the movements of one body, however necessary, can never be more than half the explanation of the conjunction. That will not produce a simple picture, but I hope it may have some approximation to the truth.

It is not, of course, suggested that these events were the key things in English history before 1642. They were not the most significant tensions, the most insoluble difficulties, or the greatest causes of anger. Their significance is more contingent than that. They mark moments when the political story took a key change of direction. It was not self-evident, or even necessarily very probable, that a crisis which began with Scots throwing stones at a bishop in Edinburgh in 1637 should lead to Englishmen fighting each other in Warwickshire in 1642. In 1637, many other resolutions of the crisis were possible, and in many cases much more probable. These key events are important because they prevented the crisis from being resolved in any of these other ways. Political passion, like a river in spate, must flow somewhere. It turned to English Civil War in 1642 because all other channels were blocked. The reasons why that was so were in part a problem for *l'histoire évènementielle*, and that story is told in *The Fall of the British Monarchies*. However, even contingent events may not always happen purely for short-term reasons. We have here seven consecutive moments when, for want of a nail, the shoe was lost. If any one of those shoes had been kept, the result would have been different. Yet, if a horse loses seven shoes in a row, we may ask what was wrong with the blacksmiths and the farriers. It is that question which leads us into the long-term issues.

2

The Problem of Multiple Kingdoms
c. 1580–1630

In 1645 the Earl of Berkshire, one of the reluctant Royalists among Charles's Privy Councillors, complained that 'noe body can tell what we have fought about all this whyle'.[1] It is arguable that his successors in the task have not done much better. The central difficulty about explaining the Civil War as a purely English phenomenon is that there does not appear to be enough head of steam to justify an explosion on the scale which resulted, and when we do find an issue which generated enough steam, it often turns out to be an issue more likely to unite the country than to divide it.

One of the moments when we may begin to see daylight on this question is when we realize that historians of the Irish Rebellion are faced with a closely parallel problem. The Irish Rebellion, like the English Civil War, was for more limited aims than its subsequent admirers have supposed: it was no more a movement for Irish independence than the English was for Parliamentary sovereignty. Like the English, it was not the result of a long and inevitable crescendo of tension, and Aidan Clarke has gone so far as to describe it as 'a startling interruption of a mood of peaceful cooperation'.[2] This is a more extreme revisionism than I have ever attempted for England. The remark perhaps illustrates that Irish standards of 'peaceful cooperation' were less exacting than English ones, but, with that qualification, Aidan Clarke's point is surely valid. It is hard to improve on his own example of it, which is the method by which the rebel leader Sir Phelim O'Neill surprised Charlemont Castle on the opening day of the rebellion: he dropped in for dinner.[3] Caulfield, the owner, was not O'Neill's only Protestant

---

[1] KAO U. 269/C 292. I am grateful to Dr J. S. A. Adamson for this reference.
[2] Aidan Clarke, 'Ireland and the General Crisis', *Past and Present*, 48 (1970), 86.
[3] Id., 'Genesis of the Ulster Rising of 1641', in Peter Roebuck and J. L. McCracken (eds.), *From Plantation to Partition* (Belfast, 1981), 35. I have not followed Professor Clarke's reservations about the use of the word 'rebellion', which relate to the intentions of the participants rather than to their actions.

friend. Rawdon, Conway's regular Irish informant, wrote that he feared the commander of the rebels was 'my friend, Sir Phill. O'Neill'.[4] The point is made again in an agitated letter from a gentleman of Kerry who wanted to shelter from the rebels in the Earl of Cork's castle, because 'my house I built for peace, it having more windows than wales'.[5] In Ireland, as in England, the 1630s had generated plenty of discontent, but this had tended to unite the country rather than to divide it: as Aidan Clarke said, 'one of the features of his [Wentworth's] administration had been the impartiality with which it had trespassed upon the interests of all and sundry'.[6] Indeed, the Irish Parliament of 1640–1 sometimes suggests that Strafford deserves the distinction of being named as the only Englishman who has ever obliterated the religious divide in Irish politics. Aidan Clarke is entitled to his argument that the participation of the Old English in the rebellion was not the result of inexorable changes in their status, but of the particular circumstances of 1641.

These quotations suggest that English and Irish historians are facing a common historiographical problem. The extent of our common difficulty perhaps suggests that we ought to take it more seriously, and that, instead of treating it as one of those awkward things we must explain away, we should make it a major premiss of our investigation. When Aidan Clarke remarked that 'the attempt to recover royal authority in Scotland weakened it elsewhere',[7] he seems to have been looking in the same direction as I am. Our common difficulty suggests two major hypotheses.

The first is the hypothesis that the main disruptive force in both England and Ireland was the problem of multiple kingdoms: both of them were first destabilized by Charles's efforts to call on them to repress his subjects of Scotland, and both of them were further divided between 1639 and 1642 by the continual intrusion of the other two into their domestic affairs. During those years, there was a constant billiard-ball effect of each of the kingdoms on the affairs of the others. To take a few examples, the troubled history of legislation by ordinance begins with its use by the Irish Parliament

---

[4] PRO SP 63/260/35.
[5] BL Egerton MS 80, fo. 6[r].
[6] Aidan Clarke, 'Policies of the Old English in Parliament 1640–1641', in J. L. McCracken (ed.), *Historical Studies*, 5 (1965), 88.
[7] *NHI* iii. 267.

as a device for evading the requirements of Poynings's Law.[8] The English Triennial Act of 1641 first surfaced in public as a Scottish negotiating proposal in October 1640:[9] since the Scots had correctly identified the English Parliament as the seat of their English friends' influence, they therefore equally correctly identified the strengthening of the English Parliament as a way of making peace with England more secure. The English proposal, advanced through the winter of 1641–2, for the great officers and Privy Council to be chosen in Parliament, was a deliberate and conscious attempt to copy the settlement Charles conceded to the Scots in September 1641.[10] The attempt during 1642 to deprive the King of his negative voice in England followed the recent practice of the Scottish Parliament, and was hotly championed by Nathaniel Fiennes, who had been in Scotland in 1639. The belief that Nathaniel Fiennes had been in Scotland in 1639 has hitherto rested only on the authority of Clarendon. As so often, the penance for disbelieving a specific factual statement by Clarendon has turned out to be a long pilgrimage to a remote archive, in this case to Traquair House. Dr Peter Donald, who has made this pilgrimage, has there discovered a letter from Traquair to Hamilton, noting Fiennes's presence in Scotland on 10 August 1639.[11] The attempt in the summer of 1641 to amend the Root and Branch bill in the English Parliament, in order to make it apply to Ireland, was made by Sir John Clotworthy, who was not only one of the Scots' best friends at Westminster, but also an Ulsterman concerned with the interests of the Scots in Ireland.[12] These examples tend to sustain the proposition that the problem of multiple kingdoms had a major influence on the daily development of the crisis which led to the English Civil War. If this proposition is correct, it would bring Britain into line with much else that was happening in Europe. The cases of Catalonia and Portugal are sufficiently familiar, though an Englishman in Catalonia might have echoed the comment of the

---

[8] Hamilton MSS 803; PRO SP 63/258/82, 259/9 and 60, 274/9; Patrick Darcey, *An Argument* (Dublin, 1764), 61–3.

[9] PRO SP 16/471/22.

[10] *Nicholas Papers*, i (Camden Society, NS 40, 1886), 52; *PJ* i. 99 and other refs. This case will be further developed in Russell, *FBM*.

[11] Peter Donald, 'The King and the Scottish Troubles 1637–1641', Ph.D. thesis (Cambridge, 1988), 305, 305 nn. I am grateful to Dr Donald for permission to quote from his thesis.

[12] BL Harl. MS 5047. fo. 30[r].

Spanish veteran from the Netherlands who said that 'only the preachers are missing to make them lose their faith along with their obedience'.[13] Mention of the Netherlands reminds us of one of the rare cases where, as in Britain, the problem of multiple kingdoms was combined with the problem of difference in religion, and both examples suggest that it was a highly volatile mixture. The basic difficulty, as Charles I and Philip II both found, was that it was extremely difficult for a ruler to permit in one kingdom doctrines which he prohibited in another. He could not handle any kingdom simply in the interests of that kingdom, without constantly looking over his shoulder at the effect on the other kingdoms. The hypothesis that the problem of multiple kingdoms was a major cause of instability in Britain looks perfectly plausible when considered in a European context.

My other hypothesis is that the Scottish crisis which began in 1637 deserves logical, as well as chronological, pride of place in the explanation of the British troubles. No one has ever argued for Scotland, as they have for England and Ireland, that there was not sufficient combustible material to explain what happened, nor that there was not sufficient depth of ideological difference. We should consider the hypothesis that until well on in the 1640s the major conflict in the British Isles was that between the King and the Scottish Covenanters and that it was the inability to resolve that conflict in any durable way which pushed the King's other kingdoms into choosing sides between them. At least one contemporary foresaw that the Scottish crisis was capable of having this effect. Hamilton in June 1638 asked the King 'how you can effect your end, without the haserding of your 3 crownes'. He warned the King that reliance on England to suppress Scotland would drive England into rebellion. To the Covenanter Earl of Rothes, Hamilton said that if this came to pass, 'he doubted if ever he sall see peace in this kingdome againe'.[14]

The brief of this chapter, concerned as it is with the origins of the English Civil War, imposes a kind of tunnel vision on any study of the British problem from 1603. Themes which would be vital in a study of the British problem in its own right become peripheral in a study of its contribution to the causes of the English Civil War. We will not, for example, be able to investigate the issues behind Lord

---

[13] J. H. Elliott, *Revolt of the Catalans* (Cambridge, 1963), 368.
[14] Hamilton MSS 327.1; Rothes, p. 137.

Chancellor Dunfermline's query of Salisbury in 1606, whether the English ambassador in Paris would represent the Scots, or the Scottish insistence in 1610 that copies of any treaties agreed in London should be deposited in Edinburgh.[15] These things are more vital as part of the long-term causes of 1707 than of 1642. War, one of the major causes of strain in multiple kingdoms, was mercifully absent for the whole of the reign of James VI and I, and for all but the first few years of the reign of Charles I. During Charles's first years, London's Castilian determination to copy Olivares's union of arms made a significant contribution to the origins of the Irish Rebellion, but did not do as much visible damage as might have been expected to Anglo–Scottish relations.[16] However, the fact that some of the bitterest English protests at billeting were aimed at the Scottish regiment of the Earl of Morton and the Irish regiment of Sir Piers Crosby is unlikely to be coincidental. It suggests that James's original aim of a 'union of love' was still a long way from realization.[17] James's on-the-whole successful resolution of the problem of distribution of offices, and the tensions surrounding his Scottish Bedchamber, will not be developed as they should be in a narrative account, since they seem to make little direct contribution to the origins of the English Civil War.[18] It should be stressed that Dr Galloway seems to be correct that there was no flood of 'hungry Scots' to London in 1604. There was significant Scottish representation in the Bedchamber, whose members, as the King's personal attendants, naturally included some who were both the King's old friends and his fellow-countrymen. Otherwise, the number of Scots appointed to office appears to be very moderate. What then becomes interesting is the undoubted existence of a contrary myth among the English. This is perhaps attributable to the shock the English

[15] *CSPD 1603–10*, vol. xix, no. 88; Jenny Wormald, 'James VI and I: Two Kings or One?', *History*, 68 (1983), 190. For a rare case of an English ambassador acting in a Scottish interest, see PRO SP 77/30, fo. 37ʳ.

[16] Secretary Coke's plan to copy the Union of Arms is in PRO SP 16/527/44. Its concrete results seem to have been the Scottish regiment of the Earl of Morton, the Irish regiment of Sir Piers Crosby, and the Graces in Ireland, on which see below, pp. 54–7, 128–9.

[17] L. O. J. Boynton, 'Billeting: The Example of the Isle of Wight', *EHR* 74/ 290 (1959), 23–40; G. E. Aylmer, 'St. Patrick's Day in Witham, Essex', *Past and Present*, 61 (1973), 139–48. I am grateful to Dr R. P. Cust for discussion of Sir Piers Crosby's regiment. It should be recorded that the Scots in the Isle of Wight were Highlanders.

[18] On the Bedchamber, see Neil Cuddy, 'Revival of the Entourage', in David Starkey (ed.) *The English Court* (1987), 173–225.

suffered at the discovery that they were not the only pebbles on the British beach. Dr Cuddy has, it is true, found tensions aroused by the King's Scottish Bedchamber, but it is hard to make such tensions into a cause of civil war, since under Charles it was their absence, not their presence, which was a harbinger of the crisis of 1637.[19]

The questions among our original seven to which this chapter is directed are why there were Bishops' Wars, why there was no settlement in 1641, why there was no dissolution of the English Parliament, and why there was no negotiation in 1642. To explain the absence of a settlement, we must explain what was perhaps the single most divisive force in England in 1641: the Scottish Covenanters' commitment to a 'Scottish imperial' vision of British unity, which involved forcing England into uniformity with the Scottish church. Since this is perhaps the hardest thing in the story for an English historian to understand, it demands the lion's share of the space. This Scottish imperial vision of the church is particularly relevant to two of our seven questions. It is particularly relevant to the failure to achieve a settlement in 1641, since the Scots, who had created the opportunity for the English to negotiate for one, also went a long way to deprive them of the chance to take advantage of it. This Scottish imperial vision is also highly relevant to the failure to achieve meaningful negotiations in the summer of 1642, since it seems that Pym and Hampden, rather than backing Northumberland's efforts to negotiate with the King, preferred to work for the Scottish alliance they were to achieve in the Solemn League and Covenant of 1643. It was this Scottish imperial vision, especially as held by Archibald Johnston of Wariston, that provided most of the Scottish interventionist sentiment with which they chose to work.[20]

The relevance of Irish affairs to the coming of the English Civil War arises mainly from the question why the Long Parliament was not dissolved. Once the Irish Rebellion of October 1641 was under way, Charles could not dissolve or prorogue the Long Parliament without sacrificing one of his three kingdoms, a prospect which he found unacceptable. The causes of the Irish Rebellion, then, are causes at one remove of the failure to dissolve the English

[19] Bruce Galloway, *Union of England and Scotland* (Edinburgh, 1986), 17; Brian Levack, *Formation of the British State* (Oxford, 1987), 61.
[20] The evidence for this judgement will be rehearsed at length in Russell, *FBM*.

Parliament, and therefore a necessary part of our story. The distinctive difficulties of James VI and I, in all three of his kingdoms, were usually in matters of money rather than of religion, and in this, we will find that the government of Jacobean Ireland is no exception. Where the Irish story is peculiar is the fact that, because of the revenue implications of the policy of plantation, attempts to improve Irish revenue were always likely to have religious implications.

In the opening years of the reign of Charles, the need to finance the war heightened all difficulties involving revenue, and in this too Ireland was no exception. In the years 1625–9 Charles's government was eager to encourage Ireland to contribute to the costs of its own defence, and in Ireland, as later in America, that issue is an important part of the background to rebellion. It will therefore be necessary, in order to understand why the Long Parliament was not dissolved, to understand some of the hopes and fears raised in Ireland by the negotiations to encourage it to contribute to its own defence.

In Scotland, by contrast, royal revenues were never large enough to become a significant part of the calculations of any British king, and for this among other reasons, Anglo–Scottish problems were always more nearly exclusively religious in character than Anglo–Irish ones. To understand the Scottish imperial ambitions of 1641, in particular, we must look at the ambivalences in the relationship between the Scottish and English churches right back to the Scottish Reformation in 1559–60. The Scottish Reformation was carried through by the pro-English party in Scotland, with English armed help, and for a long time, was guaranteed by the likelihood of English protection against any hostile French intervention.

Nevertheless, the Scots, even while in this state of semi-dependency, had achieved a fuller and more perfect reformation than their English protectors had been able to achieve for themselves. This discrepancy encouraged English reformers to look to Scotland as a pattern to be emulated, and all the more so because English intervention had brought about this wished-for result. In this, the Scots' allies of 1641 were heirs to a long tradition. Bishop Jewel wrote in August 1559 that 'the theatrical dresses, the sacrilegious chalices, the idols, the altars, are consigned to the flames: not a vestige of the ancient superstition and idolatry is left'. This passage must surely be read in the light of his voluble dismay at the failure to achieve exactly the same thing in England. A year later, Bishop Parkhurst remarked wistfully that 'the Scots have made greater progress in true religion in a few months, than we have done in many years'.[21] It can only have made the contrast more poignant that, within a dozen years, Jewel and Parkhurst themselves were being blamed for it. In the First Admonition to Parliament in 1572, the Scottish example was invoked, as it was in 1641, to support the case that bishops themselves were an obstacle to reformation, and that only a Presbyterian discipline could bring it about: 'is discipline meet for Scotland? and is it unprofitable to this realm? Surely God hath set these examples before your eyes to encourage you to go forward to a speedy and a thorough reformation'.[22]

The difference between the churches caused tension on the Scottish side of the Border too, and there, the combination of physical dependence and spiritual superiority was one which challenged the preaching mentality to show its mettle. Scottish desire to contribute to the reformation of England, as well as English desire to emulate Scotland, goes back to the 1560s, and it was a desire designed to satisfy Scottish honour, as well as godly zeal. In 1566 the Scottish General Assembly drafted a letter of protest against Parker's *Advertisements*. The task of delivering this letter was assigned to John Knox, who hoped to go to England to see his children. In 1583, after consultation with John Field the English Presbyterian, the General Assembly asked Whitgift and his fellow-bishops to 'disburden their brether of England of the yoke of ceremonies imposed to them against the liberty of the word'.[23] The Scottish Covenanters of the Civil-War period remained aware of this past, and in 1640 the Covenanter pamphlet, *The Lawfulnesse of our Expedition into England Manifested*, accompanied its promise to bring about the reformation of England with thanks for the help England had given to the Scottish Reformation, in freeing Scotland from the French.[24] It is hard to believe that this statement was made without any pleasure at the thought that the reforming boot was now on the Scottish foot.

[21] *ZL* i. 39–40, 91.   [22] Collinson, *EPM*, p. 115.
[23] Peterkin, pp. 49–50, 271. The best exposition of the context remains Gordon Donaldson, 'Attitude of Whitgift and Bancroft to the Scottish Church', *TRHS*, 24 (1942), 95–115.
[24] *Lawfulnesse of our Expedition into England Manifested* (Edinburgh, 1640), Sig. A. 4.

Because the ideal of closer union of the English and Scottish churches was already a well-established one, perception of, and even pleasure in, the obstacles in its way were also well established. The most serious of these obstacles was that England and Scotland had fundamentally opposed mythologies of what 'reformation' was. The English Reformation, at least in a legal sense, was carried through by the power of the State, and its great documents were Acts of Parliament asserting the authority of Parliamentary statute over all manner of persons and causes. To the English, the claim to clerical autonomy was one of the things the Reformation had been against, and therefore a mark of 'popery'. Thomas Becket was, and remained, the archetypal popish traitor.

The Scottish Reformation, on the other hand, was carried through in the face of the opposition of the Regent and the reluctance of the Sovereign, and was enforced by Acts of Parliament which were treated as valid although they had never achieved the royal assent. As their leaders told William Cecil, 'we have against us the established authority, which ever favoured you and Denmark in your reformations'.[25] The Scottish Reformation was the classic example of reformation without tarrying for the magistrate, and one of very few successful examples of its kind anywhere in Europe. Because the Scottish Reformation was achieved against the State and not by it, the independence of the church from the State tended to become a mark of reformation rather than of popery, and the hotter Scottish reformers located ultimate authority, not in the Parliament, but in the General Assembly of the Kirk. This enabled the Scots to draw more heavily than the English on the precedents and ideas of the conciliar movement,[26] and to drive them back on an ascending theory of power, which saw ultimate authority residing in the General Assembly because it was the 'representative kirk' of a church which was a 'perfect republick'.[27] The Scots, or at least the stricter among them, constantly bewildered such Erastian Parlia-

---

[25] Jenny Wormald, *Court, Kirk and Community* (1981), 100–23, esp. pp. 113–14, 117; also ead., *Mary Queen of Scots* (1988), 90–128. Mary's presence in Scotland does not appear to mark as clear an end to her symbolic absence as it might have done.

[26] Calderwood, iv. 10; J. H. Burns, 'Scotland and England: Culture and Nationality 1500–1800', in J. S. Bromley and E. H. Kossmann (eds.), *Britain and the Netherlands*, iv (1971), 22.

[27] Rothes, pp. 45–6. *Reasons for a Generall Assemblie* (1638), Sig. B. 1; *An Answer* (1639), 48–52; *Reasons* (1638), Sig. A. 2.

mentarians among their English allies as Saye by restricting the power of their Parliament in religion as much as they restricted the power of their King. Andrew Melville was the spiritual heir of Thomas Becket (a comparison which implies a highly favourable one between James VI and Henry II), and he and his successors could never understand any definition of 'popery' which made Becket its epitome. Melville, like Becket himself, never enjoyed the full confidence or agreement of his presbyterial colleagues. Yet like Becket, he supplied the ideal on which his successors (even some of those who thought it could be taken too seriously) were liable to fall back under stress. It was these two points, the autonomy of the church and the ascending theory of power, on which the English and the Scots remained convinced that each other's ideals savoured of popery. They were two nations divided by a common language.

The existence of each church therefore constituted a standing threat to the ideals of the other. This was the truer because in neither country was the national mythology universal. In both of them, one of the major causes of instability was the existence of a vigorous minority who preferred the system of the other country to their own. For Anglicizing Scots and for Scotticizing Englishmen, the ion of the crowns, and perhaps even more the prospect of the union of the crowns, represented both a danger and an opportunity. The readiness of these groups to seize any chance to assimilate themselves to the other country's church created alarm inside their own countries. They encouraged the dominant figures in their own churches to protect themselves against the importation of a rival system by seizing any chance to export their own.

This was not a new phenomenon in the Long Parliament. In 1641 the Scottish Commissioners, presenting their charge against Laud, alleged that

from the first time of the reformation of the kirk of Scotland, not only after the coming of King James of happy memory into England, but before, the prelates of England have beene by all meanes incessantly working the overthrow of our discipline and government.

Laud's reply simply reverses the charge:

A little change in the words answers this. For from the very first of the reformation of the church of England, as well before, as after, the coming in of King James of happy memory, the presbyters of Scotland have been by all meanes incessantly working the overthrow of episcopacy, our discipline and government: as appears most manifestly in Archbishop Bancroft's works.[28]

Both these charges are correct. In particular, they are correct in dating the first significant appearance of the phenomenon to the 1580s, the time when Protestants began to think seriously about the possible ecclesiastical implications of the union of the crowns.

The 1580s, and particularly the presence of a group of Scottish Presbyterian exiles in England in 1583–4, produced what Professor Donaldson has described as 'a curious anticipation of that alliance which, in the next century, was to produce the Solemn League and Convenant'.[29] The history of this 'anticipation', and in particular of the way it polarized opinion in both countries, can add a good deal to the understanding of what happened later. The political circumstances of the 1580s never became such as to bring these issues to a head, but the record suggests that, given the right political climate, the divisive force of these questions of Anglo–Scottish union might have become very great. The absence of the Laudian dimension in England of course helped to damp the problem down, but even without it, English resistance to the 'pretended holy discipline' would clearly have been intense. So, too, was the Scottish resistance to Anglicization, most clearly voiced by David Calderwood. Both emotions survived to plague Charles I.

The two national minorities, who wanted to import each other's ecclesiastical systems, were led by John Field the Presbyterian in England, and by Patrick Adamson Archbishop of St Andrews in Scotland. Anglo–Scottish Presbyterian links can be traced back to 1571–2, when Andrew Melville and Thomas Cartwright were in exile together at Geneva, but it was Field's relationship with the Scottish Presbyterian exiles in England in 1583–4 which bound the two Presbyterian movements together. The support given to the Scottish exiles by Walsingham, Davison, and Beale suggests that it was not only under Charles I that leading figures in England were willing to turn to Scottish influence to limit the excesses of their Archbishop, and even of their monarch.

[28] Laud, *Wks.* iii. 380. I would like to thank my wife for drawing my attention to this reference.
[29] Gordon Donaldson, 'Scottish Presbyterian Exiles in England 1584–8' (Records of the Scottish Church History Society, 14, 1960), 80. I would like to thank Dr Nicholas Tyacke for drawing my attention to this article. Also Donaldson, 'Attitude of Whitgift and Bancroft to the Scottish Church', pp. 95–115.

It was in response to their influence, and in alarm at it, that Archbishop Adamson, who came to England in the winter of 1583–4, established a rival network of Anglo–Scottish contacts. Where the Scottish Presbyterians had looked to Walsingham and Davison, Adamson looked to Whitgift and Burghley. Like Field, Adamson sailed under the banner of British uniformity. He told Whitgift that 'I shall endeavour myself to the preservation of ye true religion professit in the whole yle, and common quietnes and mutuall amitie of her majestie and our master'.[30] Adamson concentrated on the causes of episocopacy and royal authority: he asked Whitgift for a work setting out English ideas on 'ecclesiastical polity',[31] and it is tempting to wonder whether, many years later, that was exactly what he got. It is possible that Adamson had more in common with the new school of English Protestants than this, and his complaint that his opponents were fetching the office of a pastor out of the schools of rhetoric was certainly one that Bancroft and Howson would have understood.[32]

Scottish Presbyterians also suspected that Adamson's visit to England had something to do with Scottish hopes of the English succession. His behaviour on his return to Scotland strengthened this suspicion, since it was quickly followed by the Black Acts, the first attempt to change the kirk of Scotland to bring it into line with the church of England. The most important of the Black Acts was in effect a repetition of that most English of Acts, the Statute of Praemunire. Adamson was one of the Lords of the Articles who produced this Act, and he later justified it in a Declaration which included such English-sounding claims as that the King had the same power in his realm which the Emperor had in the Empire.[33] All this makes it plausible to see the programme of the Black Acts as influenced by ideas Adamson brought back from England, and probably as designed to make the King of Scots a more acceptable successor to the kingdom of England. This seems to have been the view of his opponents, who in 1591 made Adamson recant the view that 'I believed the government of the kirk to be like unto the kingdoms of the earth'.[34]

[30] BL Add. MS 32,092, fo. 79ᵛ. [31] Ibid., fo. 42ʳ.
[32] Patrick Adamson, *De Sacro Pastoris Munere* (*s.l.*, 1619), 1. See also Calderwood iv. 104 and other refs.
[33] *A Declaration* (Edinburgh, 1585), Sig. B. 3.
[34] Calderwood, iv. 50–5; *Recantation of Maister Patrik Adamsone* (1598), Sig. A. 4 and B. 1.

As always, proposals for the closer union of the two kingdoms generated their mirror image; they generated rival union proposals from the other side. In 1590, when the boot was on the other foot, John Davidson, who had been one of the Scottish exile ministers in England, came up with what sounds very like a proposal to anticipate the Westminster Assembly. He asked for the question of discipline to be decided by 'the word of God in a lawfull assemblie and brotherlie conference appointed by the supreme magistrates to that effect'.[35] Bancroft may well have been correct in believing that Cope's Presbyterian Bill and Book in the Parliament of 1586–7 should be seen in the same context.

In the 1580s, as in the 1640s, proposals to assimilate the systems of the two countries to each other created vehement nationalist reactions. English resistance to 'Scotticizing discipline' was most clearly articulated by Bancroft. In the process, Bancroft made himself the spiritual father of the Royalist party, which was created round the same cause. In Scotland, the suspicion of creeping conformity with England was most clearly articulated by David Calderwood, who made it one of the central themes running through his History of the Kirk. Calderwood was not merely one of the spiritual fathers of the Covenant, but lived to write in its support. The dangers attendant on moves towards closer union in religion between the two countries were therefore clear for all to see well before the union of the crowns in 1603. The Commissioners of the Scottish synods summed up the problem in 1604: they said the two realms could not be united 'without unioun and conformitie of the kirks, government and worship: how could the kirks be united, unless one gave place to the other?'[36]

These fears were ones that the Covenanters had not forgotten. A Covenanter pamphleteer in 1640, possibly Johnston of Wariston, explained how 'the Lord has followed the back-trade of our defection', by which he meant much the same as John Le Carré means by 'taking back bearings'. The conclusion was that 'this back trade leadeth yet further, to the prelacy in England, the fountaine whence all these Babylonish streams issued unto us: the Lord therefore is still on the back trade, and we following him cannot yet

---

[35] John Davidson, D. Bancroft's Rashnes (Edinburgh, 1590), 29: my italic.
[36] Calderwood, iv. 257–8.

be at a stay'.[37] This passage illustrates the fact that the 1580s are relevant in more ways than as a high-risk period in Anglo–Scottish relations. They also made a vital contribution to the growth of Covenanter mythology, and supplied a pattern of fighting English policy by co-operation with English allies of which the Twelve Peers in 1640 were very ready to take advantage.

Those who had learnt this lesson by 1603 appear to have included James VI, and for this reason among others, fears for the independence of the English and Scottish churches, though still present, were less acute during the debates of 1603–7 than they had been in the 1580s. It was not until Charles was on the throne, and appointed himself the heir of Patrick Adamson, that the pattern of the debate of the 1580s was revived. The characteristic anxieties of 1603–7 centred on another question which was to add to the tensions over the Scottish National Covenant: the question of how to merge two legislative sovereignties. This question also inevitably raised the problem of the relations between one King and two Parliaments. It was this question which caused anxiety to such men as Sir Edwin Sandys and Nicholas Fuller, anxieties which can only have been made worse when Francis Bacon told the English Parliament that this treaty was 'a notable opportunity to mend our state'. Any English members who knew that these plans included the introduction of the Scottish Lords of the Articles to control Parliamentary proceedings might be forgiven their anxieties.[38]

Much of the English discussion in 1603–7 centred on alternative models of union, of which the British Isles provided three. The first was that of the union with Wales, which involved none of the problems of multiple kingdoms, since England and Wales were a unitary state, with one law, one Parliament, one church, one Privy Council, and one judicial system. The attractions of such a union to the English were obvious, but the very same things which made it attractive to the English did (and do) make it unattractive to the Scots. The second form was that with Ireland, a relationship more complicated than that with a pure colony, since Ireland had its own Privy Council, Parliament, and legal system. Nevertheless, Ireland was clearly in a subordinate relationship to England, a subordination

[37] *Lawfulnesse of our Expedition into England Manifested*, Sig. A. 3 (STC 21, 923).
[38] *CJ* i. 182; *Jacobean Union*, ed. Bruce R. Galloway and Brian P. Levack (Scottish Historical Society, Edinburgh, 1985), pp. xxxviii–xxxix.

symbolized by Poynings's Law, which made it impossible to introduce any bills in the Irish Parliament unless they had been approved in England, in practice by the English Privy Council. According to the French Ambassador, many Scots feared this pattern might be applied to them.[39] The third type of union, which actually existed between England and Scotland, was like the union between Castile and Aragon. It was a union of the crowns of two sovereign and independent states, with two Privy Councils, two Parliaments, two legal systems, and two churches. England and Scotland might be unequal in terms of size, power, population, and wealth, but in terms of legal sovereignty, they were two equal and independent states. It is arguable that much of the difficulty the English did (and do) suffer from the Union has resulted from their reluctance to accept the fact of Scottish legal and cultural separateness.

The only institution common to both states in 1603 was the King, and even he had to go to court in Calvin's Case to answer the famous question repeated by Dr Wormald, whether he was two kings or one. This was, literally, the issue in Calvin's Case. The question on which Calvin's claim to English nationality came to hang was whether English and Scottish allegiance were one allegiance or two. This in turn came to hang on the question whether allegiance was due to the laws, which were several, and produced two different citizenships, or to the King, who was single, and therefore attracted a single allegiance. The decision that allegiance was due to the King and not to the law highlights the fact that such men as Fuller and Sandys were not irrational in fearing that the Union might increase the King's power against that of a law and a Parliament which any full union would reduce to provincial, instead of national, status.[40]

James, while stopping well short of perfect union, nevertheless wanted a sacrifice of name, and therefore of some independent identity, on both sides. It was the issue of the name, and the closely related issue of union of laws, which caused alarm in the English Parliamentary session of 1604. Any plan for the union of laws would involve, as they put it, 'erecting a new kingdom', and therefore new laws. 'If a new name, a new kingdom, as of an island

[39] *Jacobean Union*, ed. Galloway and Levack, p. xxv n.
[40] Wormald, 'James VI and I', pp. 187–209; Sir Edward Coke, *Seventh Report*, 4–10. See also the remarks of Sandys in PRO SP 14/7/63 and Bowyer, pp. 258–9. For Fuller, see Bowyer, pp. 265–6.

discovered; of a conquered kingdom'. As Nicholas Fuller said, 'nolumus leges et nomen Angliae mutare'[41]—a feeling which made a considerable contribution to the drafting of the Apology of the Commons. Moreover, as Sandys pointed out, neither the Parliament of England nor the Parliament of Scotland could legislate for the new United Kingdom, and the result would be to strengthen the Crown as the only British institution.[42] If, as Thomas Hedley feared, the King met this situation by using his prerogative to create new Parliamentary constituencies in order to summon the Scots to the Westminster Parliament, he would gain the power to control the Parliament by controlling its membership—a fear which may not be irrelevant to the case of Goodwin v. Fortescue.[43] All this created a strong desire in the English Parliament to assimilate the pattern of the union with Scotland to the pattern of the union with Wales. Thus, as Sandys put it, 'the government of other countries shall be brought to ours', and, in Justice Warburton's words, Scotland should become 'parcel of England'.[44]

These points might sound well to English lawyers, but, as the Earl of Mar twice warned Cecil, they sounded a lot less well in Edinburgh.[45] Scottish fears about the Union centred on the remark attributed by Polydore Vergil to Henry VII, that 'the greater will draw the less'. It was this fear which made the Scots resistant to any proposal for union of laws, and encouraged them to identify Scottish identity with the survival of a separate system of Scottish law and of a separate Scottish church. Russell, an Edinburgh lawyer, insisted that the union was a union of equals, 'not of Scotland as subalterne to Ingland, quhilk wil be na unioun, but ane plaine discord—Thairby ancienne Scotland to loss hir beautie for evir! God forbid!' He feared Scotland might be made a 'pendicle' of England, a word which occurs constantly at moments of maximum Scottish anxiety. Russell feared Scotland might sink to this status if it lost its church or its legislative sovereignty, and that so England would gain what they had failed to gain by conquest.[46] This fear of loss of legislative

---

[41] Brian Levack, *Formation of the British State* (Oxford, 1987), 38; *CJ* i. 957.
[42] PRO SP 14/7/63.
[43] Levack, *Formation of the British State*, pp. 37–8; Galloway, *Union of England and Scotland*, p. 41.
[44] Levack, *Formation of the British State*, pp. 27, 39; *CJ* i. 952.
[45] PRO SP 14/8/9 and 10.
[46] *Jacobean Union*, ed. Galloway and Levack, pp. 27, 84, 98.

sovereignty became increasingly central in Scottish thinking about the Union.

The Scots, on the whole, were remarkably realistic in accepting the status of junior partner because they were the smaller and poorer kingdom, and the less regular seat of the king's residence. Yet the very effort they made to be realistic about the extent of English superiority made them the more insistent on the one place where they had always claimed primacy: they had the better reformed church. As Russell put it, 'as to religioun (praysit be God) thair is na reformit kirk in Europe injoyis the puritie of the evangell in greater sinceritie than Scotland. It war to the great advantage of England the lyik were thair'.[47] For many Scots, any suggestion of religious union with England both threatened their one claim to primacy and called their legislative sovereignty in question. For that reason, religious union, as Dr Galloway has said, 'raised offensive implications of inequality between the two nations'.[48] The Scottish Parliament of 1604 aimed to confirm their security by passing an Act (later rehearsed in the Scottish National Covenant) depriving the Commissioners for the Union of power to alter anything in the Scottish church, or any Act relating to it. This provision was repeated in the Act of Union of 1707, so Parliamentary inability to alter the Scottish church may be a unique exception to the principle that an Act of Parliament may do whatever it likes. Since the Act of Union was in its original form a treaty, it may at least be said that any attempt to alter it revives the issue of Scottish legislative sovereignty.[49]

It was a misfortune to James that the Moderator of the General Assembly in office in 1604 happened to be James Melville, and, as anyone who knew James Melville might have predicted, he thought attack the best form of defence. When Patrick Galloway's report of the Hampton Court Conference was read to the Presbytery of Edinburgh, James Melville happened to be among those present. He instantly asked his colleagues to pray for the brethren of England, 'who having expected a reformation are disappointed and heavily grieved', and at the same time exhorted them to 'take heed that no perell or contagioun come from our neighbour kirk'.[50]

---

[47] *Jacobean Union*, ed. Galloway and Levack, p. 88.
[48] Galloway, *Union of England and Scotland*, p. 74.
[49] *APS* 4. 264; Levack, *Formation of the British State*, pp. 124, 134–5.
[50] Calderwood, vi. 246–7.

Melville had identified the safety of the Scottish church with the reformation of the English, and in this he was the true spiritual ancestor of Johnston of Wariston and the Covenanters of 1641. Melville kept up his English Presbyterian contacts, and in 1607, while in exile in England, was offered a bag of money from his English brethren by the committed Presbyterian Edmund Snape. The fact that Melville refused this money on the grounds that the Scots were suspected of coming to beg tells us volumes about Scottish sensitivity to loose English talk.[51] Yet, though Melville kept his contacts, he and Snape never represented any significant threat to James VI and I after 1603. James VI proved he could detach moderates from extremists as skilfully as James I, and the period from 1603 to 1625 was one of almost continuous defeat for the Melvilles and their ideals. Yet their ideals were not forgotten, and were there ready for reviving when they were again needed in 1637–8.

For many Scottish Jacobeans, such as Robert Pont, the consolations of the union included the prospect of increased Scottish influence in Ireland, 'so that the savadg wildnes of the Irish, and the barbarous fiercenes of the other ilanders, shall easily be tamed'.[52] This prospect was welcomed from the New English perspective in Ireland, and Sir Henry Docwra wrote to Cecil asking him to settle the state of the country by sending some Scots to inhabit it. This idea was not universally popular, and some people were found protesting that 'we will not have a Scot to be our king'.[53] Nevertheless, by James's death, there were some 8,000 adult male Scots resident in Ulster, and James had planted what was to become a major British problem in its own right.[54] Nevertheless, though the plantation of Ulster contributed heavily to the Irish Rebellion of 1641, it did not lead to any major explosion during the reign of James VI and I.

If we are to assert that the problem of multiple kingdoms was a major cause of the crises of 1637–42, we must explain why, if it was so difficult to handle, it did not lead to a major explosion earlier. If we make the more limited assertion that Charles failed to handle the problem of multiple kingdoms, we must still examine how James

[51] Ibid. 660.
[52] *Jacobean Union*, ed. Galloway and Levack, p. 18.
[53] *CSP Ire.* 1603–6, vol. ccxv, nos. 29, 48.
[54] David Stevenson, *Scottish Covenanters and Irish Confederates* (Belfast, 1981), 11.

did handle it, in order to see wherein Charles's failure consisted. Either way, we must understand the British policies of James VI and I. He certainly enjoyed a calm period in this area. In Anglo–Irish relations, the calm period runs, with an interruption in Ulster in 1607–8, from 1603 to 1625. In Anglo–Scottish relations, it runs from about 1587 to 1625. In both cases, it coincides with James's period of power. The correlation is too close for it to be likely that it is purely coincidental, and suggests that in this field, as in so many others, what James deserves to be praised for is what did *not* happen during his reign. He should be remembered as the prince of dogs in the night-time.

James had Anglo–Scottish problems, and he had Anglo–Irish problems, but, largely because he lacked his son's energy, he seems to have avoided, sometimes by a narrow margin, a three-cornered British problem of the sort which caused so much trouble to his son. In Scotland, as in Catalonia, such a problem came to a head when the troops of one partner in a multiple kingdom crossed the border of another in order to enforce their will. That was the act which invited retaliation with any weapon to hand, and which, by threatening the balance within multiple kingdoms, brought the anxieties of all partners in a multiple kingdom to boiling-point. Under James, *rex pacificus*, such an event was rarely imaginable, and was thought of on a small scale only in the Ulster rising of 1607–8.[55] It was also a common pattern that war, by creating a driving need for revenue, led to pressure which upset the balance of multiple kingdoms, and here James, like Philip III and Lerma, benefited from the period of European peace that followed the end of the Anglo–Spanish war in 1604. In the absence of war, the biggest threat to the stability of multiple kingdoms was likely to come from religion, and religion was the area of James's greatest interest and of his greatest success. There is food for thought in Robert Cecil's exhortation to James to 'expose yourself to as many painful days for enriching your estate as you have done for rectifying the church and commonwealth'.[56] The church was James's priority area, and the king who appears in the pages of Calderwood is one who is not easily reproached for laziness. It was the area where James tried hardest, and the one where he was most

[55] *CSPD 1603–10*, vol. xxviii, nos. 65, 66.
[56] 'Collection of Several Speeches . . . of the Late Lord Treasurer Cecil', ed. Pauline Croft, *Camden Miscellany* (Camden Society, 34, 1987), 293–4.

successful. In the British field, the success resulted from his ability to give security to Protestants, without thereby threatening Catholics with extinction. It also resulted from his Walpolean ability to let sleeping dogs lie.

After a brief running-in period from 1604 to 1607, James abandoned most of his ideas for institutional change, which had, even originally, been less far-reaching than they are usually taken to be. He abandoned some ideas, such as the creation of a British Council, along the lines of the Spanish Council of State, which might have been useful to his successor.[57] The result was that the legal and institutional separateness of both kingdoms was left unaltered, which was perhaps the wisest policy so long as both viewed the prospect of any such change with such profound suspicion.

James's biggest success was in the area of Charles's biggest failure, the relationship between the English and Scottish churches. James's first comment on this issue was to tell his English Parliament in 1604 that the kingdoms were already united in religion.[58] This was an essentially bluffing assertion, but it drew the support of a surprisingly varied collection of people, including Lord Chancellor Ellesmere and Robert Pont, a former Moderator of the General Assembly.[59] He tried to sustain the bluff by a largely cosmetic series of adjustments to both churches, and by following in both the policy of separating moderates from extremists so well described for England by Dr Fincham and Dr Lake.[60] In other words, the dominant influence in each church went to those least likely to denounce the arrangements of the other. In England, James enjoyed natural support in this process from all those worried at the implications of the professionally anti-Presbyterian divinity which had been growing up under the encouragement of Richard Bancroft.[61] In Scotland, he enjoyed the natural support of all those who believed, like the Temporizer in James Melville's dialogue, that the discipline was not of necessity while men had liberty to preach the word.[62] These people seem to have been a larger

[57] *Jacobean Union*, ed. Galloway and Levack, p. xv.   [58] *CJ* i. 143.
[59] PRO SP 14/7/74; *Jacobean Union*, ed. Galloway and Levack, pp. xxxix, 5–7.
[60] Fincham and Lake, pp. 169–203. James VI and the James I described in this article are definitely one king.
[61] Lake, *A. & P.?*, *passim*, esp. pp. 244–50.
[62] Calderwood, iv. 302.

proportion of the Scottish church than is often realized. For example, David Lindsay, Robert Pont, Patrick Galloway, and Peter Blackburne were all former Moderators of the General Assembly, all good Jacobeans, and all but Galloway either accepted or considered offers of bishoprics. Between them, they represented a larger strand of the Scottish church than the two Melvilles did, as Calderwood reluctantly testifies. For such men, the essentials were true doctrine and freedom from idolatry, and if they were secure of these things, they would accept considerable flexility in issues of government and discipline.[63]

James's efforts to adjust the two churches towards each other were not confined to the years after 1603. He seems to have always anticipated the possibility of the English succession, and there is no implausibility in believing, as many Scottish Presbyterians did, that a programme designed to make the English succession easier was in place as early as 1584. The problem in 1584 is how far the policy can be considered to be James's. The extent of his responsibility for policy in 1584 is hard to discover, and the man credited (or discredited) with the ecclesiastical policies of 1584–5 was Patrick Adamson Archbishop of St Andrews. All we can say with confidence is that the ideas produced by Adamson in 1584–5 were ones with which James, when fully of age, was later in agreement. From 1584 James's policy ran, by slow stages, to the Parliamentary ratification of the Five Articles of Perth in 1621. This was a thirty-seven-year programme, with long gaps in the middle, giving people time to drop their defences, and never going far enough at any one stage to make it quite worth whole-hearted resistance. It is a policy worthy of Job himself.

We can now see that James's programme was made up of a series of items, sometimes pursued by changes so small that at the time they barely appeared worth comment. His first aim appears to have been to gain control over the calling of General Assemblies. He began this programme in 1586 by a request so small it would have been footling to refuse it. He asked the Assembly to adjourn to the afternoon of the same day. According to an English observer, they thought this was done to infringe their privileges, but thought it unwise to refuse.[64] His next request, in 1588, was one no self-

---

[63] See *Jacobean Union*, ed. Galloway and Levack, pp. 7–10, for Pont's distinction between essentials and inessentials.

[64] Calderwood, iv. 548. BL Add. MS 32, 092, fo. 88ᵛ; another copy in NLS MS 6.1.13, fos. 33–5.

respecting Presbyterian could refuse, and least of all at that date: he asked for a special assembly to combat the danger of popery. In 1591 he asked to move the General Assembly to Edinburgh, to make it easier for him to attend.[65] In 1605 at the first assembly due after the union of the crowns, he moved further. A mix-up over procedure, which Calderwood suspected was not accidental, resulted in a small group of ministers convening without permission. James, to the dismay of Lord Chancellor Dunfermline, had them convicted for treason.[66] He then called the Melvilles and a few of their key allies to Hampton Court, where they were subjected to a peculiarly high-powered series of sermons, including one from Lancelot Andrewes, arguing from the Biblical power of Moses to the general proposition that at all times and in all places, the power to call ecclesiastical assemblies belonged to kings. In 1610 the General Assembly at Glasgow at last conceded the point.[67]

Andrewes's sermon illustrated how much the English notion of the Royal Supremacy had to offer to a king plagued with Melvilles, and it seems that the next of James's aims was to obtain some form of Royal Supremacy. This aim is perhaps visible with the second of the Black Acts in 1584, which showed a remarkable resemblance to the English Statute of Praemunire. It might be fair to say that this brought James as near the Royal Supremacy as Henry VIII had been in 1515. From there on, he advanced by a series of pinpricks. After the abortive Assembly of Aberdeen, he exacted an oath from the ministers that he was 'supreme ruler of the kirk under Christ'. The use he made in Scotland of the Oath of Allegiance raises the question how far it may have been designed against Scottish Presbyterians, as well as English papists. The Act anent the King's Prerogative, of 1606, consolidated this gain. In 1612 he obtained an Act of Parliament acknowledging him as 'supreme Governor'.[68] For

[65] Peterkin, pp. 323–7, 352.

[66] Calderwood, vi. 326; *Faithfull Report of Proceedings anent the Assemblie of Some Ministers at Abirdeen* (s.l., 1606), *passim.* For Dunfermline's views, see PRO SP 14/18/31.

[67] Lancelot Andrewes, *Sermon preached before the King's Majestie at Hampton Court* (1606). It is a mark of how far Charles moved from his father's position that it was to this sermon that Baillie appealed in 1638, to establish the point that Charles was not entitled to introduce the Scottish Prayer Book without consulting a General Assembly: Baillie, i. 2. For the Glasgow Assembly, see Peterkin, p. 587.

[68] Calderwood, vi. 391–2, 436, 495–7; *APS* 3. 281, 292–3, 469–70. For a paper collecting these precedents for Charles's use, probably in 1639, see JRL Crawford MSS 14/3/45.

James's life, that was where the issue of the Royal Supremacy rested, and it was a Supremacy which was something of a Cheshire Cat. One of Charles's major errors was believing that James had carried the Royal Supremacy far enough in Scotland for him to treat it as an established and recognized fact. By the time Charles had finished, not even the grin was left.

The longest and most visible of James's struggles in Scotland was to breathe life into the shell which was all which was left of Scottish episcopacy. He was scrupulous in offering the title of bishop to good preachers, often former Moderators of the General Assembly, of whom a considerable number took it. James and the General Assembly then engaged in a long debate about how the kirk should be represented in Parliament, which ended in a compromise at the Assembly of Montrose in 1600. Calderwood, possibly with the aid of hindsight, commented: 'thus the Trojan horse, the episcopacie, was brought in, busked and covered with caveats'.[69] James's greatest triumph was at the General Assembly of Linlithgow in 1606, when he achieved agreement that bishops should be permanent moderators of synods—twenty-two years after the idea had first been suggested by Archbishop Adamson.[70] James risked a great deal at Linlithgow, since in the grey area of compromises between episcopacy and presbytery, it was arguably the difference between permanent and temporary moderators of synods which constituted the watershed. If James's objective was to make English episcopalians accept the church of Scotland as a lawful church, he had his reward. No one in England had criticized Scottish church government more passionately than Archbishop Bancroft. Yet a few months after Linlithgow, Bancroft, talking to Andrew Melville of all people, said that 'we differ onlye in the forme of government of the church, and some ceremoneis; but as I understand, since yee came from Scotland, your church is brought to be almost one with ours in that also'.[71] Bancroft, no doubt, enjoyed rubbing salt in Andrew Melville's wounds, yet even so, his remark, grudging though it clearly was, represented a major victory in James's struggle to bring his two churches closer together. England's most prominent critic of Presbyterianism had recognized the government of the Scottish church as legitimate, and that, perhaps, was the

[69] Calderwood, vi. 20.
[70] Ibid. iv. 54.
[71] Ibid. vi. 642.

object for which James had risked so much political capital at
Linlithgow. In 1610, to block any future attempt by English
bishops to unchurch the Scots, James had three Scottish bishops
consecrated by the typically Jacobean trio of George Abbot,
Lancelot Andrewes, and James Montague. The absence of the
English archbishops from this ceremony is interesting: it represented, not the doubts of Bancroft, but those of Spottiswoode
Archbishop of St Andrews. As a good Scot, Spottiswoode would not
be consecrated by an English archbishop, for fear of reviving
English claims to a metropolitan primacy over Scotland. The
incident was a reminder of how easily any threat to the independence
of the Scottish church could bring fears for Scottish nationhood to
the surface.[72]

Both in Scotland and in the Channel Islands, the issues on which
James seemed likely to encounter the greatest resistance, and the
ones he left to the last, were those of ceremony and liturgy. The
issue of ceremony was left till his return to Scotland in 1617,
followed by the Five Articles of Perth in 1618. The Five Articles
were chiefly concerned with kneeling at communion, and with the
celebration of Christmas and Easter. James called on the aid of his
English bishops for this campaign, and Buckeridge's *Discourse on
Kneeling* and Morton's defence of the ceremonies were both timed
in its support. Their support was relevant: the Covenanters later
described the Five Articles as 'Five Articles of conformity with the
church of England',[73] and the description is more or less exact.
James, after a vigorous campaign to secure subscription to the
Articles, did not do much to ensure that they were actually
observed. Anyone who calls this sloth or failure to carry through a
policy mistakes James's objective. He was not concerned to make the
Scots kneel, but to prevent them from calling the English idolaters
for doing so. As with the issue of bishops, he was concerned to
prevent his two churches from unchurching each other—to bring
them to extend each other diplomatic recognition. A Scot who had
subscribed the Five Articles of Perth might never kneel again, but
he could no longer condemn the English for doing so without
condemning himself as a perjurer.

James, as Charles later reminded everyone, had also contemplated a
Scottish liturgy, and had even induced Patrick Galloway to secure

---

[72] C. V. Wedgwood, *History and Hope* (1987), 147.
[73] NLS Adv. MS 33.4.6, fo. 144ᵛ.

approval in principle for such a notion from the General Assembly in 1616.[74] This time James decided to backtrack before provoking any more opposition, and it seems to have been on this issue that he told Laud he would fain bring all things to a pitch of reformation floating in his own brain. After the Parliamentary ratification of the Five Articles of Perth, James seems to have promised that no further ecclesiastical change would be forced on Scotland. He had pushed Scotland to the limit, but not over it.

That he had not pushed the Scots over the limit was partly because he was asking both countries to accept adjustments, and not just one. It was also because the issue on which he asked the English to do the adjusting was the one on which his Scottish Protestant subjects were most fully united. The quid pro quo James offered the Scots was the encouragement of Calvinist doctrine south of the Border. As Dr Wormald remarked, 'the Calvinist church was utterly clear about doctrinal unity, and on that point, James and Melville were at one'.[75] For Russell, the Edinburgh lawyer, free will was one of the heresies of popery. For Robert Pont, it was because the churches agreed in 'fundamentall doctrine' that unity was possible in spite of some differences in discipline.[76] For most Scots, this unity in doctrine, together with James's unquestioned fondness for preaching, were the main reasons for overlooking changes in government and discipline which many of them found uncongenial, though not intolerable. As the price the Scots paid for union was permanent moderators in synods, so the price the English paid was the silence of the Arminians on issues of justification and election.

At Hampton Court, when the Conference took the decision, congenial to Calvinists, to ban baptism by midwives, it was bringing the English church into line with a decision of the General Assembly in 1583.[77] James could no more afford a baptism which was not recognized in all his dominions than a modern ruler can afford passports which are not recognized in all his dominions. In 1607–8, immediately after Linlithgow, Thomas Rogers published a confession of faith dedicated to Bancroft, in which the doctrine of the church of England was said to be 'the very same, which both his

---

[74] Peterkin, pp. 595–6; Calderwood, iv. 145; *Large Declaration*, 19 Feb. 1638 (1639), 15–18.

[75] Wormald, *Court, Kirk and Community*, p. 130; W. R. Foster, *Church before the Covenants* (Edinburgh, 1975), 2; Calderwood, v. 77.

[76] *Jacobean Union*, ed. Galloway and Levack, pp. 7, 112.

[77] Peterkin, p. 276.

highness, and the whole church and kingdom of Scotland, yea and the primitive church, professed.'[78] Here, perhaps, the Scots had their quid pro quo for Linlithgow. James after 1603 put his name to three confessions of faith. The Scottish Confession of 1616 sugared the pill for agreement to a Scottish liturgy. The others were the Irish Articles of 1615 and the Confession of Dort of 1618. All were impeccably Calvinist, and James was entitled to claim that 'what I tell you three times is true'. James had often sailed very near the wind in adjusting Scotland to England, and fundamentalists such as Calderwood already protested that 'conformity with England is intended'.[79] The silencing of the English Arminians was essential to convincing the Scots that the English were taking their share of the adjustments too. It made the vital difference between a programme of mutual adjustment and a programme of English domination.

One way to test whether these things added up to a policy is to test them against James's policy in another of his multiple kingdoms—the Channel Islands.[80] There, as in Scotland, James was faced by a fully-fledged Presbyterian system which had satisfied Cartwright and Snape when they were exiles there. Once again, James's key aim was to secure a token acceptance of the episcopal principle. As in Scotland, he relied on the power of preferment, using the bait of a Deanery for the most conformable of the local ministers. Once again, argument centred on the question of a permanent or temporary moderator. In Jersey, as in Scotland, James got his way, this time after thirteen years of careful probing. In Guernsey, having failed to achieve the necessary division between the leading laymen and the ministers, he prudently backed off, leaving a Presbyterian church to vex Laud after him. In the Channel Islands, as in Scotland, it was the liturgy which was the main area of resistance, and in the Channel Islands, as in Scotland, James was prepared to sacrifice it as an inessential. The key points of Jacobean policy were avoidance of the obvious *casus belli*, careful lip-service to legal forms and consultation, and a concern that no nation should be made to follow the will of another, but that there should be a half-loaf for all. Charles's abandonment of Calvinist

[78] Thomas Rogers, *Faith, Doctrine and Religion* (Cambridge, 1607), pref.
[79] David Calderwood, *Defence* (1620), 40.
[80] A. J. Eagleston, *Channel Islands under Tudor Government* (Cambridge, 1949), 128–42. I would like to thank my wife for drawing my attention to this work.

doctrine removed the coping-stone from this edifice. In the process, it brought all the Scottish fears of 1604 back to the surface.

Charles's attempt in 1639 to enforce his religion on Scotland by English conquest shattered an incipient Scottish Royalist party, and convinced the Covenanters that so long as the provocative difference between the kingdoms persisted, 'our reformation, which has cost us so dear, and is all our wealth and glorie, shall againe be spoyled and defaced from England'.[81] The Scottish imperial policy of 1641 was the only way of permanently removing this danger that they could think of.

Kings in all ages have tended to have an occupational bias towards judging religions in terms of their attitudes to civil authority rather than of their doctrines. This is a tendency to which a king emerging from late sixteenth-century Scotland was unlikely to be an exception. James had had no great objection to the theology of the Melvilles; his concern was with the extent to which they were prepared to accept his civil authority. This was a concern which many Catholics in Ireland were prepared to go some way to meet. Many of them, especially among the Old English, held attitudes not yet fully imbued with Counter-Reformation principles: in Aidan Clarke's words, they believed 'that temporal and spiritual allegiance could be separated without inconsistency, and that a true community of secular interests between subject and prince was a sufficient guarantee of loyalty without the added cement of religious conformity'.[82] Archbishop Lombard, head of the Catholic hierarchy in Ireland, recommended bishops to the Pope on the ground of their loyalty to James. Francis Nugent, who was largely responsible for the introduction of the Capuchins into Ireland, said that 'seeing I am a bound vassal to his Majesty, though I differ from him in points of religion, I owe him all fidelity and service, and I will spare no pains, in my ways to give true demonstration of the respect I bear . . . to him and his royal issue'.[83] Remarks such as these must have been music in James's ears.

James had lived with Catholics in Scotland, and was aware that, if not his mother's partisans, they were capable of being loyal subjects. Consequently, though he was not prepared to allow any official toleration of Catholicism, he was prepared to say that 'though he

---

[81] NLS Advocates' MS 33.4.6, fo. 145^r.

[82] Aidan Clarke, *Old English in Ireland* (1966), 22.

[83] Id. 'Policies of the Old English in Parliament', p. 85.

would much rejoice if the Irish Catholics would conform themselves to his religion, yet he would not force them to forsake their own'.[84] This statement, like a penal statute, should be construed strictly: it did not commit James to toleration of Catholic worship, even in private, even though it did dissociate him from those, like Sir John Clotworthy, who looked forward to the 'extirpation' of popery. It was a position which was misunderstood in Ireland at the time. In 1614 he told an Irish delegation that he did not intend 'to extort any man's conscience'. One of those who heard him reported that he did not mean to have the laws against recusancy enforced, and found that James was extremely angry with his misunderstanding. He had, as Dr Clarke and Dr Edwards put it, 'interpreted a declaration of respect for private beliefs as a promise of public toleration'.[85] The misunderstanding indicates a thin line which was crucial to Jacobean ecclesiastical policy.

There were those among James's subjects in Ireland who did sympathize with the view that popery should be 'extirpated'. They tended, more than James ever did, to see a threat to political loyalty in the very fact of popery. Such men as Sir William Parsons, who saw himself as a representative of an 'English empire',[86] tended to this view. So did some of the Ulster settlers, including some of the Scots. For them, fear always tended to be a spur to such thinking. One undertaker in County Fermanagh remarked that 'although there be no apparent enemy, nor any visible main force, yet the wood-kern and many other (who have now put on the smiling countenance of contentment) do threaten every house, if the opportunity of time and place doth serve'. Colonists at Londonderry were said to live 'as it were with the sword in one hand and the axe in the other'.[87] The fears of the planter and of the anti-papist were capable of blending.

From James, such people would get little support for their fears, but a great deal of indulgence where their own methods of worship were concerned. Until the arrival of the Scottish army in 1641, Scottish Protestants in Ulster seem to have worshipped in the same churches as the English, and even ministers from Scotland felt no need to organize a separate Presbyterian church.[88] From James, they got a Protestant church dominated by James Ussher, ultimately

---

[84] *NHI* iii. 190.   [85] Ibid. 216–17.

[86] Ibid. 235.   [87] Ibid. 205.

[88] Stevenson, *Scottish Covenanters and Irish Confederates*, pp. 12, 118.

promoted to the Archbishopric of Armagh. It was Ussher, in the Irish Convocation of 1615, who was responsible for the drafting of the Irish Articles, an impeccably Calvinist production which 'catered usefully for the doctrinal preferences of the Scots in Ulster'.[89] Ussher held a relaxed attitude to ceremony, and a moderate view of the episcopal office remarkably like the ideas agreed on at Linlithgow in 1606. Few people could have been better suited to the task of persuading Scots that episcopacy was not a threat to fundamental Protestant principles. It seemed a useful basis for a policy of keeping Protestants happy in their own worship, while leaving Catholics in peace.

Where the anti-popery forces were more able to gain a response from James was the issue of money. In all James's kingdoms, it was money and not religion which was his Achilles heel, and Jacobean government in Ireland suffered particular difficulties in matters of money. The Elizabethan regime had been no better at maximizing income in Ireland than it was in England, and in the last years of her reign, the war in Ireland had done severe damage to Irish revenues. The result was that Ireland, to the great dismay of Robert Cecil, was heavily dependent on the English Exchequer.[90] The plantation of Ulster, which should perhaps be seen in part as the privatization of garrison duty, did something to reduce this dependence, but in the later part of the reign, Ireland was still costing the English Exchequer £20,000 a year—a substantial part of the English deficit.[91] James therefore was, and remained, wide open to any proposal which could be presented as designed to increase Irish revenue.

In addition, James suffered in Ireland, as he did in England, from an excess of servants demanding rewards that he could not afford to give them. Any proposal which involved the combination of a grant to a private individual with an opportunity to raise new revenue for the Crown could therefore harness a considerable number of regular Jacobean concerns. These things directed the attention of suitors to the confused state of Irish land tenure. English lawyers, led by Sir John Davies, were trying to establish the principle of feudal tenures, by which all land should ultimately be held, mediately or immediately, of the Crown. With feudal tenures came wardships, and with wardships came revenue.

[89] *NHI* iii. 229. See also Tyacke, p. 23.
[90] See ch. 7 below.   [91] *NHI* iii. 230.

Moreover, since heirs gaining livery of their lands after a wardship could be required to take the oath of supremacy, with wardship came the opportunity to strike a blow at popery. It could thus be serious enough if the Crown or its agents could find a feudal tenure.

It might on occasion be more serious if they could not, since, if there was no feudal tenure produced, English lawyers were capable of finding that no one had valid title to the land, and thus the opportunity for a plantation could be created. From the Crown's point of view, a plantation, by creating new feudal tenures and reserved rents, could create new revenue. It could also, by creating a new Protestant landowning class, do much to reduce the potentially exorbitant costs of Irish defence. From the point of view of the individual suitor, there was the opportunity to pick up a valuable estate at a bargain price. It is no surprise to anyone familiar with Jacobean England that the hunt for concealed feudal tenures became big business in Jacobean Ireland.[92] These operations increasingly created an atmosphere of insecurity for Catholic landholders in Ireland, first for the native Irish, and later for the Old English as well. Even the Earl of Ormond was threatened by a plantation, and reacted by protesting that he was the first Englishman to be treated as if he were Irish.[93] It was this growing insecurity of Catholic land tenure, rather than any direct measures of persecution, which increasingly created fears for Catholicism in Ireland. These things were remembered, and a confederate pamphlet issued from Kilkenny during the Rebellion recalled how the government

gave way to certain projectors, monopolers and probing fellows (the instruments and factors of some ministers of state) to vex them with strange and unknown suits for concealments, intrusions, alienations, and some monopolies were set on foot to their great impoverishment . . . so that a man might see they were resolved to bear anything, if they might but enjoy their religion and lands.[94]

Much of this description might have come from Jacobean England: the peculiarity of Ireland is the threat to the country's religion implicit in this pursuit of private profit.

In England, a reaction against this sort of operation came to a head in the Parliaments of 1621 and 1624, and ultimately led to

[92] Ibid. 206–8.   [93] Ibid. 242.

[94] *Discourse between Two Councillors of State*, ed. Aidan Clarke (Analecta Hibernica, 26, Dublin, 1970), 163.

legislation in the Parliament of 1624. The key Act, from an Irish point of view, was the English Concealment Act of 1624, which made sixty years' possession confer a valid title against the Crown.[95] The adoption of such a principle in Ireland, if it could be achieved, would restore security to Catholic landholders, put a stop to the policy of plantation, and consequently make Ireland secure for Catholicism. It may therefore be imagined that this Act exercised a strong appeal to many Old English landowners, and a corresponding repulsion to many New English interests with connections with the Dublin government.

All these issues were brought to a head in 1625 by the onset of Charles I's war with Spain. Memories of 1601, as well as elementary strategy, indicated that the defence of Ireland should be a high priority in English military planning. However, England in 1625 was in no position to finance its own defence, let alone Ireland's. This made the thinking associated with the Union of Arms, whereby Ireland would pay for its own defence, peculiarly attractive to Charles I and his Council. When the English Council met at Southampton on 2 September 1625, they accepted a proposal to recruit Old English into the trained bands. It is not coincidental that this proposal was moved by the Lord Treasurer. This proposal was promptly obstructed by the Irish Privy Council, because 'thereby we should have put arms into their hands of whose hearts we rest not well assured'. In other words, they saw it as their task to defend Ireland against papists, not by them.[96]

Charles, whose pursuit of the war was utterly single-minded on both sides of the Irish Sea, overruled these objections, and proceeded to negotiate a series of major concessions to the Old English, in return for consent to finance an army of 5,000 foot and 500 horse. The concessions, known as the Graces, involved a long series of measures designed to restore security of land tenure, of which the most important was the application to Ireland of the English Concealment Act.[97] These proposals appeared to most parties to make Ireland safe for Catholicism, and led Archbishop Ussher to protest that they were a proposal to sell Christ for thirty pieces of silver. In 1628 Charles reached agreement with an Old English delegation for confirmation of the Graces in return for

[95] On this, see Russell, *PEP*, pp. 110 and nn., 156, 157, and 191–2.
[96] Clarke, *Old English in Ireland*, pp. 33–6.
[97] *NHI* iii. 234–5.

£40,000 a year for the army for three years, plus more 'from time to time'.[98] Thus the pressure of war appeared to have reversed the whole pattern of Irish politics, forging an alliance between the King and the Catholic Old English against the government in Dublin.

Before the Graces could be confirmed, Charles's war had ground to a halt, and his need for them had disappeared. This enabled the Dublin government to reassert both the danger of tolerating papists, and the threat to royal revenue implicit in the abandonment of the hunt for concealed lands. The Crown's policy rapidly reverted to something like what it had been before, leaving the recovery of the Graces as a major Irish objective for many years to come. In 1634 Strafford rudely described the Concealment Act as 'their Delilah', and told them they had already had more concessions 'than their six little subsidies were worth'.[99] Strafford, like previous English rulers, was heavily influenced by the need to prevent Ireland from becoming a drain on the English Exchequer. Irish Catholicism was being slowly sacrificed, not so much to English anti-popery, as to the poverty of the English Exchequer. It could perhaps have been foretold that in 1640–1, when Strafford was removed and Charles's authority collapsed, the recovery of the Graces would go straight to the top of the Irish agenda. It might also have been foreseen that when they did, since political crises are bad for revenue, the same story would happen all over again.

---

[98] Clarke, *Old English in Ireland*, pp. 39–40.
[99] *Two Councillors*, ed. Clarke, p. 166.

3

The Church, Religion, and Politics
The Problem of the Definite Article

ON 2 August 1642 the Lords and Commons told the country that the Royalists 'come . . . to crown their work, and put that in execution which was first in their intention, that is the changing of religion into popery and superstition'. On 19 September the King told his assembled troops outside Wellington that 'you shall meete with noe enemyes but traytors, most of them Brownists, Anabaptists and atheists, such who desire to destroy both church and state'.[1] Both these statements contain an element of mythology, but in the Civil War, as in most other major conflicts, mythologies recruited as many troops as facts. To understand the war, it is necessary to understand the mythologies. We are likely to find that when they are fully understood, the genuine element in them is rather larger, and the mythological rather smaller, than at first sight might appear.

For the next three chapters, we will be concerned with issues involving religion, and we must say which of our initial list of questions they are designed to answer. Above all, they are designed to explain the division into parties, since that appears to have happened largely, though never exclusively, on religious lines. When we have said this, we have not necessarily said that they were fighting for religion. Some undoubtedly were, such as Lord Brooke, who exhorted the House of Lords, of all ill-chosen audiences, to 'proceed to shed the blood of the ungodlie'.[2] Many of those who fought for religion, like Lord Brooke himself, were in the vanguard of those who helped to get the war started, but they were not necessarily a majority. Others, in choosing a side, chose the lesser of two evils, and identified that as the side where their friends were, and their friends might be their co-religionists. Many

---

[1] *LJ* v. 258; BL Harl. MS 163, fo. 749ᵇ.
[2] *Two Speeches* (1642), BL E. 84(35), p. 7. I am grateful to Dr J. S. A. Adamson for this reference.

other reasons apart from zeal might lead a man to side with his co-religionists.

To say the parties were divided by religion is not the same thing as to say religion caused the Civil War. In explaining how these two parties came to fight each other, we are at once faced by a paradox. Many aspects of the division over religion can be traced back to 1559. Others, which made the quarrel a much more fundamental one, can be traced back to the York House Conference of 1626, and yet, right up to 1639, religious divisions in the country did not appear to be generating a bitter enough *odium theologicum* to make them a likely cause of war. Religious division generated plenty of ill-will, but it coexisted with a high degree of local social tolerance. In 1639 Brilliana Harley told her son she would have sent him a newsbook, 'but your father leaft it at the bischops'.[3] Admittedly Bishop Coke of Hereford was one of the few remaining Calvinist bishops, a fact without which the story would be incomprehensible, but this and many similar stories still do not point to a community about to fight for religion. Many hot Protestants were prepared to argue that 'some of my best friends are papists'. D'Ewes, for example, objected to the inclusion of his friend the Count of Egmont in a list of papists drawn up in November 1641, saying "'tis true hee is a papist, but a presbiteriall one, and one that hates the Jesuits, and therefore I desire that wee may rather doe him all the honour we cann, than offer him anie iniurie.'[4] This is on a level with the exclamation heard in a modern London street: 'that's not a coloured man: that's the doctor'.[5] Neither story suggests a society so instinctively intolerant that it was about to tear itself apart.

The English Civil War did not begin with a great uprising in the country: it began with a breakdown of government at the centre, symbolized by the fact that from January 1642 King and Parliament did not dare be in the same place as each other. Religion undoubtedly determined many people's reactions to that break-down, but if it helped to cause the breakdown itself, it must have done so by providing some of the answers to other questions on our checklist. How far did it do so? In the first place, religion

---

[3] *Letters of Lady Brilliana Harley*, ed. T. T. Lewis (Camden Society, 58, 1854), 27.

[4] D'Ewes (C.), p. 174. I am grateful to Professor M. J. Mendle for this reference.

[5] I owe this story to Lord Pitt of Hampstead, whom I would like to thank for permission to reproduce it.

undoubtedly contributed heavily to the outbreak of the Bishops'
Wars. It contributed to the English defeat in the wars, by building
up a party in England whose sympathies were on the Scottish side.
The contribution of the Bishops' Wars to polarizing English
opinion was the bigger for the fact that everyone agreed that the
wars were a bad thing, and therefore that heavy blame rested on
those responsible for their outbreak. James Machison of Burnham,
Bucks said that 'I care not for my Lord of Canterbury, for he has
been the occasion of this strife between the Scots and us, and I care
not if he heard me', while on the other side Robert Sibthorp the
Laudian insisted that they should not be called the Bishops' Wars,
but '*rebellio Puritanica*'.[6]

By creating pro- and anti-Scottish parties, religion made a major,
but indirect, contribution to the failure of the settlement. Without
the existence of a large party ready for religious reasons to back the
Scots against the King, the Scottish invasion could not have had the
effect it did, yet it was the Scottish invasion which gave England
the major constituent of a true opposition: an alternative source
of power. It was the Scots who insisted on terms so unpalatable to
Charles that they raised the question whether the country had to be
governed with the King's consent, and it was that question on which
Charles nailed his colours to the mast. Religion was an important
part of the reasons why Charles's consent was not forthcoming, but
for Charles, as usual, the ultimate sticking-point was his 'authority':
the point where his religious convictions and his political power
met. Among the individual issues on which the settlement broke
down, the execution of Strafford was not mainly a religious issue.
Root and Branch was, but for most of the junto, with the possible
exceptions of St John, Fiennes, and Hampden, Root and Branch
was not a fundamental issue of principle: it was first a commitment
to Scottish allies, and then a way of preventing Charles from
recovering power to control the church. It was an issue on which
British problems, religious convictions, and theories of government
could never be separated for more than a few seconds at a time. The
third issue on which the settlement failed was the issue of the
Queen's Mass, and her right to be served by a Catholic secretary.
This, at least for the commoners in the junto, was a matter of

---

[6] *CSPD 1639*, vol. ccccxxii, no. 113 (Samuel Hull to Laud); Huntington
Library Stowe Temple MSS. I would like to thank Professor P. Collinson and Dr
R. P. Cust for the latter reference.

fundamental religious conviction, and the fear of popery it reflected was a cause of the Civil War.

The issue of royal marriages is one on which religious tension had been liable to cause difficulties ever since the Reformation. It was the fundamental point about Tudor and Stuart ideas on marriage that it should be without 'disparagement', that is, between social equals. This was an idea which applied at least as strongly to royal marriages as to private ones, and which was reinforced through the early Stuart period by the need for a dowry which was likely to be worth more than any foreseeable Paliamentary subsidies. The case for a marriage without disparagement led directly to a Catholic marriage. When James in 1621 said that the House of Commons had advised for 'the match of our dearest son with some Protestant (we cannot say princess, for we know none of these fit for him)', he made a fair point.[7] Only France and Spain could offer either an adequate dowry or a bride English self-esteem could accept without a sense of disparagement.

This meant that any likely marriage would have to be with a Catholic, creating a fear of a *'Gaping Gulf'* ready to swallow up England's hard-won and tenuous conversion to Protestantism. It also necessarily meant some sort of dispensation for the Catholic spouse and his or her household to worship according to their consciences, and therefore raised, in a highly visible form, the problem of the limits of the dispensing powers of the Crown. Any likely royal marriage, then, would have been likely to raise, not only the problem of religious division, but also the problem of the just limits of law and prerogative. These problems were visible as far back as Elizabeth's marriage negotiations with the Archduke Charles and the Duke of Anjou, but time seems to have made them harder, and not easier, to solve. When the King and the Houses struggled over whether Henrietta Maria should be allowed any priests, they were heirs to the *damnosa hereditas* of Henry VIII. James's famous advice to Prince Henry, that two religions should not lie in his bed, had been sound advice, but it was advice a King of Scots could give, but a King of England, for reasons of status, could not.[8]

[7] J. R. Tanner, *Constitutional Conflicts of the Reign of James I* (Cambridge, 1960), 284.
[8] See Wallace T. MacCaffrey, 'The Anjou Match and the Making of Elizabethan Foreign Policy', in Peter Clark, Alan G. T. Smith, and Nicholas

The breakdown of the settlement was in the area where religious conviction and political power met, and in the area where they were so closely involved together that it is not even a meaningful question to ask which was which. We have to explain, then, not only why some people might fight for religion, but also why, in the normal seventeenth-century structure of authority, it was normal to find religion and politics as closely intertwined as economics and politics are today.

Together with those who fought for religion, we should include those, like George Digby, who fought against religion out of a deep distaste for having the other side's creed enforced on them, and more generally, in disgust at the construction of any further clerical hoops for laity to jump through. When Digby complained that the Etcetera Oath was objectionable for the same reasons as the Scottish Covenant, he was expressing a position which was more anti-religious than religious.[9] In 1642 an Oxford man living in Holywell, 'being desirous to look back to the garlic and onions of Egypt', set up a maypole, and decorated it with a picture of a godly College manciple, at which he began shooting. To say this man was preparing to fight for religion would perhaps be misleading, but to say he was preparing to fight because of religion would not be. He never had the opportunity to do so, because he fell down laughing at his own achievements, and suffered a stroke, from which, our godly source tells us, he had not yet recovered.[10]

Yet, when all the qualifications are allowed, the fact remains that many people, and very many of the first activists, did fight for religion, and that the breakdown of the political process at Westminster happened at the point where ideas of religion and of political authority were almost closely interwoven. To make these things appear plausible to the twentieth century, it is necessary, not only to recount the story, but to investigate its philosophical

Tyacke (eds.), *English Commonwealth 1547–1640: Essays in Politics and Society Presented to Joel Hurstfield* (Leicester, 1979), 59–75; and Susan Doran, 'Habsburg Marriage Negotiations 1558–1568', *EHR*, civ/413 (Oct. 1989), 908–26. I am grateful to Professor N. M. Sutherland and Mr David Venderbush for many helpful discussions of this issue, and particularly grateful to Dr Doran, who first drew it to my attention. It is an issue on which the lines seem to have hardened with the passage of time.

[9] Rushworth, III. i. 31–2. This remark is typical of the Erastian anticlericalism which divided the English Royalists from Charles I.

[10] *True New News* (*s.l.*, 1642), BL E. 239(7), pp. 2–3.

underpinnings. The late twentieth century is, in historiographical terms, about the hardest society to which to explain religious intolerance that has yet existed. Religious intolerance to the twentieth century, like arbitrary government to the nineteenth, is that from which we are beginning to hope we can pride ourselves on having escaped, and our historiographical judgements often show a need to testify to our freedom from it. Many passages in works published since 1945 refer to the religious intolerance of their heroes in terms rather of apology than of search for understanding. It does not help that the word 'religion' has slowly changed its meaning with the retreat of the State from religious enforcement, and that what takes place outside the South African Embassy may sometimes be nearer to seventeenth-century meanings of 'religion' than what takes place inside St Martin-in-the-Fields. In Professor Collinson's phrase, 'religion was a public duty, not a private opinion or a voluntary profession'.[11] The word 'religion', both by common usage and by prevailing etymology, meant first and foremost rules which were to be enforced. The medieval religious were those who lived under a rule. Hobbes was therefore right that 'he that pretends to teach men the way of so great felicity, pretends to govern them'.[12] Under these circumstances, it was as ludicrous to talk of separating Protestantism from politics as it would be now to talk of separating Socialism from politics.

One of the major difficulties of seventeenth-century England was that it was a society with several religions, while still remaining a society with a code of values and a political system which were only designed to be workable with one.[13] This was such a constant source of difficulty that one should perhaps be impressed by the strength and stability of a society in which it caused as few problems as it did. In the first place, religion was widely regarded as the sole source of morals. John Donne once remarked: 'there is no virtue, but religion',[14] and the view was widely shared. When we read of an unhappily married couple, for whom 'nothing but the power of religion could make them live as man and wife',[15] we are looking at

[11] Collinson, *EPM*, p. 25.
[12] Thomas Hobbes, *Leviathan*, ch. 36.
[13] *Political Works of James I*, ed. C. H. MacIlwain (Cambridge, Mass., 1918), p. xvii.
[14] John Donne, 'To Rowland Woodward', line 16, in *Complete English Poems*, ed. A. J. Smith (1971), 207.
[15] Keith Wrightson, *English Society 1580–1680* (1982), 101.

a definition of religion unfamiliar to the twentieth century. William Gouge thought we owed the capacity to love to the power of religion: 'there is in us by nature no spark of love at all, if Christ by his loving of us did not first instill love into us'. Man acquired the capacity to love 'as the aire heated by the sunne is hote, and a wall on which the sun-beames smite, giveth a reflexion of heate back againe'.[16] Religion was almost the invariable means of coming to terms with the frequent experience of premature bereavement; when Cottington was deeply dismayed by the death of his wife, Garrard, the epitome of conventional wisdom, remarked: 'he hath been much troubled by it, but God's will must be done, and I doubt not but he will bear it as becomes a wise man and a good Christian'.[17] To those who took these ideas seriously, the ignoring of religion could appear to lead to a Iago-like descent from one sin to another. When Mervin Audley Lord Castlehaven was on trial for having a homosexual affair with his page, and then assisting his page to rape his wife, prosecuting counsel could not resist the opportunity for a homily: 'he was constant in no religion, but in the morning would be a papist, and go to Mass, and in the afternoon a Protestant, and hear a sermon. He believed not in God, he feared not God, he left God, and God left him to his own wicked way, and then what might not he run into?'[18]

To anyone influenced by this vision of chaos, the case for enforcement of religion was very difficult to resist. It was difficult to resist in the name of conscience, for many people defined conscience as a divine voice in a way which made the notion of an erroneous conscience a fertile source of problems: Immanuel Bourne said conscience was 'of a divine nature, being placed in the middest, as an ambassador betweene God and man, and given by God unto him for a perpetuall companion: it is like thy shadow'.[19] This doctrine did leave room for an erroneous conscience, but it did not leave very much. It is always a temptation to refuse to recognize unexpected

[16] William Gouge, *Domesticall Duties* (1622), 412–13. I am grateful to the Rev. Dr Daniel Doriani for bringing this passage to my attention, and for much helpful discussion of these issues.
[17] Knowler, i. 206.
[18] Conrad Russell, 'Arguments for Religious Unity in England 1530–1650', *JEH* 18/2 (1967), 210. The family seems to have been a disturbed one: Lord Audley's sister was the notorious Lady Eleanor Davies. *CSPD 1633–4*, vol. cclv, no. 19.
[19] Immanuel Bourne, *Anatomie of Conscience* (1623), 13.

consciences, and such definitions did not make that temptation any easier to resist.

These beliefs supplied part, but not all, of the background to the key belief which made religion a political issue: the belief that it must be enforced. This belief was defended by an inherited and unchallenged creed that the spiritual welfare of subjects was one of the ends of government. When James I in 1604 was presented with a summary of the Royal Supremacy, he was told he was 'ordained to beare the sword with full power and authoritie to commaund that which is good and forbid that which is evil.' William Perkins agreed that the magistrate 'beares the sword specially for the good of men's soules'. It was his duty 'to urge men to the keeping of the commandments of the First Table, to a practise of pure religion, and to the keeping of the Sabbath day'.[20] The *Homilies* told rulers they were much to blame 'if for lack of correction they wilfully suffer God to be offended, and they for whom they govern to perish'.[21] The enforcement of religion was as unquestioned in the list of the purposes of government as the need to defend the country.

Self-preservation might encourage rulers to discharge this duty, since religion was also the ground of theories of political obligation. As Laud said, 'no laws can be binding if there be no conscience to obey them: penalty alone could never, never do it. And no school can teach conscience but the church of Christ'. Dod reminded all those in subjection that their governor 'stands in the place of Christ unto thee', and was to be obeyed accordingly. Hooker drew attention to the extent to which religion did duty for the lack of any detective force: 'inasmuch as those laws have no further power than over our outward actions only, whereas unto men's inward cogitations, unto the privy interests and motions of their hearts, religion serveth for a bridle'.[22] Every time a government relied on an oath in lieu of detection to discover offences, it was strongly reminded of the point. The Earl of Manchester, speaking in the Star Chamber in 1637, said that

your lordships well know that every man's state, every man's credit, his possessions and livelihood, much depends upon oaths; for if not upon the

---

[20] PRO SP 14/6/46; William Perkins, *Treatise of Callings*, in *Works*, i. Cambridge, 1612 edn. 764.   [21] *Sermons or Homilies* (SPCK, 1938 edn.), 69.
[22] Laud, *Wks.* i. 112; John Dod, *Plaine and Familiar Exposition of the Ten Commandments* (1606 edn.), 184; Richard Hooker, *Laws of Ecclesiastical Polity*, ed. Keble (Oxford, 1836), ii. 21–2 (V. ii. 3).

jurors yet the witnesses in any case of evidence, be it for matter or title or matter of fact . . . if they be caused to swear against their consciences, and that tye be taken away whereby they stand obliged before God and men to give right to the truth, no man is sure of any thing he enjoys.

To a seventeenth-century audience, it would have strengthened Manchester's case, rather than weakening it, that he was speaking on a perjury charge. The vision of an irreligious world was of one in which perjury would become the normal state of affairs.[23]

So long as governments enforced religion in a divided society, they put perpetual strains on the system. They also daily exposed what was almost a contradiction in the prevailing code of values. That code invoked Romans 13: 'let every soul be subject unto the higher powers. For there is no power but of God; the powers that be are ordained of God. Whosoever resisteth the power resisteth the ordinance of God: and they that resist shall receive to themselves damnation'. On the other hand, it equally upheld Acts 5: 29, 'we ought to obey God rather than man'. The 'Homily of Obedience' itself said that 'we ought not to obey kings, magistrates, or any other (though they be our own father) if they would command us to doe any thing contrary to God's commandments. In such a case, we ought to say with the Apostle, we must obey God rather than man'.[24] When there was general agreement what God commanded, this was a workable pair of doctrines, but when there was not such agreement, it made the duty of disobedience alarmingly widespread.

Since husbands, fathers, and masters were officers of local government, this was a problem for the little commonwealth of the family, as well as for the State, and it is in the context of the family that some of the bravest attempts to tackle the potential divergence of these texts were made. William Gouge urged husbands to approach the issue with extreme care: 'to command a thing unlawfull, or forbid a thing which ought to be done, is to bring his owne authority into opposition with Gods: in which case he bringeth his wife into this strait, either to reiect God's commandment or his'. He stressed that the wife was bound to follow her conscience, even if erroneous, for the conscience was subject only to God: 'if it be forced, it will be fearfull horror, and a hell in that party whose conscience is forced: she that doubteth is condemned, if she doe that whereof she maketh doubt'. The husband had to try to resolve his

[23] *ST* iii. 789–90.
[24] *Sermons or Homilies* (1640 edn.), i. 74.

wife's conscience, but if he failed he had to decide, on his own judgement, whether her refusal was due to 'obstinacy' or to 'weakness'. If it was obstinacy, he should stand on his power, and if it was weakness, he should not. He was to stand on his power if his wife insisted on going to hear Mass, or not going to hear the Gospel.[25] These arguments help to understand why husbands tended to fear that division in religion would mean that they would never again have control of their families, and all the arguments applied to the little commonwealth of the family may be applied by correspondence to the State.

The official resolution of these dilemmas involved a psychological knife-edge so sharp that few could be expected to rest on it: it was required that people should have the courage to disobey commands contrary to God's, and then that they should have the further courage to make no attempt to protect themselves, but to take their punishment without complaint. It does not seem to have been expected that many people would perform both parts of this duty: either they would lack the courage to disobey, or they would take the further step from disobeying to resisting, agreeing with Lancelot Gobbo that 'the fiend gives the more friendly counsel'.[26] William Perkins told those with the misfortune to be married to idolaters that the idolatry was no excuse for dissolving the marriage, but that if the idolatrous spouse should attempt conversion, it might become necessary to 'omit the dutie of marriage'.[27] The question was not theoretical: when Mrs Hazzard, founder of the Baptist church at Bristol, resolved on ecclesiastical separation, she had to be absent herself from services conducted by her husband, who was a church of England minister, and a collection of Job's comforters hastened to tell him that 'ye next thing that followed would be that she would forsake the bed alsoe'.[28] Any husband whose wife was a recusant might find his authority and standing diminished, like the unfortunate mayor of York, who was called before the High Commission and told 'that he is unmete to governe a cittie that can not governe his owne howsehold'.[29] Occasionally those in this

---

[25] Gouge, *Domesticall Duties*, pp. 374–6.
[26] Shakespeare, *Merchant of Venice*, II. i. 29–30. Gobbo was justifying flight rather than rebellion, but the theological arguments were the same.
[27] Perkins, *Idolatry of the Last Times*, in *Works* (Cambridge, 1603 edn.), 839.
[28] *Records of a Church of Christ at Bristol*, ed. Roger Hayden (Bristol Record Society, Bristol, 1974), 93.
[29] David Palliser, *Age of Elizabeth* (1983), 63.

position might ask inconvenient questions, like the candidate for Mayor of Appleby in 1634, who said he did not see why he should be disqualified, since divers Privy Councillors and the King himself had wives who were recusant. Archbishop Neile could not understand why the King and Laud were reluctant to prosecute in this case.[30] In the Short Parliament election for Norfolk, Sir John Holland, who was married to a recusant wife, suffered damage from a whispering campaign based on the slogan that 'ther ar too many religons in Holland'.[31]

In this context, the belief that religious division led to trouble and disloyalty could only remain a self-fulfilling prophecy. Those who wished to make a distinction between religious and political loyalty, as many often did, could only make the distinction effective if authority would allow them to do so, which it would never admit to doing. In Ireland in 1603, a number of people reacted to the death of Elizabeth by attempting to claim liberty of conscience to hear Mass, claiming that they had no intention of disloyalty. One of the Englishmen who witnessed this phenomenon reported that they were making 'frivolous and slight demands to have liberty of conscience with free use of their popish religion', and that they were 'poisoned with blind zeal towards the Pope and his counterfeit religion'. He said the proper remedy was for the English to build a citadel in the town at the townsmen's expense.[32] If Catholicism had not been disloyal before, it was made so afterwards. So long as enforcement remained the automatic assumption, the only way to escape from it was to become one of the enforcers instead of one of the enforced. John Cosin, celebrating his triumph at the York House Conference, said that 'if the faction had conquered, they had shewed no mercy; now they are subdued, they show no patience'.[33] He knew perfectly well he would show no more mercy, and would have shown no more patience, than they did: that was why he and Richard Montague had approached the conference with such intense anxiety. It was, as major religious disputes usually were, an issue of political survival.

We must add to this the normal urge of those with power to prohibit whatever they take to be self-evidently wrong. John Dod,

---

[30] Bodl. MS Clarendon, vol. 6, no. 388.
[31] Clive Holmes, *The Eastern Association in the English Civil War* (Cambridge, 1974), 25.
[32] *CSP Ire. 1603–6*, vol. ccxv, no. 58 and other refs.   [33] Cosin, ii. 74.

discussing the duty of a master to prevent the stranger within his gates from profaning the sabbath, said that 'no man is so savage, that if he see a blinde man running into a well, wherein hee may be drowned, will say, let him go, I care not, he is none of my familie, nor of my friends'.[34] D'Ewes, the Parliamentary *ingénu*, remarked that 'the verie inquisition of Spaine had a good couler in the first institution: being only intended against Moors and Jews, but is now turned to the ruine of the godlie Protestants'. His objection to the High Commission, to which he was working up, was not that it punished people, but that it punished hardly any but the pious and innocent.[35] Behind this hankering for certainty was a deep fear of moral relativism, and of the threat to faith which might result from admitting such a thing. Laurence Chaderton asked: 'do we not see in all places diversity of opinions. Shall we therefore call in question the foundation of religion? God forbid'.[36] This fear of relativism became more explicit after 1642, when toleration became a greater danger, but the later remarks only make explicit what had been implicit before. Samuel Rutherford the Covenanter, in a satirical Independent prayer, wrote: 'grant that thy holy spirit may bestow upon my dark soul more sceptical, conjectural and fluctuating knowledge, to know and believe things with a reserve, with a leaving of room to believe the contrary tomorrow of what I believe today'. He thought such belief would turn the word of God into a 'nose of wax', which could give no certain guidance.[37] Matthew Newcomen in 1644 thought that if every man was left to the liberty of his own religion 'it will open a door to Turcisme, Judaisme, atheisme, polytheisme, any monster of opinion'. He insisted that 'it is most certain, he that admits contrary religions beleeves neither of them'.[38] This dislike of relativism was reinforced by a readiness to deny the names of 'religion' and 'Christian' to rival claimants. Archbishop Heath in 1559 referred to all princes 'whether they be Protestants or Christians', and Christopher Goodman described the Spaniards as 'a people witout God'.[39] Cornelius Burges, preaching on 5 November 1641, described the papists as striving to 'abolish

---

[34] Dod, *Ten Commandments* (1610 edn.), 167.

[35] D'Ewes (N.), p. 288.   [36] Lake, *MP*, p. 129.

[37] Russell, 'Religious Unity', p. 224.

[38] Matthew Newcomen, *Sermon tending to set forth the Right Use of . . . Disasters* (1644), 36, 38.

[39] Hartley, p. 14; Christopher Goodman, *How Superior Powers ought to be Obeyed* (Geneva, 1558), 96.

religion', and even Charles I, not the most famous anti-papist in his kingdom, described the Irish Rebellion as 'horrid and odious to all Christians'.[40] The ultimate fear was of a society of unfettered consumer choice in religion. At least one Elizabethan MP was quite happy with this 'consumer' image. Mr Gates in 1572 said: 'that uniformitye never hitherto obtained, nor ever to be looked for in the church. Not possible any one meate could like the tastes of all us here present'.[41] Yet as such a society seemed to come nearer, and more and more supposed 'fundamentals' were called in question, fear of the moral relativism it seemed to imply grew more intense. The example of the Dutch did not always make such a society seem encouraging, and as Andrew Marvell had it,

> Hence Amsterdam, Turk–Christian–Pagan–Jew,
> Staple of sects and mint of schism grew,
> That bank of conscience, where not one so strange
> Opinion, but finds credit, and exchange.[42]

Whenever anyone might have been inclined to let these questions recede into the background, the terms of the debate with Rome brought them back into the foreground. In that debate, two premisses were accepted without question on both sides. One was that Christ, by his promise that he would be with us even to the end of the world, had committed himself to preserve a continuous, visible, Christian church as long as the world should endure. Christian baptism and Christian ordination, like university degrees, could only claim to be valid if they were conferred by a continuous, visible, and lawful succession from the days of the founders, in this case the Apostles. This meant that the first reformers relied on the Roman church for the lawfulness of their baptism and ordination, and consequently that of all their successors. When Perkins faced the charge that the first reformers' preaching had been against their calling, and that 'if they had no calling, neither have we that are their followers', he answered 'that by virtue of their oathes at their ordination, they were bound onely to the Catholike and apostolike church, and not to the present church of Rome'.[43] This was why it was so important to maintain the distinction between the Catholic

[40] Cornelius Burges, *Another Sermon* (1641), 20; *CJ* ii. 454.
[41] Hartley, p. 368.
[42] Andrew Marvell, 'Character of Holland', ll. 70–4.
[43] Perkins, *Treatise of Callings*, in *Works* (Cambridge, 1612 edn.), i. 760.

church, to which every Protestant who recited the creed claimed to belong, and the popish church, so called because it was false rather than Catholic. It was necessary to assert that the popish church was false, because the other belief which was common ground was that separation from a church which, even if corrupt, was lawful, was the sin of schism, the second worst sin after heresy. Francis Hastings, in a draft will written before 1585, wrote that:

I beleeve that we all oughte to keepe the unitie of the churche of Christ by joining togeather in a Christian communion, and submitting ourselves to the common instruction and yoke of Christe: and that wheresoever in all the worlde God hath ordained a true order of a Christian churche and congregation, it being established must be holden for holye; in which churche the pastors that are assigned to teache must be reverently hearde and obeyed.[44]

The fact that it was thought so sinful to leave the church only made it appear the more necessary to control it.

Even the hottest of orthodox Protestants, when they considered the questions of the visible church and the lawful ministry, had to derive their title to both from the church of Rome. John Winthrop, in a memorandum possibly aimed at Roger Williams, asked:

if Christes churches were so utterly nullified, and quite destroyed, then I demande when they beganne againe and where? Who beganne them? That we may know by what right and power they did beginne them: for we have not heard of any new Jo. Baptist, nor of any other newe waye from heaven, by which they have begunne the churches a newe.

He said that any argument which denied the continuity of the visible church denied Christ's promise that the church would not fail, 'and that foule assertion, that dothe denye the people of God in England or els where to be visible church Christians is verye offensive to all godly and tender hearted Christians'. He accused those who said such things of suffering from a pride which 'will not give them leave, to distinguishe betweene corrupt churches and false churches'.[45] Yet if Winthrop classified the Roman church as a corrupt church and not as a false church, he laid himself open to all

---

[44] *Letters of Sir Francis Hastings*, ed. M. Claire Cross (Somerset Record Society, 69, Frome, 1969), 115.

[45] *Winthrop Papers*, iii (Massachusetts Historical Society, Boston, Mass., 1943), 11–13.

the arguments developed by Calvin and others against leaving a church which was not false.

Because it was so clear that succession was necessary, and that schism was a sin, Protestants had to assert that the Roman church before Luther was true enough to give them valid baptism and orders, while false enough to free them from the sin of schism in leaving it. For everyone who engaged in Protestant polemics, this passage between Scylla and Charybdis was raked with Roman artillery, and few if any Protestants completed the navigation with complete safety. A Jesuit, replying to a Laudian bishop, pointed up the dilemma:

If he say the Roman church erred fundamentally, he will not be able to shew, that Christ Our Lord had any visible church on earth when Luther appeared, and let him tell us how Protestants had, or can have, any church which was universall, and extended herselfe to all ages, if once he grant that the Roman church ceased to be the true church of Christ, and consequently, how can they hope for salvation, if they deny it to us.[46]

It hardly needed adding that if Protestants conceded that the Roman church had not ceased to be the true church of Christ, they should rejoin it.

With this Scylla and Charbydis came two different ideas of what the church of England was, encapsulated in an exchange between D'Ewes and Hyde on the Root and Branch Bill. Hyde claimed that episcopacy had continued in the church many hundred years, to which D'Ewes replied that in *this* church it had continued rather less than one hundred.[47] D'Ewes's was exactly the opposite approach from the one used by Laud, who insisted that 'we live in a church reformed, not one made new'.[48] Both then and subsequently, the church of England has been racked by the fact that behind Laud's ecclesiology lies the spectre of popery, and behind D'Ewes's lies the spectre of separatism. Whichever of these was right, it tended to follow that the other had no lawful baptism and no lawful sacraments, and therefore was no church at all. This was a severe fate, and one we can understand their desire to avoid.

---

[46] Edward Knott, alias Matthew Wilson, *Charity Maintained* (*s.l.*, 1634), 16. It serves to underline the point that the BL copy belonged to Sir Kenelm Digby, who was converted to Rome.

[47] BL Harl. MS 163. fo. 626[a–b].

[48] Laud, *Wks.* iii. 341. I would like to thank my wife for bringing this passage to my attention twenty-seven years ago. We have been debating it ever since.

The knowledge of these difficulties adds an extra dimension to our understanding of the fear of popery, and may sometimes tempt us to imagine that even some of the hotter sorts of Protestant were not always free of fear that they might have committed the sin of schism. The discomfort shows, for example, behind Jewel's reply to Harding: 'you saye, it standethe not with Goddes promise to forsake his church a thousande yeeres. It is mutche for you, M. Hardinge, openly to break Goddes commaundementes, to defile his Holy Sanctuarie, to turn light into darknesse, and darkness into light: and yet nevertheless to bind him to his promisse'.[49] This sounded good, but it was not, of course, an answer to Harding's point. Any Protestant who was impaled on this hook had to ask himself why Christ's promise had been so nearly broken, and why the church had so nearly failed. This question prompted others: why popery had been so powerful, and so tempting, that it had nearly prevailed, and, worse still, could it happen again?

One of the consequences of recent work on the conversion of England has been to push back the dates of conversion to Protestantism, often well into the later part of Elizabeth's reign. This information helps to understand why, for hot Protestants of the 1640s, the people's need to clear themselves of the guilt of schism was often still a live emotional force, and therefore may help to understand why it was necessary to magnify the evils of Rome to the point where divorce was the only possible remedy. For many of them it can only have heightened this tendency that the 'popery' from which they had separated was represented by a senior family member within their own memories. William Whitaker and Robert Bolton were both the sons of Lancashire papists, and their conversion represented a choice for the values of their universities against those of their parents. Sir Robert Harley's paternal grandfather John was a recusant, and had been in trouble in 1577 for reading loudly from the Latin primer during divine service. Sir Robert himself was praised in his funeral sermon (in 1656) for being 'the first that brought the Gospel into these parts'. Even Sir Thomas Barrington, who came from as established a Protestant family in as thoroughly converted a county as could well be found, probably remembered the popery of his grandmother. Her presentation as a recusant in 1581 was before his birth, but his

---

[49] J. E. Booty, *John Jewel as Apologist of the Church of England* (1963), 134.

father's success in melting down her gold crucifix, and making it
into rings with inscriptions contrasting 'false devotion' and 'true
religion' was probably well within his memory.[50] The continuing
assertions of such men that Rome was anti-christian should perhaps
be seen in part as continuing replies to charges of schism they faced
or had faced from older generations of their own families. One may
sometimes wonder whether their fear of popery sometimes included
a continuing fear of a nagging unease in their own consciences.

These questions accounted for a great deal of the fear which
appeared so constantly in attacks on popery, and account for some
of the tendency to magnify the power of popery to seduce true
Christians. The fear of popery is vital to the coming of the Civil
War, and if we are to understand the fear of popery, it is essential
to understand exactly what was being feared. In the 1580s almost
every Elizabethan Protestant feared popery, for it was an immediate
and physical danger. Mary Queen of Scots and the Spanish Armada
between them represented a recognizable physical threat to
England, which was not easily ignored. The anti-popery of such
cool Protestants as Lord Chancellor Hatton was very clearly and
recognizably directed at this physical target. After 1587 and 1588,
however, this physical danger slowly receded into the background.
Domestic papists, though still far from a negligible group even into
James's reign, slowly diminished in number, and began to seem less
obviously dangerous. As the physical threat receded, so a divergence
slowly appeared between the reactions of some Protestants to the
notion of a popish threat and those of others. It is essential to
understand this divergence if we are to make sense of why in
1641 some Protestants were filled with a fear of popery, and others
were not.

We have perhaps been impeded from taking the fear of popery as
a cause of the Civil War as seriously as we should have done by John
Selden's famous remark that 'we charge the prelatical clergy with
popery to make them odious, though we know they are guilty of no
such thing'.[51] Selden should have spoken for himself: he knew the
prelatical clergy were not guilty of popery, but in fact he was one of

[50] Lake, *MP*, p. 54; C. M. Dent, *Protestant Reformers in Elizabethan Oxford*
(Oxford, 1983), 170; Jacqueline Levy, 'Harleys of Brampton Bryan', Ph.D.
Thesis (London, 1983), 46, 322; *Barrington Family Letters 1628–1632*, ed.
Arthur Searle (Camden Society⁺, 28, 1983), 11–12. I am grateful to Dr Levy for
permission to quote from her thesis.
[51] John Selden, *Table Talk* (1887), 135.

the few prominent Parliamentarians who never charged them with it, and therefore a highly untypical member of the group. It should not be assumed a priori that Selden understood what those who charged the Laudian clergy with popery really meant.

Before we can judge the validity of a charge of popery, still more its sincerity, we need to know what the speaker meant by 'popery', and that was as protean a charge as 'Puritanism'. Perhaps the first question which arose was whether only those guilty of communion with the church of Rome could be described as 'papists'. When William Whitaker Master of St John's College, Cambridge, charged one of his Fellows with popery, Burghley and Whitgift both dismissed the charge as soon as they heard that he came to church: for them, a papist was necessarily someone who was in communion with the church of Rome.[52] Many members of the Long Parliament, of whom Culpepper and Seymour were the most prominent, held to this narrow definition of popery, and, almost without exception, they were Royalists. They might dislike popery as cordially as anyone else, but holding to a narrow and legal definition of it, they did not fear it, because they did not regard it as powerful enough to be dangerous. Looking back we may see such Arminians *avant la lettre* as Samuel Harsnett as coming into this category: Harsnett cordially disliked popery, which he viewed in much the same way as Ben Jonson did alchemy, as a sort of fairground con-trick. Yet Harsnett was no more frightened of popery than Jonson was of alchemy: he did not credit it with enough spiritual power to be dangerous.[53]

It was a very different matter for those who were concerned to discover why the church had so nearly failed, and went on from that concern to look for, as they saw it, the inward and spiritual dangers of which the lapse into popery had been merely the outward and visible sign: for them, it was necessary to look for the corrupting principles which had made it possible for popery to come so near success, and then to root out those principles so thoroughly that they could never grow again. They believed in unconscious popery, much as many people now believe in unconscious racism. For them, a church-papist who had conformed and come to church had not

[52] Lake, *MP*, pp. 171–80. I am grateful to Dr Lake for many interesting discussions of this case and the themes it raises.

[53] Samuel Harsnett, *Declaration of Egregious Popish Impostures* (1603), 20 and *passim*.

thereby ceased to be a papist until he was genuinely converted. For them it was necessary, in the words of the 1544 instructions for the Council of the North, that they should make people truly renounce the Bishop of Rome, 'whose abuses they shall so beat into their heads by continual inculcation as they may smell the same, and perceive that they declare it with their hearts and not with their tongues only for a form'.[54] Until this happy state was achieved, they were still papists.

For those who thought in this way, it was possible to see behind the phenomenon of church-popery a risk of a situation parallel to that so well described by Blair Worden in the Rump Parliament, in which the desire of a new regime to draw in conformists led to a situation in which the conformists outnumbered the revolutionaries, and were able to run things their own way. At times, Elizabethan evidence might suggest that such fears were valid. In the diocese of Norwich after the death of Parkhurst, the Queen sent in Bishop Freke with instructions to enforce full conformity, and he soon found that these were so unpopular that the Catholics became the main supporters of full conformity on the Norfolk and Suffolk benches. It is possible that at this point some Protestants began to wonder whether the church-papists would have the last laugh in the end.[55] When Martin Marprelate asked: 'how many bishops are there in England which have not either said masse or helped the priest to say masse or been present at it?',[56] he was appealing to these fears, and his case was weakened (or strengthened?) only by the fact that he himself had probably once been present at Mass. The tensions such cases might create on a local level are illustrated by the story of a Fellow of Merton called Henry Ledsham, suggestively from the diocese of Chester. Mr Ledsham was considered for a Fellowship in April 1571, and some objections were made against his morals and his religion, so his probation was continued until All Saints' Day. In August the College decided to elect him to a Fellowship, but required of him a 'sincere confession' renouncing the authority of the Pope, and transubstantiation and the authority of

[54] G. R. Elton, *Tudor Constitution* (Cambridge, 1960), 206. I would like to thank my wife for drawing my attention to this passage and to its implications.

[55] Collinson, *EPM*, pp. 187–8; A. Hassell Smith, *County and Court: Government and Politics in Norfolk 1558–1603* (Oxford, 1974), 208–25; Diarmaid MacCulloch, *Suffolk and the Tudors* (Oxford, 1986), 193–7.

[56] Martin Marprelate, *O Read Over D. John Bridges* (1588; repr. Leeds, 1967), Epistle, p. 16.

the Mass, and upholding clerical marriage.[57] In spite of a stormy career, including a dramatic quarrel with the Warden, he remained a Fellow for five-and-a-half years. The statutes required a Fellow to give up his Fellowship on receiving a richer benefice, or on marriage, and in 1577 the majority of the eight senior Fellows pronounced him no Fellow because he had two richer benefices, 'and moreover, he has married a wife'.[58] In Ledsham's case, the phrase 'the attractions of conformity' should perhaps be given a literal interpretation, and he does not look very convincing as a vicar in a committed Protestant church. The Long Parliament majority, and especially Pym, showed a constant concern for detecting church papists 'for the preventing of feigned conformity',[59] which suggested that they feared most of the recent changes in the church had been the work of those who, as they put it, were 'more earnest in the Protestant profession, than in the Protestant religion'.[60] They feared the Ledshams would have the last laugh.

The danger stretched beyond conscious church-papists, to all those who were corrupted by the same principles that had led to the Roman backsliding. If these principles could be identified, it was then reasonable to regard those who were seduced by them as papists in spirit, even if they were unaware of the fact. Many of the hotter Protestants therefore devoted great effort to discovering those things which were not merely the defining qualities of popery, but also its seductive elements. Perhaps the one invoked most often by Parliamentarians and those whose books they read was idolatry, which concerned Cornelius Burges so much that he said that wickedness 'primarily is the sin of idolatry'.[61] The danger of idolatry was that, as the Old Testament had taught, it was so exciting: the desire of hot Protestants to destroy images and ceremony was not because they were not attracted to them, but because they were: these things encouraged them to worship stocks and stones, instead of confining worship to God, who was its only proper object. The 'Homily on the Peril of Idolatry' said that

---

[57] *Reg. Ann. Coll. Mert. 1567–1603*, ed. J. M. Fletcher (Oxford Historical Series, NS 24, Oxford, 1976), 36–8.

[58] Ibid. 46, 47., 64, 81, 82, 85, 90, 178. He was not allowed to catechize the Postmasters.

[59] *LJ* iv. 691.

[60] Rushworth, III. i. 586.

[61] Cornelius Burges, *Two Sermons* (1645), 5.

the nature of man is none otherwise bent to worshipping images (if he may have them and see them) than it is bent to whoredome and adultery in the company of harlots. And as a man given to the lusts of the flesh, seeing a wanton harlot, sitting by her, and imbracing her, it profiteth little for one to say, beware of fornication! . . . even so, suffer images to be set in churches and temples, ye shall in vaine bid them beware of images.[62]

When John Dod spoke of Jeroboam setting up 'infectious idols', he was not speaking metaphorically.[63] Other features of 'the beauty of holiness', such as music, might be rejected in church because they did give pleasure, and not because they did not. When the Parliamentary army occupied Hereford in the opening weeks of the Civil War, 'sabbath day, about the time of morning prayer, we went to the Minster, where the pipes played, and the puppets sang so sweetly that some of our solidiers could not forbear dancing in the holy quire, whereat the Baalists were sore displeased. . . . Not satisfied with this human service, we went to divine'.[64] ·In discussing the argument that it was possible for a Protestant to attend Mass as a social courtesy, Dod said that ministers refrained from doing so because they 'feare their owne weaknesse and frailty'.[65] He seems to imply that he did not trust himself to attend a Mass without being converted to popery: a truly remarkable tribute to the power of the Mass. Jewel said: 'this it is to have once tasted of the Mass. He who drinks of it is mad'. Brasbridge, Elizabethan vicar of Banbury, said Rome caused men 'to revolte from the Christian religion unto idolatry'.[66] When the Commons divided on a clause in the Grand Remonstrance, passionately supported by Pym, which condemned the bishops for having ushered in idolatry, it was carried by 124 votes to 99. All those who voted in the majority could perfectly sincerely, on their own premises, accuse the Laudian bishops of popery. For Pym, for example, the possession of altars was sufficient proof of idolatry, and it was therefore quite legitimate to describe those guilty of altar-worship as papists.[67]

---

[62] *Sermons or Homilies* (1640 edn.), 61.
[63] Dod, *Ten Commandments* (1606 edn.), 57.
[64] *CSPD 1641–3*, vol. ccccxcii, no. 32.
[65] Dod, *Ten Commandments* (1606 edn.), 60.
[66] ZL i. 24; Barton J. Blankenfeld, 'Puritans in the Provinces: Banbury, Oxfordshire 1554–1660', Ph.D. thesis (Yale, 1985), 68. I am grateful to Dr Blankenfeld for permission to quote from his thesis.
[67] D'Ewes (C.), pp. 151–2. For Pym, see *Verney's Notes of the Long*

A closely related, and indeed overlapping, principle of popery was the belief that 'will-worship', the devising of worship by human authority, was legitimate. For many, rejection of popery meant the rejection of will-worship: in the words of Burges, preaching to the Long Parliament 'let no worship be thrust upon him, which himselfe hath not prescribed'. The Irish Articles of 1615 upheld this rejection of will-worship, contradicting the English Articles in the process: 'all worship devised by mans phantasie, besides or contrary to Scripture (as wandring on pilgrimages, setting up of candles, stations and *iubiles*, pharisaicall sects and fained religions, praying upon beades, and such like superstition' was unlawful,[68] and a central principle which had made the construction of popery possible. If this definition of popery were valid, the Articles of the church of England, which decreed that 'the church hath authority to decree rites and cermonies', were themselves popish, and the church of England actually was a popish church. Anyone who charged the Laudians with popery for this reason was charging them with something they actually believed. The point in dispute then becomes whether this was a valid definition of popery or whether, as Laud said, it implied that 'the external decent worship of God could not be upheld in this kingdom, without bringing in of popery'.[69]

Others, again, gave Calvinist doctrine so central a place that for them it became a part of the definition of Protestantism. This is the only possible ground on which Sir Thomas Roe could have defined the church of the Palatinate as the only clear Protestant church of Germany.[70] John Dod, who has a special importance because he was acting as Pym's minister for much of 1638–9, said that papists 'would . . . deprive all others of the comfort of perseverance, making this a certaine point of their religion, that no man stands certain of salvation and by this meanes they hinder men from cheerfull obedience, and cut off all sound thankfulnesse'.[71] This is one of many passages which may make us wonder whether assurance performed the same psychological functions for Calvinists as belief in the perpetual visibility of the church did for Catholics, and

Parliament, ed. John Bruce (Camden Society, 31, 1845), 123: 'alter-worship is idolatry, and that was injoyned by the bishops in all there cathedrals'.

[68] Cornelius Burges, *First Sermon* (1641), 72; *Articles of Religion* (1629), Sig. C. 3.

[69] Laud, *Wks.* VI. i. 44.   [70] *CSPD 1633–4*, vol. cclix, no. 64.

[71] Dod, *Ten Commandments* (1615 edn.), 20.

whether attachment to predestination was in part because it gave
some people back that certainty of which departure from Catholicism
had deprived them. This definition of popery is peculiarly clear in a
draft from the diocese of Hereford for the Ministers' Remonstrance
of 1641, which asked for all those to be classified as papists who
would not take an oath against popery and Arminianism, and in
favour of the doctrinal part of the Thirty-Nine Articles, the Irish
Articles, and the Lambeth Articles. They then underlined the
selective definition of orthodoxy by insisting that no one be made to
subscribe anything else whatsoever.[72] In 1604 when John Reynolds, at
Hampton Court, attacked popish books, he was pressed to define
popish books, and replied that he meant 'free will books'. In 1614
Robert Abbott the Archbishop's brother had publicly denounced
Laud as a papist in points of free will, justification, and certainty of
salvation.[73] In the face of beliefs such as these, it is not surprising
that when Fuller, vicar of St Giles Cripplegate and Dean of Ely,
maintained that there was no difference in substance between the
church of Rome and the church of England, but only in
circumstance, he should be called a papist, nor that John Buckeridge
should be so called when he asserted, at York House, that the
Council of Trent had never erred in fundamentals.[74] What is at
stake in these disputes is not the objective question whether those
accused were papists, but the subjective question how the accusers
defined popery.

This is even clearer with those, from John Field and Martin
Marprelate to Lord Brooke, who thought a key point of popery was
belief in superiority among ministers.[75] This belief, which had the
great advantage of establishing common ground with the stricter
Covenanters, was one whose holders ought to define the church of
England as popish, for if that was popery, the church of England
was in fact popish. This is a conclusion from which Field and
Martin Marprelate seem to have held back, though Martin has left
a certain ambiguity on the point. If they held back, they were

---

[72] BL Loan MS 29/172, fo. 364^{r-v}. I would like to thank Dr Jacqueline Levy
for bringing this MS to my attention, and Dr Levy and Dr Peter Donald for
valuable discussions of it.

[73] BL Add. MS 38, 492, fo. 83^v) Peter Lake, 'Calvinism and the English
Church 1570–1635', *Past and Present*, 114 (1987), 50.

[74] D'Ewes (C.), p. 98; Cosin, ii. 69.

[75] Collinson, *EPM*, p. 101; Marprelate, *O Read Over D. John Bridges*, p. 6
and other refs; Lord Brooke, *A Discourse concerning Episcopacy* (1642), 31.

influenced by the doctrine of marks of the true church, a doctrine relied on as a touchstone in deciding when it was lawful to leave a church and when it was not. On this subject, Calvin, Bancroft, and the Thirty-Nine Articles speak with a single voice: if a church contains anywhere within it the word of God duly preached, and the sacraments duly administered, then it is a true church, and those who can worship with these things should not separate from it. On the other hand, those who cannot find these two things should leave the church immediately, for it would then have become sinful to remain there. Field and his allies tried to erect discipline as a third mark of the true church, but it never obliterated the first two. In the primacy of Archbishop Whitgift, the first two were not threatened: his doctrine was not in dispute, and, save for the particular accident of kneeling, the celebration of the sacrament seems to have caused little dispute. It is then perfectly logical that the godly of the 1580s did not accuse Whitgift of popery, whereas their successors of the 1630s, facing free will and altars, did accuse Laud of popery: on their definitions of popery, they were perfectly right to do so. The question, which Laud unerringly asked them, was whether their definition was mistaken: 'perhaps that which some of them call popery is orthodox Christianity, and not one whit the worse for their miscalling it'.[76] The question, in fact, was whether in rejecting popery, they had thrown out the baby with the bath-water.

Laud's proposition perhaps provides a clue to the rival Royalist mythology, much repeated by Charles and Laud among others, which accused their opponents of being 'separatist'. When applied to such men as William Prynne, the charge seems at first sight as patently absurd as the charge of popery applied to Charles, yet perhaps we need to bring to the one charge as much as to the other an understanding of what it meant to those who made it. For Laud, Cosin, and their allies, the things the godly rejected as 'popery' were the essential characteristics of the church: what they called 'idolatry' was what Laud called a 'decent external order'. What they called 'will-worship' was no more than the words of Article XX: 'the church hath power to decree rites or ceremonies', which the Laudians were surely entitled to regard as the official doctrine of the church. For men like John Cosin, rather than superiority of ministers being a mark of popery, a perpetual episcopal succession was a necessary

---

[76] Laud, *Wks.* iii. 379–80. I would like to thank my wife for bringing this passage and its implications to my attention.

guarantee of a true visible church and of a lawful ministry. What the godly called an adherence to popish and Arminian doctrine, the Laudians regarded as proof that they had not rejected the true Catholic doctrines of the primitive church, as they believed them to be set out by the Fathers. For the Laudians, in fact, all these 'marks of popery' were essential parts of the church's claim to be regarded as a lawful and apostolic institution. If these things were of the essence of the perpetual visible church, then they were surely as entitled to think that those who rejected them were separatists even if they did not know it as the godly were to think that those who held them were papists even if they did not know it. What was really at stake behind these rival charges of popery and separatism was that within the church of England there were two churches struggling to get out. This was uncomfortable to both sides, since they all agreed that there was only one church. It therefore became daily more necessary to them, in order to prove that they did belong to that one church, to prove that the others did not. The proposition that outside the church there was no salvation was as true in politics as it was in theology, and it is natural enough that both parties should have shown a considerable determination to ensure that whoever ended up outside the church, it was not going to be them. It makes sense, then, that they should have sought to control the commanding heights of English theology.

4

The Church of England 1559–1625
A Church designed by a Committee?

'THE Devil take him, whomsoever he be, that had a design to change religion'.[1] These words were part of Charles I's off-the-cuff reply when presented with the Grand Remonstrance, and they mark out the ground on which he and the majority in the House of Commons joined issue. They agreed that there could be only one church and only one religion, and they agreed that it was a crime to alter or innovate that religion. Granted their agreement that this was a crime, they were forced to join issue on the question which of them was guilty of that crime. Since what was at stake was the claim to lawful succession, innovation was necessarily one of the major charges to be substantiated: as Laud said at the trial of Burton, Bastwick, and Prynne, 'they, which are the only, or the chief, innovators of the Christian world, having nothing to say, accuse us of innovation'.[2] Since it was a rule of the contest that the more persuasive claim of orthodoxy won the debate, it was necessary to claim it at all points. Even Anthony Lapthorne, Dr Fincham's favourite bad penny, was described in 1642, when installed as lecturer in the parish from which the High Commission had deprived him in 1617, as 'an orthodox divine'.[3]

We may get some hint of how divisive such rival claims to orthodoxy might be from the cause of Maidstone, where in February 1642 the House of Commons installed as lecturer 'Thomas Wilson, an orthodox minister', 'and Mr. Barrell, curate of the said place, is hereby required to give way thereunto'. Thomas Wilson had been suspended from his living at Maidstone by Laud for refusing to read the Book of Sports and for refusing to read an

---

[1] *CJ* ii. 330.
[2] Laud, *Wks.* VI. i. 42.
[3] *CJ* ii. 577. I would like to thank Dr Fincham for a great deal of information about the previous stormy career of Anthony Lapthorne. See also Russell, *FBM* for his possible links with the Scots during the Bishops' Wars.

'arbitrary prayer' against the Scots.[4] Robert Barrell's ecclesiastical complexion may be guessed from the fact that the rector to whom he was curate was none other than William Laud, and that he had been complained of for 'causing the communion table to be sett up to the wall at the east end'. The sharing of a pulpit between him and Wilson may have been a local civil war in its own right, and it is no surprise to find in July 1642 that Barrell was summoned before the Commons for seditious words against the Scots.[5]

The contest between Wilson and Barrell is a microcosm of one which was repeated all round England, and it cannot be stressed enough that it was not a contest between a church and its opponents, but a custody battle between two rival claimants for control of that church. It cannot be described as one between 'Anglicans' and 'Puritans' without begging every question which was at issue. The word 'Anglican' was not known in England until 1635. It is now becoming increasingly clear that the complex of ideas described by the word 'Anglican' did not exist in the Elizabethan church, any more than the word did: Peter Lake, in an important new book has argued that Anglicanism 'came to exist . . . largely because Hooker invented it'.[6] It took a long time for Hooker's invention to become popular. It did not acquire a claim to be authoritative until accepted by Charles I, and it is a serious point, and not a word-play, to say that one of the things at stake in the Civil War was whether the church of England was to be an Anglican church or not.

To say that the church of England was not divided between Anglicans and Puritans is not to say that it was a harmonious church peacefully enjoying a Calvinist consensus: a phrase neither Dr Tyacke nor I have ever used, though both of us have been accused of it. The church of England, all through the period, was a deeply divided church, but the division was not between the orthodox and the unorthodox: it was between rival claimants to the title of orthodox, and therefore between rival criteria of orthodoxy. In 1615 when George Abbot Archbishop of Canterbury and John Howson Dean of Christ Church and later Bishop of Oxford confronted each other before James I, their encounter was as far from consensus as anything can well be: the only things they agreed about were that, to win the debate, one of them would have to prove

[4] *CJ* ii. 427. Alan Everitt, *The Community of Kent and the Great Rebellion 1640–1660* (Leicester, 1966), 59, 77; Bodl. Microfilm 39, p. 31.

[5] Tyacke, p. 203; *CJ* ii. 698.   [6] Lake, *A. & P.?*, p. 227.

himself to be more orthodox, and more on James's side, than the other. This appears, for example, in the determined attempts of both parties to appropriate the memory of Archbishop Bancroft, Abbot claiming he had regarded Howson as a papist, and Howson claiming he had regarded Abbot as a Puritan.[7] The word 'Puritan' was a polemical weapon in this debate: it was used by Howson to attempt to associate Abbot's admitted predestinarian theology with an unsoundness, which he did not admit, on questions of ceremonial conformity. In fact, the word was used with intent to deceive. It is the purpose of the word to deny orthodoxy to those whose title to it is sometimes superior to that of their accusers. It is because the attempt to deceive is in the very nature of the word that it is best avoided where possible, except in discussing the accusers rather than the accused. Charges of popery and charges of Puritanism are both weapons in a struggle for power, and tell us a great deal more about those who used them than they do about those against whom they were used. This is why I have preferred throughout to describe the hotter sort of Protestants by their own preferred title of 'the godly'. The charge that Pym was a 'Puritan' served the same function as the charge that Laud was a 'papist', and historians who accept either of these charges at face value will not understand the mixture of truth and falsehood which made them such useful weapons to those who used them.

In taking the contest of 1642 as a contest between two rival claims to orthodoxy, we avoid any need to study a supposed correlation between 'Puritanism and Revolution'. So long as there was only one church, anyone in danger of being thrust out of it was liable to fight back and attempt to thrust out his accusers. It was therefore always a danger, as contemporaries said, that those who did not agree with the religion in force might find themselves turned into dissidents. We may agree with Stephen Marshall: 'I suspect, in case the tables were turned, and we had a king endeavouring to take down the bishops . . . the world would hear another divinity'.[8] If James's Calvinist daughter had succeeded him, it is perfectly possible that Laud, whom she cordially disliked, could have anticipated the

---

[7] Nicholas Cranfield and Kenneth Fincham, 'John Howson's Answers to Archbishop Abbot's Accusations', *Camden Miscellany*, XXIX (Camden Society+, 34, 1987), 319–41, quotation from p. 338. I would like to thank Dr Cranfield and Dr Fincham for letting me see this text before publication.

[8] Collinson, *RP*, p. 7; W. Lamont, *Godly Rule* (1969), 57.

schism of the non-jurors, and left subsequent historians to write learned essays on the revolutionary potential of Arminianism. Many godly preachers deserve Professor Collinson's description of Samuel Ward: 'as factious and subversive as the *Homily of Obedience*'.[9] The loophole in this description is that where it followed Acts 5: 29, even the 'Homily of Obedience' was subversive: it exhorted its readers to obey God rather than man. It was only the truly fortunate who believed that they did not have to make the choice.

In fighting for the claim of orthodoxy, the two sides were forced, even if with some degree of reluctance on both sides, to join issue on the interpretation of the settlement of 1559, which was the legal basis of the church in which they lived. The problem we have to tackle is how it was possible for two such diametrically opposite groups of people to believe, or hope they believed, that they were heirs of the same settlement. Part of the blame for this state of affairs must rest on the settlement itself: its ambiguity, which was its short-term political strength, was equally its long-term political weakness. In May 1640 the Laudian canons defended the placing of the holy table at the east end, as ordered by Queen Elizabeth's Injunction, while in November the Long Parliament, arranging its first communion, directed that the communion table be brought down into the middle of the church, 'according to the rubric'. Both parties were quoting, and both parties were quoting the same source: Queen Elizabeth's Injunction, which directed that the table be kept at the east end, and brought down into the body of the church at service time.[10] Since it was not to be imagined that churchwardens would engage in a lengthy furniture-moving session every Saturday evening, it is hard not to suppose that a local option was the result the Queen had intended. Even more plainly, contradiction emerged from the requirement of the Queen's Injunctions that wafers should be used for communion, taken beside the requirement of the Prayer Book and the Act of Uniformity for 'common bread'. Everyone who took communion had to disobey one of these requirements.

However, the greatest ambiguity is not here, but between the settlement of 1559 itself and the people appointed to administer it, for a high proportion of the bishops appointed to administer the

[9] Collinson, *RP*, p. 177.
[10] Laud, *Wks.* v. 625; *CJ* ii. 32; Tyacke, pp. 200–6. I would like to thank Dr Anthony Milton for advice about Laudian attitudes to 1559.

settlement were men who, to put it no higher, had a limited faith in the settlement they were supposed to enforce. In Professor Collinson's words, 'that she committed episcopal authority to men of conviction rather than time-servers, to men whose outlook was in many ways so unlike her own, is a conundrum which underlies much of the ecclesiastical conflict of the reign.'[11] It also underlies much of the ecclesiastical conflict of 1642. Since much of the working apparatus of the church was constructed by these men after they were in office, and much was constructed by Queen and Council before they were in office, the Elizabethan Settlement also represents two deeply conflicting bodies of people. Indeed, it may be seen as two settlements. The Acts of Supremacy and Uniformity, and the Book of Common Prayer, were put together in 1559, before any bishops were named, and, as Jewel bitterly complained, '*we* are not consulted'.[12] On the other hand, because the responsibility of the clergy for doctrine was so deeply ingrained in received thinking, the Thirty-Nine Articles had to wait until the first Protestant convocation, of 1562–3. They and the *Book of Homilies* represent, even if imperfectly, the minds of those same reformed clergy who were not consulted on the making of the settlement of 1559. This is how the church of England acquired its peculiarly hybrid character: its discipline and its doctrine came out of different·minds, and therefore represented ideals of the church which were at least potentially divergent. It is not surprising that there were a number of people in the church who owed a stronger allegiance to one than they did to the other. Since the bishops who accepted office in this imperfect settlement naturally hoped to reform it further, their hopes helped to give rise to the deepest ambiguity of all, between the Queen, who was 'resolved . . . to alter nothing which she had once settled', and those who regarded the settlement as the beginning of a 'continuous further reformation'.[13] It is this second ideal of 1559 which was followed by Strickland in 1571, offering a reformation of the Book of Common Prayer which was 'a reformacion not contrariant but directly personant to our profession'.[14] Oliver St John in 1641 was surely following the same ideal when he claimed, during the debates on the Root and Branch Bill, that the Prayer Book of 1559 had only been intended to be temporary.[15]

[11] Collinson, *EPM*, pp. 61–2.   [12] *ZL* i. 23.
[13] Collinson, *EPM*, pp. 14, 35.   [14] Hartley, p. 200.
[15] Bodl. MS Rawlinson D. 1099, fo. 56[v].

At the beginning of the Elizabethan church, those who subscribed to the ideal of 'further reformation' included a considerable number of its bishops. Jewel, writing to Martyr about 'that comical dress', and other such things, said that 'these are indeed, as you very properly observe, the relics of the Amorites. For who can deny it? And I wish that sometime or other they may be taken away and extirpated even to the lowest roots'. Sandys, who was 'rather vehement in this matter', hoped that the copes, the 'popish vestments' 'will not last very long', and even Richard Cox, not one of the hottest reformers among the episcopate, complained about the crucifix in the Queen's chapel that 'the Lord must be entreated that this stumbling block may at length be removed'.[16] It is not surprising that with bishops who felt so little enthusiasm for the ceremonies they were supposed to enforce, when it came to the enforcement of conformity, the episcopal trumpet gave forth an uncertain sound. Grindal, writing to the preacher to the Merchant Adventurers at Antwerp, told him to use the Prayer Book, but as much or as little of it as the elders of his congregation liked. He was to place the communion table as the local reformed churches did, and need not insist on the surplice or kneeling at communion. Bishop Bentham, addressing the man who was to be minister to Sir Robert Harley's mother, was equally Nelsonian: 'for the cross in baptism, I will never require it of you, and for the surplice, if you will wear it but sometimes, or but twice or thrice, or if you will wear it but once, I will urge you no further.'[17] This is how the church of England acquired a divergence, which lasted right through to the Civil War, between what was legally required and what authorities treated as normal and acceptable practice. When D'Ewes in 1641 described Bishop Wren's requirement of reading the whole of the Prayer Book service as an innovation, he was not altogether without excuse.[18] To require the church of England to work to rule was to disrupt it.

When this first generation of bishops asked themselves why they accepted this imperfect settlement, the answer was normally that they did so for the sake of the doctrine, in which they were allowed a comparatively free hand. Grindal, excusing himself for the Advertisements, told Bullinger that in 1559 they had been unable to

[16] *ZL* i. 52, 74, 65, and other refs.
[17] Collinson, *EPM*, pp. 67–8.
[18] BL Harl. MS 164, fo. 890ª.

prevail 'either with the Queen *or the Parliament*', but had decided to accept office 'since the pure doctrine of the Gospel remained in all its integrity and freedom'.[19] Jewel, while protesting that 'as to ceremonies and maskings there is a little too much foolery', consoled himself because 'the doctrine is everywhere most pure'.[20] The belief that the English church was acceptable because of the purity of its doctrine might restrain people much more radical than Jewel and Grindal: Walter Travers the Presbyterian said that 'true doctrine as the elder sister is recovered let us not hinder her to affect also discipline with her health'.[21] Sir Francis Knollys in 1584 called on Whitgift, 'to open the mouths of all zealous preachers, being sound in doctrine, although they refuse to subscribe to any traditions of man',[22] and William Perkins said that 'our owne churches in England hold, beleeve and maintaine, and preach the true faith, that is, the ancient doctrine of salvation by Christ, taught and published by the prophets and apostles, as the book of the articles of faith agreed upon in open Parliament doth fully shew'.[23] To those who accepted the doctrine of marks of the true church, this was a compelling reason for continued membership of the church, and Robert Browne the separatist recalled those who told him, when he contemplated separation, that the bishops had the word and sacraments, and therefore must have the true church.[24]

For Perkins, and for many others, a predestinarian version of true doctrine was also vital to their ability to rebut Catholic arguments about the succession of the visible church. John Foxe, in his *Book of Martyrs*, provided a doctrine of the succession of the church through an underground succession of true believers, including the Albigenses, Wycliffe, and Hus. The definition of the church which resulted from this doctrine of succession was inevitably not a very institutional one, and Archbishop Abbot, who followed Foxe, rendered the promise of the perpetual visibility of the church as a promise 'that the congregation of God's saints shall continue'.[25] This did not lead to a denial of the doctrine of a visible church. It did lead to a doctrine of low visibility from which only

[19] Collinson, *EPM*, p. 33; *ZL* 168–9: my italics.
[20] *ZL* i. 55.   [21] Lake, *MP*, p. 65.
[22] *CSPD 1581–90*, vol. clxxi, no. 23.
[23] R. T. Kendall, *Calvin and English Calvinists* (Oxford, 1979), 54.
[24] Collinson, *EPM*, p. 133.
[25] G. Abbot, *Treatise of the Perpetuall Visibilitie and Succession of the True Church* (1624), 9.

Presbyterian discipline seemed to offer an escape. Bishop Morton, who also followed Foxe, said that the unregenerate were only as much members of the church as spittle of the body.[26] It was very tempting to any Protestant who drew his notion of the church from Foxe to shift the emphasis of Christ's promises on the church from the institutional visible church to the invisible church of true believers. This turned Christ's promise that the faith of the church would not fail into the tautological statement that the faith of those whose faith would not fail would not fail. Morton was retreating to safe ground when he maintained that 'the Catholike church doth essentially consist only of persons regenerate in this life, and predestinate to life everlasting'.[27] Perhaps inevitably, it was Perkins who developed this approach to its utmost logical extent.

He too pinned his identification of the church on predestination. He said there were two sorts of members of the visible church, 'members before God, and members before men', but it was of course the first that interested him. They, who gave identity to the church, were the elect: 'nowe to beleeve the church is nothing els but to beleeve that there is a companie of the predestinate, made one in Christ, and that withall we are in the number of them'. The church, in fact, could be defined as 'a peculiar companie of men, predestinate to life everlasting, and made one in Christ'. These were the people Perkins defined as 'the family of God'.

There remained the problem of identifying the ecclesiastical communities in which these people were to be found. It was difficult to do this by succession, since the church had so long been concealed, and 'lay hidde under the chaff of poperie'. The 'popish assemblies' had been no true or sound members of the Catholic church. Perkins, then, did what the first Protestants had perforce had to do: he identified the church by the truth of its doctrine, rather than by its visible succession: 'and whereas they [the papists] plead for themselves that they have succession from the apostles, the true answer is that succession of person is nothing without succession of doctrine, which they want, and we see that heretikes have succeeded lawful ministers'. Without true doctrine, it was not a true church: 'the preaching of the doctrine of the prophets and apostles, ioyned with any measure of faith and obedience, is an infalliable mark of *a* true church'. It was true that baptism had descended through the

[26] T. Morton, *Grand Imposture of the (Now) Church of Rome* (1626), 11–12.
[27] Ibid. 10.

popish church, but it had not belonged to the papists, but to 'another hidden church of God, which he hath in all ages gathered forth of the middest of them'. This view left any church which suffered changes in doctrine dangerously liable to an identity crisis.[28] For Perkins's successors, then, the loss of the doctrine of predestination would deprive them, not only of their reasons for conforming to an imperfect church of England, but also of any viable doctrine of the church whereby to justify their separation from Rome.

There is no need to claim that the spectrum of reformers from Cox to Perkins took up the whole of the Elizabethan church: it seems improbable that this can have been the case. Yet it is this part of the spectrum which provides most of the leaders of the church, most of the dominant figures in the universities after the initial purges, and most of the published work. In later generations, the Laudians were to experience difficulties in tracing their visible succession through the dark days of Elizabeth's reign. When Peter Heylin maintained that under Leicester's Chancellorship, Oxford had been so much altered that 'there was little to be seen in it of the church of England', he provided an amusing, and possibly deliberate, echo of Foxe on the dark days of popery.[29] Dr Lake's list of those who challenged Calvinist orthodoxy before the death of Elizabeth consists of Corro, Barrett, Baro, Hooker, Overall, and Harsnett. From an earlier generation, we should add Bishops Cheyney and Guest, who were described by Thomas Norton as heretics, because Lutherans and free-will men.[30] Harsnett's Paul's Cross sermon of 1584, on the well-chosen text, 'as I live, saith the Lord, I delight not in the death of the wicked', is a superb anti-Calvinist production, including a very early attempt to brand Calvinists as 'puritans'. Yet the two important points about this sermon are that it was preached in 1584, and that it was printed in 1656.[31] It is rash to commit ourselves to an interpretation which stresses either of these facts more than the other. At the time, Harsnett was silenced by the Archbishop, while Overall was

[28] William Perkins, *Exposition of the Creede*, in *Works* (Cambridge, 1603 edn.), 365, 362, 343, 365, 367, 368, 366, 368: my italics.
[29] Conrad Russell, *Crisis of Parliaments* (Oxford, 1971), 209.
[30] Peter Lake, 'Calvinism and the English Church 1570–1635', *Past and Present*, 114 (1987), 34–5; Collinson, *EPM*, p. 206. I am grateful to Dr Tyacke for reminding me of Bishops Cheyney and Guest.
[31] *Three Sermons*, printed by Dr Richard Stewart (*s.l.*, 1656), BL E. 1629 (1), p. 165 and *passim*. Also BL Harl. MS 3142, fo. 54ʳ.

dismissed by him as 'factious and inclined to that sect that loveth to pick quarrels to the present state and government of the church'.[32] Corro and Baro were foreigners and Barrett later a convert to Rome, and if this is taken for an 'Anglican' succession, not even the presence of Hooker is enough to make this into a very impressive list. It is perhaps a more serious difficulty for any notion of a continuous 'Anglican' tradition that there is no defence of the disputed ceremonies before Hooker which gives them any positive content, or advances beyond the bare and negative assertion that they are not unlawful. This 'religious vacuum at the heart of the conformist position', as Peter Lake calls it,[33] is well illustrated in the will of Archbishop Sandys, drawn up in 1587. He wrote:

concerning rites and ceremonies by political constitutions authorized amongst us, as I am and have been persuaded, that such as are now set down by public authority in this church of England, are no way either ungodly or unlawful . . . so I have ever been and presently am persuaded, that some of them be not so expedient in this church now, but that in the church reformed, and in all this time of the Gospel (wherein the seed of the scripture hath so long been sown) they may better be disused by little and little, than more and more urged.[34]

So long as ceremonies which remained a requirement of conformity were defended with no more enthusiasm than this, those who defended them could not complain if they were regarded as the cooler sort of Protestants. Dr Lake's remarks are meant to apply to the clergy, and specifically to published work. Among the laity, we can find two members of Parliament whose remarks suggest they may have had a view of the church institutional and sacrament-centred enough to be recognized by Howson or Buckeridge. These are Francis Alford and James Dalton. Alford, after a complaint that 'our shepe will teach their sheppard', protested that 'I like not of these verball sermondes'. Dalton asked, if unqualified ministers were thrust out, 'what becomes of the sacramentes, baptism, buryall?' Alford replied: 'it willbe come of buryall as on did that threw him into the earth and said "farewell Anthony"'.[35] These are

[32] M. Claire Cross, *Royal Supremacy in the Elizabethan Church* (1969), 206. This is a good example of the all-purpose usefulness of the slur of 'Puritanism'.

[33] Lake, *A. & P.?*, p. 66.

[34] Edwin Sandys, *Sermons* (Parker Society, 1842), 448.

[35] J. E. Neale, *Elizabeth I and Her Parliaments*, ii (1957), 80; BL Lansdowne MS 43, fo. 164ʳ.

views of the functions of the church which Richard Hooker would have recognized. For these two members, these were not new ideas of the 1580s. They had advanced similar arguments against the bill for tolerating French and Dutch reformed services in 1572. Alford said that 'he thinketh the preferrers of this bill had a zeale but no science. He thinketh the matter longeth best to divines, and therefore would have the matter first treated of in the Convocation house . . . neither we to follow the example of other realmes, having more learned men in England then any other dominion which he hathe beene in.' Dalton supported his objection to following the continental example, urging that it was 'a derogation to the learned men of England' to argue that we should follow the practice of other places. The stress on the sacraments rather than preaching, the rejection of the continental example, and the belief that religious matters should be settled by the clergy, all make these men ancestors of the Caroline church of England, but they are part of a lonely and often submerged group, not of the mainstream Protestantism of Elizabethan England. They did the same service for later Anglicans' notions of the continuous succession of their church that Wycliffe and Hus had done for Protestants' belief in their succession through the fourteenth and fifteenth centuries.[36] No doubt these two members are the tip of an iceberg, but it is an iceberg too invisible for us to know even whether it was a Protestant or a Catholic iceberg.

The dominance of the church by those with a limited attachment to its discipline and ceremonies was strengthened, rather than weakened, by the limited success of Whitgift's subscription campaign of 1584. After this campaign had provoked protests from all the lay members of the Privy Council except Sir Christopher Hatton, it became painfully clear that if the church of England should ever seriously attempt to exclude all those who would not give it full ceremonial conformity, it would barely have a church left. The power and influence of prominent laymen with limited sympathy for Whitgift's efforts would alone have been enough to ensure that. When Robert Beale Clerk of the Council told Whitgift that he used the Prayer Book 'according to the right rules of Christian libertye', the Archbishop cannot have been in much doubt what he meant.[37] He meant he was leaving large parts of it out.

[36] Hartley, pp. 362, 369.   [37] BL Add. MS 48,039, fo. 3ʳ.

When Whitgift told two Oxford Fellows that he intended to enforce the wearing of the surplice in University College, they said, perfectly correctly, that to agree would be to derogate from the authority of their Visitor the Earl of Leicester, who also happened to be Chancellor. Leicester's co-operation was unlikely, and, they reported, 'we were lett go'.[38] The patchwork quilt of local jurisdictions which made up Elizabethan England made it unlikely that standards of orthodoxy would ever cease to be subject to local variation. In Northampton, for example, the mayor claimed in 1610 that the surplice had not been seen in forty years, and when it appeared, it was almost bound to be regarded as an innovation, as, locally, it was.[39]

This limited and compromising definition of conformity had become so entrenched that in the 1630s, when stricter conformity was being aimed at, Archbishop Neile complained bitterly of the use of the word 'conformable' to apply to any people who used parts of the Prayer Book, rather than only to those who used it in full.[40] The Laudians were demanding not only innovations, but also a stricter enforcement of rules already in existence. The distinction was neatly encapsulated by one of John Winthrop's correspondents in the 1630s, who distinguished between those deprived for breach of the 'old conformity' and those deprived for breach of the 'new conformity'. Since he listed himself among those deprived for breach of the 'old conformity', his distinction should be taken as honest.[41] Yet, by pre-1625 standards, even full enforcement of the 'old conformity' might legitimately be regarded as innovation.

If nature abhors a vacuum, ambitious young graduates in search of a bishopric abhor it even more, and it is remarkable that this vacuum at the heart of the conformist position took so long to fill. The first signs that things were changing began to come early in the 1590s. This was in part, as Dr Lake stresses, the result of the debate with Presbyterianism, which made it possible to organize the arguments for the church in a quite new way, and above all, put an end to the situation in which the most Protestant argument could be assumed to be the best. The defeat of the threat from Mary Queen

---

[38] BL Add. MS 38,492, fo. 80ʳ.

[39] W. J. Shiels, *Puritans in the Diocese of Peterborough* (Northampton, 1979), 8.

[40] *CSPD 1633–4*, vol. cclix, no. 78; also *CSPD 1629–31*, vol. cliii, no. 45.

[41] *Winthrop Papers*, iii (Massachusetts Historical Society, Boston, Mass., 1943), 380–1.

of Scots and the Spanish fleet in 1587–8 was another reason why things began to shift. For those for whom the threat of popery was external and physical, it became possible to argue that the hotter Protestants were 'afraid of papistry more than is the cause'.[42] This remark came, significantly, from an opponent of the Lambeth Articles of 1595, for it was the failure to achieve confessional status for the Lambeth Articles which gave a green light to those with alternative views of the nature and functions of the church. The Calvinists remained in control for a long time after the Lambeth Articles, but because they had been denied monopoly, therefore, as Peter Lake says, their 'claim to represent the sole fount of orthodoxy in the church of England was definitively discredited'.[43]

For a long time, those with alternative views were a small voice, though often not a very still one. When Archbishop Abbot in 1615 accused Howson of not preaching against papists, Howson replied that the reason was that 'in my time there were never above 3 or 4 att once, that were suspected of popery, and there were 300 preachers whoe opposed them by sermons and disputacons: contrary wise there were ever 300 supporters of puritanisinge, and but 3 or 4 to oppose'.[44] No doubt there is a considerable element of rhetorical exaggeration in these words, but a representative of a creed securely in the saddle would not have chosen that particular exaggeration.

During the twenty-five years between the publication of the first part of Hooker's *Ecclesiastical Polity* and the synod of Dort, Hooker, Howson, and their colleagues rapidly built up an alternative ideal of the church, which made it no longer necessary for conformists to portray themselves as a pale shadow of their nonconforming opponents, holding the same beliefs but not being as serious about them. We are meeting, for the first time, a defence of conformity which does not stop at regarding it as an absence of vice, but can argue it to be a positive virtue. For Hooker, the starting-point of this new construction was the rejection of the Foxeite view of the succession of the true church as based on a collection of individual true believers: for Hooker, it was a succession of 'a sensibly known company' of professing Christians, sharing 'one Lord, one faith, one baptism'. This means that the church of

---

[42] Lake, 'Calvinism and the English Church', pp. 47–8. For the argument about the effects of the debate with Presbyterianism, see Lake, *A. & P.?*, *passim*.
[43] Id., *MP*, p. 236.
[44] Cranfield and Fincham, 'John Howson's Answers', p. 330.

England necessarily derived its succession from Rome, of which it was, in Dr Lake's phrase, 'a reformed continuation'.[45] This meant, in turn, that Hooker had to concede that Rome, though corrupt, nevertheless remained a true church, which they were continuing even while reforming its 'decayed estate'. From this he proceeded to the proposition that it was necessary to retain as much, and not as little, of the old foundation as we could. When he added the proposition (anathema to Perkins) that we had to rely on the authority of the church to know that the Scripture was God's word, he had created an ideal which, even if it might be hundreds of years old in Christianity, was perhaps being heard for the first time in Protestantism.[46]

This changed attitude to the succession from the Roman church conferred a limited legitimacy on the pre-Reformation church, since it became part of their ecclesiastical pedigree. This led to a sharply diminished enthusiasm for the abolition of things which had been abused in days of popery, and brought in instead a readiness to distinguish between use and abuse. John Howson, preaching at Paul's Cross in 1597, said that 'they have to doo with the reformation of the church or common-wealth, may learn not to take away the use of good things, because they be abused, but remoove the abuse, and restore the thing to his proper nature and first institution.'[47] George Digby, speaking on the Root and Branch Petition in 1641, turned to the same argument:

but what have we here? A multitude of allegations, a multitude of instances of abuses and depravations of church-government: and what inferred from thence? Let the use be utterly abolished for the abuses sake: as if they should say, that because drunkenness and adultery are grown so epidemical, as is alleged in the petition, let there be no more use of wine nor of women in the land.[48]

This is a fundamentally different attitude from that which argued that the use led necessarily to the abuse, and took, for example, bishops and images for marks of popery, because they had been abused under popery, and therefore were likely to be abused again.

---

[45] Lake, *A. & P.?*, pp. 155-6.

[46] Ibid. 157, 153-4. For Perkins's view, see *Exposition of the Creede*, in *Works* (Cambridge, 1603 edn.), 364: 'We knowe and are resolved that Scripture is Scripture, even by the Scripture it selfe'.

[47] John Howson, *Sermon preached at Paules Crosse* (1597), 16.

[48] Rushworth III. i. 171.

This changed attitude to physical continuity followed logically from the changed attitude to institutional continuity from the church of Rome.

From concern about the visible church, they turned naturally to concern about the physical state of the church as a building: John Howson, at Paul's Cross, complained that in country villages 'the churches are almost become . . . little better than hogstyes',[49] a phrase we should hesitate to take as a figure of speech, since Wren, in his 1636 visitation in the diocese of Norwich, discovered a church which actually was being used as a hogsty.[50] It was not only in country villages that churches were so irreverently treated: in the 1630s a man from Bedfordshire (hardly one of 'the dark corners of the land') was found pissing in St Paul's, and when challenged, replied that 'he knew it not to be a church'.[51] It is easy to understand why cases like these might have provoked a need to reassert that a church was a holy place, and to mark out that fact by ceremonial furnishing. Howson complained that churches were 'not like the palaces of princes, as they were in the primitive church . . . but like a country hall, faire whitelimmed, or a citizen's parlour, at best well wainscotted; as though we were rather Platonists than Christians'.[52]

Sir Edwin Sandys, the Archbishop of York's son and Richard Hooker's pupil, followed his tutor rather than his father, and even contrasted Protestants unfavourably with papists in this point. He wrote, in terms which would have bewildered Tyndale or Latimer: 'the one thing I cannot but highly commend in that sort and order; they spare nothing that either cost can performe in enriching, or skill in adorning the temples of God, or set out his service with the greatest pompe and magnificency that can bee devised'. Sandys knew that many of his fellow-Protestants rejected such arguments, but 'notwithstanding I must confesse, it could never sincke into my heart, that in proportion of reason, the allowance for the furnishing out of the service of God should be measured by the skant and strict rule of meere necessity'. He endorsed what was later to be a key Laudian argument in claiming that outward state could increase devotion: 'even as in princes courts, so in the service of God also,

[49] John Howson, *Second Sermon* (1598), 27.
[50] R. W. Ketton Cremer, *Norfolk in the Civil War* (1969), 72.
[51] Patrick Collinson, *Archbishop Grindal* (1979), 157.
[52] Howson, *Second Sermon*, p. 27.

this outward state and glory being well disposed, doth engender, quicken, encrease and nourish the inward reverence and respectfull devotion which is due unto so soveraigne majestie and power'.[53]

With the concern for the material church came a concern for the damage a hundred years since the Reformation had done to the material status of the clergy: Matthew Sutcliffe complained that a cobbler could live at more ease and in more reputation, and keep more servants than a minister,[54] and John Howson Vice-Chancellor of Oxford protested that it was no excuse to say that learning was its own reward, for that would mean that gentlemen only would be learned. In this, the new churchmen could make common ground with clergy as different from them as Walter Travers and Cornelius Burges. What is distinctive about this group is the readiness with which they linked their own material concerns with concern for the church as a consecrated place, and with its need for 'rich and sumptuous ornaments, great treasures and large revenwes'.[55] Jeremy Taylor, preaching at Uppingham in the 1630s, brilliantly linked the ideas together in his claim that the clergy of the church of England had mourned in black for four-score years. When we find that in the same sermon, he had inveighed against Luther, Calvin, Wycliffe, and the Waldenses, it does not take much imagination to suppose that, like Hooker, he had begun his reconstruction from rejecting Foxe's doctrine of the succession of the visible church.[56] For Richard Montague also, rejection of the Foxeite succession was a central principle: he told Cosin in January 1625 that he did not fear 'any lineal deduction from, and extraction out of, Wiclif, Hus, Albigenses, *Pauperes de Lugduno*, of a visible church'.[57]

Inside this refurbished church, they wanted to play down the exclusive emphasis given to preaching, in order to leave room for worship, which, as Howson said, involved a virtue 'morall, not intellectuall'. He claimed that preachers were turning churches into schools, a complaint which was not just a rude phrase, but an expression of serious concern that an oral appeal to the understanding was being allowed to blot out worship and an appeal to the senses.[58] For John Buckeridge, Laud's tutor at St John's and then bishop of

[53] Sir Edwin Sandys, *Speculum Europae* (1638), 12–14.
[54] Lake, *A. & P.?*, p. 116.
[55] John Howson, *Sermon at Paules Crosse*, pp. 31–2; id., *Second Sermon*, p. 21.
[56] BL Harl. MS 541, fos. 110ᵛ–111ʳ.
[57] *Correspondence of John Cosin*, ed. G. Ornsby, i (Surtees Society, 55, 1872), 45.   [58] John Howson, *Sermon preached at St. Maries* (1603), 6.

Rochester, preaching was 'the doctrine that teacheth the way that leadeth to God's worship, but not properly the worship it selfe'. For Buckeridge, preaching was something which came down from God to us, but worship was something which went up from us to God, and both were essential to a properly conducted service. Preaching might 'serve to feede the understanding, and stirre up the affection; but the offering of our hearts and soules in some one kinde or other, that is indeede the worship of God'.[59] In 1629 Dr John Browning, an Arminian and Lancelot Andrewes's former chaplain, made the same distinction between preaching and worship. When complaining to Laud of the extent of support for Thomas Hooker the troublesome godly preacher at Chelmsford, he referred to 'the people hereabouts being overmuch addicted to "hearing the word", as they call it, to the neglect of God's service and worship'.[60] It rounds out our picture to find that Browning was reported to the Long Parliament for saying the Five Members were justly accused, and for being 'a notable Arminian and alter-adorer'.[61] The interest of many poets in meditation suggests that they felt that the divinity on offer was concentrated too much on the understanding and too little on the affections: one man, translating a volume of Jesuit meditations, said he did so because 'deceaved Protestants' had no knowledge of the contemplative life, because their doctrine was all definition and speculation.[62]

We should, perhaps, give some weight to the protestations of those who said these things that they were not against preaching: it is not an insignificant paradox that most of these attacks on excessive preaching are known to us through sermons, and Lancelot Andrewes, perhaps the greatest prophet of the new creed, had some claim to be regarded as the greatest preacher of his generation. Occasionally, a deeper hostility emerges. Richard Bancroft at Hampton Court, argued that in a church newly planted, preaching was very necessary, but in a church well established, such as that of England, it was less necessary.[63] In 1627 the Cambridge Heads of

[59] John Buckeridge, *Discourse Concerning Kneeling* (1618), 38–9.

[60] *CSPD 1629–31*, vol. cli, no. 12. On Browning, see Tyacke, pp. 190–2.

[61] *PJ* i. 241.

[62] L. L. Martz, *Poetry of Meditation* (New Haven, Conn., 1954), 8, also pp. 114, 171, and *passim*. I am grateful to Professor Martz for much valuable help with the literary dimension of these issues.

[63] W. Barlow, *Summe and Substance of the Conference* (1604), 53–4; but see also BL Add. MS 38, 492, fo. 83ᵛ.

Houses supported the revision of the Emmanuel College Statutes, for the same reason.[64] These incidents illustrate the extent to which the new churchmanship rested on a conviction that popery had been defeated which their opponents were quite unble to share.

In place of the emphasis on preaching, the new churchmen offered a profound emphasis on prayer: as George Herbert had it,

> Resort to sermons, but to prayer most.
> Praying's the end of preaching.[65]

When they spoke of prayer, they did not mean extempore prayer, which they regarded as an undisciplined enthusiasm: they were expressing an almost Cluniac belief in the repetition of a set and prescribed series of liturgical forms, and above all defending the Book of Common Prayer, which Richard Bancroft said had been published with so much approbation 'as that it was accounted the worke of God'.[66] Howson, in his 1619 Visitation Articles, asked whether visiting preachers read the *whole* service on Sundays and holy days.[67] One of the fullest expositions came from Buckeridge:

it is a strange noveltie, and indeed most monstrous in the church of Christ, that there should bee no prescribed forms of prayer, and administration of sacraments, but every man left to his libertie, or rather licence, to worship God after his owne fancie; and under the name of forbidding will-worship, to set out nothing but will-worship in the church, and indeed as many will-worships as there be wils, and so set up altar against altar, and worship against worship, and make the church, that is . . . a well-ordered armie, or house, or kingdome, to bee no better than a Babell, a tower of confusion.

He complained that there were some reformers 'or rather deformers' who would not even use the Lord's Prayer because it was a set form.[68]

Worship, for them, must be a physical, as well as an intellectual, act, and Buckeridge defended kneeling as 'an acte of divine and religious worship'. Here we have in a nutshell the ambiguity of who was orthodox: kneeling at communion had been officially prescribed, but a matter of dispute ever since the making of the settlement. Therefore, in a sense, it was those who believed in it who should be

---

[64] Hamilton MSS 149.

[65] George Herbert, 'Church Porch', 5–6, in *George Herbert and Henry Vaughan*, ed. Louis L. Martz (Oxford, 1986), 6.

[66] Richard Bancroft, *Sermon preached at Paules Crosse* (1588), 53.

[67] John Howson, *Articles to be Enquired Of* (Oxford, 1619), art. 16.

[68] Buckeridge, *Kneeling*, pp. 77–8.

regarded as orthodox. Yet the Elizabethan defences of it had always been on the ground that it had no spiritual content, was not an act of worship, but purely an act of external order recommended by authority. To call it an act of worship, for many Elizabethans, would only have been to admit the charge of those who condemned it that it was idolatrous.

For these men, worship concerned a visible Christian community marked by the sacraments administered by a priest. For Buckeridge, 'this sacrament is the onely proper externall dayly sacrifice of the church, without which the other two relatives cannot stand; viz, that there is no religion without priesthood, nor priesthood without sacrifice'. Between him and Peter Smart the canon of Durham, who believed that 'Christ was sent of God to be the last priest, which should offer the last sacrifice, upon the last altar, that ever the world should have',[69] was a gulf so wide that it was hard to see how they could long continue to participate in the same worship in the same church. For Buckeridge, the sacraments were that by which 'we are made one body of Christ, and one blood, and members one of another, being incorporated with Christ': 'by the force and effect of this sacrament [in this case the communion] we receive power against sinne, and Satan, the abilitie to serve God in holinesse and righteousnesse'.[70] When Bishop Morton, at York House, asked in surprise: 'what? will you have the grace of God tied to the sacraments?', he was answered with a resounding and unequivocal 'yes'.[71] With this sacramental stress came a frank desire to pitch worship to appeal to the senses, and not merely to the understanding. Buckeridge claimed that 'wee sucke his blood, and put our tongues into the wounds of our redeemer, which being made redd within and without, wee are iudged to be madd by the wise men of this world'.[72] Lancelot Andrewes, preaching on the crucifixion in 1604, was making the same appeal to the imagination: 'his blessed body given as an anvile to be beaten upon, with the violent hands of these barbarous miscreants'.[73] John Bankes the future Chief Justice, in a

[69] Ibid. 56; Peter Smart, *Downe–Fall and Vanitie Of Popish Ceremonies* (Edinburgh, 1628), 8. Buckeridge would have conceded that there was a sense in which Smart's remark was true, but it was not the sense Smart meant. There was no sense in which Smart could have conceded that Buckeridge's remark was true.

[70] Buckeridge, *Kneeling*, pp. 104–6.

[71] Cosin, ii. 61–2.   [72] Buckeridge, *Kneeling*, p. 118.

[73] Lancelot Andrewes, *Copie of the Sermon* (1604), Sig. B. 3. In this chapter, because of its chronological focus, I have deliberately restricted myself to those of Andrewes's works which were published in his lifetime.

commonplace book which drew very heavily on this sermon, added the refinement of asking himself to imagine Christ covered with 'the filthy spittle of the Iewes'.[74]

With this appeal to the senses in worship, the new churchmen combined an appeal to the reason of the learned in matters of theology. In doing so, they at least played down the Reformation emphasis on *sola Scriptura*, in favour of a defence of the authority of the church as its interpreter. Bancroft claimed that 'God hath only bour‑d himself unto his church of purpose, that men by his good directions might in this point be releeved. To whose godlie determinations in matters of question, hir doubtfull children ought to submit themselves without any curious or wilfull contradictions'. Otherwise, he said, 'if authoritie and libertie of judging shall be left to private men, there will never be anie certaintie set downe, but rather all religion will whollie become doubtfull'.[75] On this authority of the church, Howson grounded a doctrine of 'progresse in true religion either inwardly from faith to faith, and from grace to grace, or outwardly . . . from lesse to more worship, from fewer to more devout and religious ceremonies, which I have observed before to be the case of God's church, both in the Olde and New Testament'.[76] For those who took will-worship to be one of the central evils of popery, this doubtless appeared a clear exposition of the principles which had enabled the Roman church to become so corrupt. It was probably only the fact that Howson had prudently embedded these arguments in a defence of the church's authority to celebrate the Queen's accession day which saved him from serious questioning.

It should be now be apparent that we have for some time been discussing a group of people largely conterminous with the early Arminians without feeling the need to mention Arminianism, and the mere fact that it is possible to do this tells us something of importance about the group of churchmen known as the Arminians. Not all the people here mentioned were Arminian: Bancroft never was, and in his Paul's Cross sermon, went so far as to make God the author of sin. He was not the only person who was influenced by the new churchmanship while remaining a Calvinist.

[74] Dorset RO Bankes of Kingston Lacey MSS, Gospel Commentaries, p. 16. Bankes's admiration for Andrewes is plain throughout this volume.
[75] Bancroft, *Sermon at Paules Crosse*, pp. 42, 46.
[76] Howson, *Sermon at St. Maries*, p. 21.

Since these matters are contentious, it is wise to quote Bancroft's exact words:

true it is, that almightie God, if it had stood with his good pleasure, could easilie have brought it to passe in spight of the divell, that there should never have been anie such false prophets or heresies amongst us. But he saw it not to be expedient. . . . Secondly (saith St Augustine) there must be heresies because God doth see it more agreeable to his wisdome, *ex malis bona edicere quam nulla esse permittere*, to bring good out of evill, than at all to permit no evill.

These do not seem to be the words of a free-willer, and they go a long way to support Dr Tyacke's argument, drawn from Bancroft's licensing policy, that he should be classified as a Calvinist.[77] Yet it remains true, within the categories employed here, that Bancroft was a prophet of the 'new churchmen'. This fact tends to suggest that for the 'new churchmen', Arminianism was not their only, or even necessarily their first, concern.

Of those who became Arminian, not all had yet done so: Howson was still a formal Calvinist in 1602, but had become an Arminian by 1625.[78] Political circumstances obviously had something to do with the masking of Arminian commitment: censorship was always a danger, as the fate of Harsnett in 1584, and of Barrett in 1595, showed. Yet it seems that this is not the whole story: it is, indeed, one of the clearest shibboleths that separate Calvinists from Arminians that for a committed Calvinist the doctrine of pre-destination is literally, and not metaphorically, the Ark of the Covenant,[79] while for an Arminian the question how we come to be justified comes comparatively low in the list of questions to which we need to know the answer. Indeed, one may wonder whether they were sometimes more concerned to attack Calvinist predestination because it interfered with their notions of the visible church and of the regenerative power of baptism than because they found it wrong in itself. Peter Lake's remark about Hooker, that 'his main concern remained the displacement of predestination from the centre of Christian concern and its replacement by the sacrament- and prayer-centred piety set out in the *Polity*'[80] could be repeated with little

[77] Bancroft, *Sermon at Paules Crosse*, pp. 31–2; Tyacke, pp. 3, 17, 34 n.
[78] Howson, *Sermon at St. Maries*, p. 5; Tyacke, pp. 266–7.
[79] See e.g. Perkins, *Exposition of the Creede*, in *Works* (Cambridge, 1603 edn.), 343, 363.
[80] Lake, *A. & P.?*, p. 196.

alteration for Charles I, Laud, or Cosin, even if perhaps not for
Richard Montague. They were not so much concerned to deny
predestination as to stop people talking about it, in order to
encourage them to talk about other, and, as they saw it, more
profitable concerns. This is why the Arminians were content in the
Jacobean episcopate, where they could not avow their Arminianism,
but could talk with James's approval about other things they were
much happier discussing. It is one of the reasons why Charles I's
declarations forbidding controversy were perfectly tolerable to the
Arminians, and absolutely intolerable to many Calvinists, to whom
the declarations appeared as a command not to preach the Gospel.
The tendency of the Arminians to give priority to other issues also
answers Dr Sharpe's question, what use James had for the
Arminians if he did not agree with their Arminianism. On a
number of other issues, the importance of ceremony, the Royal
Supremacy and the authority of bishops, James agreed with them
and was happy to give them their head.

Under cover of their Jacobean silence on doctrine, many of their
causes advanced rapidly. In the 1630s this change appears in the
differences between the young Arminians and the old: John
Howson, in his day, had been in the forefront of the ceremonial
cause, but in the 1630s he regarded the ceremonies used by his dean
John Cosin as excessive.[81] The works of Lancelot Andrewes printed
in his lifetime give a far more restrained impression than the
collected works printed under the auspices of John Buckeridge after
his death in 1629. If we take the reflections on ordination of two
men in the same circle, who were close friends, and wrote not more
than ten or fifteen years apart, they appear to be describing different
offices in different churches. John Donne, in about 1620, wrote of
the ordination of Mr Tilman to the 'ministry', in which the chief
gift he received was the gift to preach the word. Only a daring
analogy to the Virgin reveals the ex-Catholic, and the doctrine of the
ministry is one which would have been acceptable to his old patron
bishop Morton. When George Herbert was ordained a few years
later, he was ordained to the priesthood, and the power which
registered on him was the power to make and carry God in the

[81] M. E. James, *Family, Lineage, and Civil Society* (Oxford, 1974), 120, 168;
CSPD 1631–3, vol. cciii, no. 90.

sacraments.[82] Between Donne and Herbert, two close friends, is a profound change in intellectual fashion, which clearly showed that England had two different churches existing within a common framework.

What finally brought the two churches' coexistence to an end was Charles I's decision, at York House, that only one of them should be regarded as legitimate. That decision condemned the other, either to emigrate, or to fight back with any weapon, Scottish or English, that might come to hand. Yet we must ask the question Dr Fincham and Dr Lake left us with at the end of their article on the ecclesiastical policy of James I: how long could coexistence have gone on?[83] It is clearly true that coexistence between, for example, Abbot and Howson was always going to be uneasy at best: the one thing they seem to have agreed about is that they should not have to endure being in the same church together. Dr Fincham and Dr Lake are also right about the strain placed on ecclesiastical coexistence by the Spanish match, and later by the existence of a popish Queen. The visible presence of the Mass at court constantly posed questions which drove the wings of the church even further apart, and the troubles of a popish match were always likely to tear the church of England still further apart.

After 1625, the presence of a popish consort and of the Mass at court opened up a latent crevasse which was both theological and political. It divided those who thought the Roman church was anti-christian and intolerable from those who merely regarded it as a corrupt part of the visible church of Christ. If there was one question which could be relied upon to sort the heirs of Perkins from the heirs of Hooker, it was surely the question posed by the Mass at court. It is probably not a coincidence that for un-compromising anti-papists such as Pym, the beginning of Charles's reign began to seem like the point of no return.[84] In 1641, the right of the Queen, under her marriage treaty, to hear Mass and to be attended by Catholics, became one of the sticking-points in negotiations for a settlement, and the comparative status of the law

---

[82] John Donne, 'To Mr Tilman after he had taken Orders' in *Complete English Poems*, ed. A. J. Smith (1971), 332; George Herbert, 'Priesthood', in *Herbert and Vaughan*, ed. Martz, p. 146.

[83] Fincham and Lake, p. 207.

[84] Russell, *PEP*, p. 154; id., 'Parliamentary Career of John Pym 1621–1629', in *English Commonwealth 1547–1640: Essays in Politics and Society presented to Joel Hurstfield* (Leicester, 1979), 159–62.

and the treaty became a classic issue of law versus prerogative. The scraps of debate which are recorded on this issue suggest a classic clash of rival codes of values. On 15 March 1641 Hampden argued that 'we are now in Parliament, and here are to consider what [are] the laws of the kingdom. We sit here to see the laws observed, not broken'. George Digby, on the other hand, thought the issue a fit one for political prudence: 'sometimes the timing of things are as prudential as the things themselves. Let us consider whether we are in a state to war with France in case they should quarrel with the articles. I am not against the doing of it, only whether you will do it at this instant'.[85] The next day, essentially the same clash was repeated between Sir John Strangeways and Pym:

Sir John Strangeways made a very good speech, to induce this house to leave off the debate of Sir John Winter the Queenes Secretary, for withdrawing him from the court because he is a papist, but when he had alledged the queenes great affeccion to this house, in assenting with the lords [i.e. the Twelve Peers] to desyre the kinge that he would be graciously pleased to call this Parliament, and also for the pressing his majestie to pass the triennial bill, with many other reasons. But Mr. Pim then standing up made a very excellent speech against it, and declared that we ought rather to obey God than man, and that if we doe not prefer God before man, he will refuse us, with many other good notions.[86]

Pym's and Hampden's view prevailed, and the Ten Propositions more or less explicitly demanded that no priests be allowed access to the Queen.[87] Parliamentary intransigence on an issue so essential to her went a long way to turn the Queen, and therefore the King, into hardliners.[88] The importance of the issue in 1641 tends to suggest that Dr Fincham and Dr Lake are right about the divisive force of the marriage issue in the 1620s, and also that, in the politics of 1641, views on the Christian or anti-christian character of the church of Rome were of far more than theoretical importance.[89]

[85] Maija Jansson, *Two Diaries of the Long Parliament* (Gloucester, 1984), 20–1.

[86] D'Ewes (N.), p. 493 n. The words are those of the godly diarist John Moore.

[87] S. R. Gardiner, *Constitutional Documents of the Puritan Revolution* (1889; repr. Oxford, 1979), 164.

[88] *Letters of Queen Henrietta Maria*, ed. Mary Ann Everett Green (1857), 55–6, 61, 71–3, and other refs.

[89] See e.g. [Thomas Scott?], *Boanerges* (Edinburgh, 1624), pref., where the issues of the nature of the visible church and of the dangers of a popish match are very clearly blended. I am grateful to Dr Lake and Professor Cogswell for many helpful discussions of these issues.

Since potential Protestant spouses were so few, the risk that a popish marriage might pull the Jacobean compromise apart was always real. Yet, even granted the seriousness of the risk, we may still wonder whether Charles, had he been as hot a Protestant as his sister, might have been more successful in containing it than he was.

Yet it must remain a conjectural question what would have happened if the Jacobean compromise had continued, and conjectures should not be undertaken with undue confidence. The strains were quite visible by 1621, yet it is hard to see in what way the compromise would have broken down. James, on his side, was too good a politician to make life absolutely intolerable for a large body of his subjects if he could avoid it. On the other side, it is hard to see the churchmen voluntarily shattering the compromise by withdrawal. The belief that schism was a sin was very deep-rooted indeed, and it was one where religious conviction was daily reinforced by political self-interest. There was no ecclesiastical wilderness in England, and there was nowhere to withdraw to nearer than Douai on one side or Amsterdam or New England on the other. People who felt a profound conviction that the church of England belonged to them were not likely to make such manifold sacrifices voluntarily. In the end, fortunately, we need not answer this question. We must be aware that there might have been alternative possibilities, but what we have to explain is what did happen, which was that the Jacobean compromise was killed by Charles I.

The note of 'we are the masters now', and the dependence of all these issues on ideas of succession, shows nowhere more clearly than in the Arminian triumphalism of the preface to John Cosin's *Devotions* in 1627. He proclaimed his intention to

let the world understand, that they who give it out, and accuse us here in England to have set up a new church, and a new faith, to have abandoned all the ancient forms of piety and devotion, to have taken away all the religious exercises and prayers of our forefathers, to have despised all the old ceremonies, and cast behind us the blessed sacraments of Christ's Catholic church—these men do little else but betray their own infirmities.[90]

This was the voice of those who thought, like Richard Hooker and Charles I, that the Reformation had been in danger of throwing out the baby with the bath-water. It was the voice which has since

[90] Cosin, iii. 90.

become known as the Anglican voice, but Cosin's note of triumph marks the first moment at which it could also hope to be regarded as the voice of the church of England. With the King's support, the claim stood, but it was and remained bitterly contested.

5

Religious Unity in Three Kingdoms and in One: Religion, Politics, and Charles I 1625–1642

SIR Henry Slingsby, a minor member of the Long Parliament, confided to his diary that the Long Parliament's task in negotiating an Anglo–Scottish treaty was 'like tossing three balls in one hand, which requires both the eye and hand to be very steeddy, lest one ball do enterfore with another, and all miscarry'.[1] This remark might have been made about any part of the British problem under Charles I, and what applies to the problem must also apply to its historian: whatever theme he takes up, he will be neglecting others. The story makes a highly untidy drama, constantly confused by the presence of too many actors on stage, and that confusion, because it affected the participants, was a significant cause of civil war.[2]

The purpose of this chapter is to explain how the British problem and the English domestic religious problem became merged together in one common problem, and how the result of that confusion was to raise the question which ultimately proved incapable of compromise: whether the kingdom had to be governed with the King's consent. Uniquely among these chapters, it is devoted to all seven of my initial questions, since the linking of British politics with English religion appears to have affected all seven of them. To demonstrate this point fully, we would have to outdo Sir Henry Slingsby, and keep, not seven, but twenty-one balls in the air at once. This of course cannot be done, but this chapter will keep as many as possible up for as long as possible.

It is, we may hope, unnecessary to dwell on the changes produced in the church of England by the triumph of the Arminians after York House. What this book would say on that subject would follow Dr Tyacke very closely, and perhaps we may take it as read.

[1] *Diary of Sir Henry Slingsby of Scriven*, ed. Daniel Parsons (1836), 65.
[2] I am grateful to Dr Michael Clanchy for this point.

What is important for our present purposes is the effect of that triumph on the relations between the three constituent kingdoms of Britain. The Thirty-Nine Articles, like any other official Elizabethan production, were of course ambiguous, and whether they said the same things as the Scottish Confession of Faith of 1616 or the Irish Articles of 1615 depended very heavily on how they were interpreted. In the hands of Archbishop Abbot, the English Articles were a slightly less explicit way of making the same points which had been made in the Irish Articles, the Lambeth Articles, and the Articles of Dort. To Laud, Howson and Buckeridge, on the other hand, the Thirty-Nine Articles appeared fundamentally different from the Articles of Lambeth and Dort. When they wrote to Buckingham condemning Lambeth and Dort, they maintained a prudent silence on the subject of the Irish Articles.[3] They were not allowed to do so for long. The man who first pointed out to Charles that he had not let his Irish hand know what his English hand was doing appears to be Pym, who, in the course of his attack on Richard Montague in the Parliament of 1626, said that 'he opposeth the church of England to the church of Ireland, and the articles of either to other in the poynte'.[4] The point was backed up by a shrewdly drafted Parliamentary bill, which offered to give statutory confirmation to both the English and the Irish Articles, and would thereby have made it a legal necessity to interpret them, like two places of Scripture, so that they should not be repugnant to each other.[5] In 1628 Pym extended this approach to the question of ceremonial conformity, on which there was also now a wide divergence between the relaxed practice of Ussher and the new Laudian enthusiasm in England. He said that Irish subscription to the Book of Common Prayer demanded a much less full assent than English subscription, and that practice should be uniform because 'these islands are sisters'.[6]

In the case of Scotland, divergence under Charles was now even wider, and it provided to dissidents on both sides of the Border the vital asset of an alternative model. To the small but rapidly growing party of Scottish Arminians, whose strength in Scottish universities

---

[3] Tyacke, pp. 266–7.

[4] *Debates in the House of Commons in 1625*, ed. S. R. Gardiner (Camden Society, NS 6; 1873), 181.

[5] Tyacke, pp. 154–5.

[6] *1628 Debates*, iii. 515.

was a matter of constant anxiety to the Covenanters, what was
happening in England represented a very visible utopia. Since
Charles inevitably preferred such men to the Scottish episcopate,
they were liable to become a force to press for Scotland to be
brought into line with England. On the other side of the fence,
Alexander Leighton, in *Sion's Plea against Prelacy*, offered precisely
that sort of Scottish challenge to the legitimacy of the English
church that James had put so much effort into preventing the
Melvilles from offering. In England, Peter Smart canon of
Durham found that, though he could not attack the 'idolatry' of his
dean John Cosin in a work published in England, he could easily do
so in one published in Edinburgh, where it did not infringe any
law. William Prynne's *News from Ipswich* was probably printed in
Edinburgh.[7] For many Englishmen of strong Calvinist inclination,
Scotland was becoming a dangerously attractive alternative to
England, and by 1638 Sir John Clotworthy had told a Scottish
correspondent that many 'leading persons' hoped to find 'an America
in Scotland'.[8] Moreover, as Charles's *Large Declaration* complained
in 1639, the 'Roman party' was liable to point out these
differences.[9]

   Having destroyed James's programme of British uniformity by
interpreting the English settlement in the way which made it most
remote from the Scottish and Irish churches, Charles and Laud had
to construct a new programme of British uniformity. Since their
major commitment was to those features of the English church
which were most conspicuously absent in Ireland and Scotland, this
programme for British uniformity inevitably turned into one for
English hegemony. Foreign ambassadors, who were often more
observant on British matters than the English, took the point.
Ambassadors do not use titles at random. In April 1640 the French
Ambassador said that Morton and Traquair had tried to bring the
King of Great Britain to an accommodation with Scotland, but the
King of England replied that he would lose England or punish
them.[10]

   [7] I would like to thank Ms Jane Hosking for this point.
   [8] NLS Wodrow MS Fol. 66, fo. 109ᵛ. I am grateful to Dr Peter Donald for this
reference.
   [9] *Large Declaration*, 19 Feb. 1638 (1639), 18. This work was ghost-written for
Charles by Walter Balcanquall Dean of Durham, but the work was carefully
supervised, and may be taken to represent Charles's mind.
   [10] PRO 31/3/72, p. 112.

Nothing more clearly shows that this was a programme than the extent to which, before being tried in the difficult cases of Ireland and Scotland, it was rehearsed and refined among all the minor dominions and communities subject to the King's authority. In this programme, as in so much else, Charles and Laud acted in close collaboration, with Laud, in Gardiner's words, acting 'as if he had been the King's secretary'.[11] Laud had no ecclesiastical authority in Ireland or Scotland, and was well aware of the fact, but it was perfectly legitimate for him, as for any other royal servant charged with the task, to convey the King's will. He knew he was taking risks in doing so. In 1634 he wrote to Wentworth that 'I was fain to write nine letters yesterday into Scotland. I think you have a plot to see whether I will be *universalis episcopus*, that you and your brethren may take occasion to call me Antichrist'.[12]

The first case to which Laud turned his attentions was that of the Merchant Adventurers in the Netherlands, who, he said, did not follow the set forms of prayer and administered the sacraments in 'conceived forms' of their own. In sharp contrast to Grindal, he wanted to bring them under English episcopal authority, in order to ensure their full conformity to English practice.[13] He then turned his attention to the regiments in Dutch service, and the implications of the programme were plain to see when he insisted that no one who did not use the English Book of Common Prayer should continue as chaplain to any English *or Scottish* regiments.[14] The French and Dutch Stranger churches were the next to receive attention, and here again a sharp contrast emerges with Archbishop Grindal. To Grindal, the Stranger churches were welcome, and the foreign reformed churches appeared as 'other churches of our profession'.[15] To Laud, it appeared that they 'live like an absolute divided body from the church of England established, which must needs work upon their affections, and alienate them from the state, or at least make them ready for any innovation that may sort better with their humour'.[16]

As more territories and communities came under scrutiny, it became apparent that the programme, in its full form, had a large

---

[11] S. R. Gardiner, *History of England*, viii (1891), 309.

[12] Knowler, i. 271.

[13] *CSPD 1629–31*, vol. clxx, no. 8, and *CSPD 1639–40*, vol. ccccxxxvii, no. 59.   [14] Laud, *Wks.* VI. i. 23.

[15] P. Collinson, *Archbishop Grindal* (1979), 125–52; BL Add. MS 32,092, fo. 29ʳ.   [16] Laud, *Wks.* VI. i. 25.

number of elements, among which different elements came first in different places. The full list was the Royal Supremacy, episocpacy, the Thirty-Nine Articles, a common liturgy, a body of canons, and a High Commission. In Massachusetts, it seems to have been a bishop and a High Commission which were the first items contemplated, and Governor Winthrop in reply issued orders 'to hasten our fortifications'.[17] In the Channel Islands, Laud and Charles endowed a number of closed scholarships to Oxford, in order to train ministers who understood the doctrine and discipline of the church of England, and were making plans for an assault on the surviving Presbyterianism of Guernsey when the greater troubles of Scotland distracted their attention.[18] The only territories which escaped attention seem to have been Virginia and the Isle of Man, presumably because they were not seen to pose any problems.

In Ireland, Laud noted with relief that there was no need for a liturgy, because they had the English one already.[19] The major perceived needs in Ireland were for the English Thirty-Nine Articles and for a new set of canons, and these Laud set about in 1634, with the vigorous encouragement of his protégé Bramhall Bishop of Derry. The plan seems to have nearly gone astray, and Wentworth was almost 'fatally surprized' by a committee of the Irish Convocation who drew up their own canons, which, instead of confirming the English Articles, would have confirmed the Irish under pain of excommunication.[20] Wentworth's alarm may be measured by his temper: he said an Ananias had sat in the chair of that committee, 'with all the fraternities and conventicles of Amsterdam', and complained 'how unheard a part it was for a few petty clerks to presume to make articles of faith without the privity or consent of state or bishop'. He feared complaint in England, and 'how I shall be able to sustain myself against your Prynnes, Pimms and Bens, with all the rest of that generation of odd names and natures, the Lord knows'.[21]

[17] Gardiner, *History of England*, viii. 167–8; H. R. Trevor Roper, *Archbishop Laud* (1940; repr. 1960), 257–62; E. S. Morgan, *Puritan Dilemma* (Boston, Mass., 1958), 196.
[18] A. J. Eagleston, *Channel Islands under Tudor Government* (Cambridge, 1949), 141–2 and other refs.
[19] Laud, *Wks*. VI. i. 354.
[20] *CSPD 1633–4*, vol. ccxliv, no. 48; Knowler, i. 187. I would like to thank Martin Flaherty for explaining this revealing episode to me.
[21] Knowler, i. 343. The reference to 'Bens' possibly represents the familiar anti-Puritan charge of 'judaizing'.

It was perhaps in order to avoid being 'fatally surprized' by Scottish resistance as they had almost been by Irish that Charles and Laud produced the Scottish canons and Scottish Prayer Book without any Scottish consultation except with a limited number of the Scottish bishops. The Scottish canons, which were an almost verbatim copy of the Irish canons, and therefore largely irrelevant to the Scottish church, were issued 'by our prerogative royal, and supreme authority in causes ecclesiastical', and the service book was issued by proclamation. There was no repetition of James's care to get his Scottish measures carried through a General Assembly and a Parliament. That Charles believed he was able to do this was because he thought that, as the Scottish canons put it, the Royal Supremacy gave him 'the same authority in causes ecclesiastical, that the godly kings had among the Jews, and Christian emperors in the primitive church'.[22] He had some English authority for this phrase, which came from Canon II of 1604, but its application to Scotland was new. Charles's ideas about the Royal Supremacy led him into a lot of trouble both in Scotland and in England, and they are worth understanding. They are summarized in a memorandum drawn up by Lord Herbert of Cherbury, the historian of Henry VIII, dated just in time for the preparatory work on the Scottish canons, which has a note on the dorse that it is to be shown to the Archbishop by the King's command: an interesting way round. This memorandum does not quote a single statute law, English or Scottish, and grounds the Royal Supremacy exclusively on biblical texts, mostly from the Old Testament.[23] It is a claim to supremacy *jure divino*. Whether Charles was supreme head of the church of Scotland by Scottish law was a point open to dispute: Charles had some excuse for believing he was, but many Scots had as much excuse for believing he was not. It seems that to Charles, who took the declaratory preamble of the English Act of Supremacy seriously, it did not matter whether he was supreme head of the church by Scottish law: the powers were inherent in all kings whether Scottish law recognized them or not. This, naturally, was a view which did not commend itself in Scotland. The King also seems to have agreed with his English Attorney-General that, in words close to the Act in Restraint of Appeals, 'the kingdom of England is an absolute empire and monarchie successive by inherent birthright, consisting of one

[22] Laud *Wks.* v. 585–6; E. Cardwell, *Synodalia* i (Oxford, 1842), 166.
[23] PRO SP 16/288/88.

head, which is the king, and of a bodye, which the law divideth into tow severall ptes, that is to say, the clergy and the laity: both of them next and immediately under God, subject and obedient to the head'.[24] As Charles used these ideas, they implied the existence of two entirely separate spheres of temporal and spiritual authority. These were the ideas hinted at in the Proclamation of 1626, which began the attempt to extend the English Articles to Ireland: it was issued, not by the advice of his Privy Council, but by the advice of his 'reverend bishops'.[25] Charles believed that in ecclesiastical matters he was bound only to consult a limited number of people whom he had appointed, and might thereafter promote. It was therefore one of the attractions of bishops to Charles that they represented a channel for the effective and unfettered enforcement of his own will on his church. This, of course, is an important part of the reasons why, as his reign progressed, the number of Scots and Englishmen who wanted to abolish bishops increased with such alarming rapidity. The more Charles defended them as an essential part of his 'authority', the more sharply he spotlighted the reasons why other people thought they had to go, or at least to be strongly restrained. The Earl of Traquair Lord Treasurer of Scotland bluntly told Hamilton that churchmen 'are not fitting for such great and weighty employments', and asked 'yt his matie may be pleased to hear some of the laytie'.[26]

By attempting to alter Scottish law in what many Scots thought an idolatrous direction, without employing any of the processes his father had thought necessary to Scottish lawmaking, Charles revived all the Scottish fears of 1604 at the same time. Robert Baillie protested that in England 'the leist ceremonie never appointed but in the convocation', and said that

had we been truly, as once we were falsely allegit, but a pendicle of the dioces of York, yet more than a missive letter would have been writ to have movit us imbrace a whole book of new canons, and more than an Act of Councell to have mad us recev a new form in the whol worship of God, prayer, sacraments, mariag, buriall, preaching and all.

---

[24] Dorset RO, Bankes of Kingston Lacey MSS, vol. M, pp. 1, 8.
[25] *Stuart Royal Proclamations*, ii, ed. J. F. Larkin (Oxford, 1983), 91. I would like to thank Dr Tyacke for drawing my attention to the wording of this proclamation.
[26] Hamilton MSS 1497 (n.d.).

He invoked the sermon preached to the Melvilles at Hampton Court by Andrewes, 'the semigod of the neu faction', to prove that church laws and canons had always been made in church assemblies.[27] Baillie was not a man who took his religion lightly, but it was not necessary to share his religious convictions to share his fear that the introduction of the service book by proclamation was a threat to Scottish legislative sovereignty, and risked reducing Scotland to colonial status.

The Covenanter Earl of Rothes said they were being asked to take a pattern from those inferior to them in reformation.[28] The veteran David Calderwood revived all his fears of being pressed to conformity with England, while 'they would not yield anything at all to us'.[29] The fear of creeping Arminianism was loud and articulate, and when Rothes was asked to justify his assertion that the new Prayer Book was doctrinally unsound, the example which came immediately to his mind was that it declared infants regenerate after baptism.[30] The prospect of false doctrine and idolatry caused many people who had before been able to consent to the Five Articles of Perth to cease to do so: Robert Baillie, for example, decided that 'I was not minded, on any hazard whatsomever, to practice kneeling, so long as the danger or feare of their late novations did remaine'.[31] The threat to Scottish legislative sovereignty, particularly in the ecclesiastical context where it had been most jealously guarded, was a threat to Scotland's identity, and one of the Covenanter pamphlets claimed, with some truth, that it threatened 'no lesse than that wee should no more bee a kirk or a nation'. Baillie thought it would reduce them to 'ane English province'.[32] These fears could affect those who cared nothing for idolatry or superstition, and it is no surprise that Traquair soon had to tell Charles that the power simply did not exist in Scotland to enforce this book.

Charles's reaction to this information shows qualities in him which are important to his fortunes on both sides of the Border. He was simply unable to accept the fact that his authority, like that of every other ruler in history, was bound by the limits of the possible. He told Hamilton that 'I will rather dye, than yield to these impertinent and damnable demands'. He said he would be reduced

[27] Baillie, i. 1–2.   [28] Rothes, p. 15.
[29] [David Calderwood], *Queries* (1638) (STC 4362), 9.
[30] Rothes, p. 10.   [31] Baillie, i. 68. See also Rothes, p. 91.
[32] *Intentions of the Army* (*s.l.*, 1640) (STC 21, 919), 5; Baillie, i. 66.

to the status of a Duke of Venice, which he would rather die than suffer; Hamilton was reduced to replying that they would rather die too. Hamilton said mildly that 'all that I shall say is humlie to intreat your mattie to take in consideration whatt the consequens of this may be'.[33] To Charles, this was an improper question. If he retreated, he thought, he 'will betray that trust, which the King of kings hath reposed in us for the maintenance of religion and justice amongst all his people whom he hath committed to our charge'.[34] It is the voice of one of nature's martyrs.

Another characteristic from which Charles suffered on both sides of the Border was his inability to understand that he could so much as appear to be guilty of innovation or illegality. He assured the Covenanters many times that 'we never intended the least alteration' in Scottish religion.[35] The first time he did this, one of the Covenanter leaders optimistically took it as a signal that he intended to abandon the service book.[36] The Covenanters did not make this mistake again. He also repeatedly assured them that nothing would be done against law, and that he would only press the service book 'in . . . a fair and legall way'. He expected the Covenanters' opposition to evaporate when they understood that the service book was not innovatory, and showed no sign of understanding the argument that even Hamilton advanced, that its introduction was 'not iustifiabill by the lawes of this kingdome'.[37] Charles, because he suffered from an allergy to the type of religion the Covenanters represented, seems to have been simply blind to any evidence in their favour, even on technical points. He asserted that their claims of religion were only a pretence, and so was fatally unable to understand what he was up against. It is exactly the same mistake Pym was to make in Ireland.

As they came to understand these facts about Charles, the Covenanters learnt that they could not win security through Charles's concessions, not because they would be insincere, but because he would retain the interpreting of them. Baillie perceptively compared Charles's declarations against innovation with his declaration against controversy after the 1629 Parliament in England: 'the King's declaration of his minde in religion was the stop of all process

---

[33] Hamilton MSS 10,484, 10,492, 10,491, and 327.1. See also ibid. 10,487.
[34] *Large Declaration*, p. 5.
[35] *RPCS* vii. 74.
[36] Ibid. 546–7; Hamilton MSS 394.   [37] Hamilton MSS 326.1.

against those who were like to be censured for innovating therein'.[38] Rothes and his colleagues wondered how they could be 'secure in tyme comeing from the re-entry of these innovations'.[39] Baillie noted that 'whatever the prince grants, I feare we presse more than he can grant'.[40] This meant they had not merely to secure concessions, but to procure an irreversible shift of power, so that those concessions could not be interpreted away. This was why they were converted to the abolition of bishops, because, in Rothes's illuminating phrase, their complying with the King was 'fitter for the servants of a persone than of a state'.[41] This cult of an impersonal State, in which authority was exercised collectively, was one to which all Charles's opponents were ultimately driven.

Many Covenanters seem to have been slowly and painfully converted to Presbyterianism by the logic of the struggle with Charles, rather than representing a continuous Presbyterian tradition surviving from the reign of James VI. One of the clearest examples is Robert Baillie. In 1637, when advising a friend to accept a bishopric, he wrote: 'bishops I love', but by 1641 he was willing to dismiss even clergymen prepared to consider the mildest form of modified episcopacy as 'rabbies'. The Covenanters' need to make Charles's concessions irreversible shows plainly in Rothes's demand to 'have religione so established, as men might not alter it at their pleasure heirinafter, as they had done heirtofoir, and to enjoy the libertie of the lawes of the kingdome'.[42]

Abolishing Scottish bishops might help them to control the Scottish state, but from late in 1638 onwards, the threat to the Covenanters was not Scottish: it came from the prospect of invasion from England and Ireland. It therefore became necessary to them, in order to preserve the security of their Scottish arrangements, to bring about an irreversible shift of power in England and Ireland, so such a threat could not be repeated. They immediately identified an English Parliament, rather than the English King, as that part of the English system where their support was likely to be concentrated, and as early as 1639 they were claiming that if an English Parliament could be convened, it would be so far from censuring

[38] Baillie, i. 43.
[39] Rothes, p. 149.
[40] Baillie, i. 49.
[41] Rothes, p. 70.
[42] Baillie, i. 2; Rothes, p. 137. See also *Large Declaration*, p. 102.

the Scots, that it would rather petition the King for them.[43] After the Short Parliament, this reasoning was confirmed, and it is no surprise that the English Triennial Act of 1641 began its career as a Scottish negotiating demand. The Scots refused to negotiate with Charles after Newburn until Charles agreed that the negotiating team should be commissioned by the English Parliament as well as the English king, thereby putting English diplomacy under Parliamentary control.[44] Their thinking emerges most clearly in their proposal to appoint a set of conservators of the peace to keep the peace between England and Scotland 'in the intervall betwixt the Parliaments', and to be answerable, not to the King, but to the next Parliament.[45] It was a proposal Simon de Montfort would have understood.

The Scots were interested from the beginning in exporting their reformation to England, and hoped that 'our happines should emitt the rayes of its example to our so nearlie intire and beloved neighbours'.[46] This, of course, was precisely what Charles was afraid of, and why he could not leave the Covenanters secure in power. By the time their army entered England in 1640, their aim was avowedly to reform England:

> the reformation of England, long prayed and pleaded for by the godly there, shall be according to their wishes and desires perfected in doctrine, worship and discipline; papists, prelats and all the members of the antichristian hierarchy, with their idolatry, superstition and humane invention shall pack them hence; the names of sects and separatists shall be no more mentioned, and the Lord shall be one, and his name one, throughout the whole iland.[47]

Yet, however zealous the language in which the Scots expressed this aim, their underlying concern was a hard-headed desire for Scottish security. As they told the English negotiators in 1641, without it peace would not be durable, as they hoped it might be.[48]

[43] *Information* (Edinburgh, 1639), 11. There is an MS copy of this work in the papers of Sir Robert Harley. BL Loan MS 29/46/30. See PRO SP 16/447/19 for Loudoun's hope that the Short Parliament would take the Scots' cause into consideration, and Charles's hasty reply that the Parliament would have nothing to do with the business of Scotland.
[44] BL Harl. MS 457, fos. 3ᵛ–9ʳ.
[45] BL Stowe MS 187, fo. 41ʳ.   [46] JRL Crawford MSS 14/3/33.
[47] *Lawfulnesse of our Expedition into England Manifested* (Edinburgh, 1640), Sig. A. 4.
[48] BL Stowe MS 187, fo. 47ʳ.

Some of the English warmly welcomed such a prospect, even to
the point of supporting the Scots against the King. The existence of
this group was one reason why the English lost the Bishops' Wars,
since even those who had no sympathy with the Scots regarded it as
unwise to fight with one eye over their shoulders. In May 1639 the
Countess of Westmorland, in a very able political assessment,
warned Secretary Windebank to pull back from the war, because
(among other reasons) 'they know our divisions and the strength of
ther owne combination, and yt they have a party amongst us, and we
have non amongst them.'[49] The sort of troubles this fact might lead
to were suggested by incidents such as the one at the Green Dragon
tavern in Bishopsgate Street in the summer of 1640, where two
soldiers about to go off to the war fell into conversation with two
clothiers from Dedham in Essex. The clothiers expressed sympathy
with the Scots, and one of the officers, in reply, called them
Puritans. One of the clothiers then asked the officer 'if he could
tell what a Puritan was, whereat he flew into such a rage he threw
a trencher, and hit him on the head'.[50] When the issue was so
instantly divisive, the Scottish propaganda being distributed in
Essex, urging that 'your grievances are ours: the preservation of
religion and liberties is common to both nations: we must now stand
or fall together', was liable to secure a hearing and to lead to
trouble.[51] The fear of a fifth column was therefore always likely to
sap English will to fight.

After Newburn, with the Scots established in England, the fifth
column came into their own. In November 1640 an English MP
who may have been either Francis Rous or Isaac Pennington wrote
in delight to the Covenanter Earl of Lothian that 'the hierarchie
shakes, and if this Parliament continue, they are gone roote and
branch'.[52] Others such as Saye and Fiennes had from the beginning
anxieties about the clericalist tendencies of Scottish discipline, but
hoped that the Scots might prove more manageable than Charles I.
For whatever reason, the group that produced the Petition of the
Twelve Peers from the beginning threw in their lot with the Scots,
asking them in the week after Newburn to let them know what

[49] PRO SP 16/420/70.
[50] Ibid. 16/465/31, 2; 16/466/113, 114; 16/467/14.
[51] Ibid. 16/464/79.1; 16/465/4.
[52] JRL Crawford MSS 14/3/76; also ibid. 14/3/77. The author was a member
of the committee dealing with the case of Alexander Leighton: for the short list of
possible authors, see *CJ* ii. 24.

the Scottish army was doing, so that they could co-ordinate their efforts.[53] Written to the leaders of an invading army, this letter was surely treasonable. At first, it seems that the commitment of the English junto to Root and Branch was somewhat reluctant, and more a matter of political convenience than of political or theological conviction. What they did commit themselves to by their alliance with the Scots was an attempt to coerce Charles, 'to reduce the King to a necessity of granting'.[54]

Coercion is a dangerous game, and in the Army Plot of April and May 1641 Charles attempted to meet coercion with coercion: if his opponents could coerce him by means of the Scottish army, maybe he could coerce them through the English army. It seems to have been the Army Plot which convinced Pym and his fellows that they had gone too far to draw back, that they, like the Covenanters, could only procure their own security by an irreversible shift of power. It is after the Army Plot that, for the first time, the junto showed a vigorous and united commitment to Root and Branch. In these circumstances, it was not only a religious programme: it was a constitutional one, whose major object was to deprive the King of power to control the church. They thus challenged Charles on the one point of all others where he was most inflexible: where his religious commitment and his sense of his own authority met. It is suggestive that Williams, author of a major scheme to save episcopacy by concessions, hoped to preserve bishops by taking the power to appoint them out of the King's hands, and giving it back, in good medieval style, to the cathedral chapters.[55] For Charles, such a scheme was entirely beside the point. From May 1641 onwards, both sides in England negotiated by means of threats designed to secure compliance: the object was to secure the compliance, not to carry out the threat, but the object was not achieved. The unbridgeable gulf was between Charles's determination to govern, and his opponents' determination to bypass him as effectively as Henry VI had been bypassed during his insanity. This was the issue on which it became necessary to fight.

[53] NLS Advocates' MS 33.1.1, vol. xiii, item 28. For a discussion of the surviving versions of this document, see Peter Donald, 'The King and the Scottish Troubles 1637–1641', Ph.D. thesis (Cambridge, 1987). I am deeply grateful to Dr Donald for the generosity with which he has placed his findings at my disposal.

[54] *Two Speeches*, (1642), BL E. 84 (35), p. 6.

[55] House of Lords Main Papers, 1 July 1641.

The junto's plans to coerce Charles were always intended to work by isolating him, leaving him facing a united country and preferably a united Privy Council as well. They failed lamentably in this objective, because, by committing themselves to the Scots' programme for a Presbyterian settlement, they also gave Charles the opportunity to gather a party. Arminianism had not dropped roots, but some of the Arminians' concern for decency and order in the church struck a chord across a much wider spectrum than any of their theological doctrines. Above all, plans for a Scottish Reformation of England fell foul of an overwhelming reluctance to go through yet another new settlement in religion, or to jump through yet another series of clerical hoops. The attempt to impose a Scottish Reformation on England, though it had vigorous supporters, aroused as wide and as intense a hostility as Laud himself had ever done. It is not just Charles's obstinacy which made such a settlement impossible: it is doubtful whether he could have made it work even if he had tried.

In fact, Charles put himself at the head of this body of resistance, and exploited it with considerable skill. The first emotion to which Charles and his leading ally the Earl of Bristol could appeal was an intense nationalist reluctance to let the Scots impose a reformation on England. On 9 April 1641 the Scottish treaty commissioners reported to Edinburgh that

we had in the treatie yesternight a verie hard rencounter about the paper concerning uniformitie of church government, a poynt which some of the Inglish commissioners cannot indure should be touched by us, . . . but they thinck it intollerable that we should come into this kingdom and presse them with a reformation of religion againes the fundamentall lawis of the kingdome, againes practice of 1500 yeare, and at this tyme when there is such a comotion in the cittie and country about the government of the church that they have no other end but to stirre sedition and make trouble.

This was beginning to sound comically like some of the complaints the Scots had made in 1637.[56]

The case that bishops had had a continuous existence in the church for 1500 years appeared persuasive to many middle of the road people, and in 1606 it had been repeated to Andrew Melville by

[56] Edinburgh University Library, MS Dc 4. 16, fo. 94ʳ.

James Montague, Dean of the Chapel Royal, the man who preached
William Perkins's funeral sermon.[57] As offered in 1641, it was not
a defence of the Laudian bishops: indeed, every Royalist petition
except the one from Surrey began its defence of bishops by
disowning the Laudians. What they offered was a defence of visible
continuity. The Somerset petition, while admitting that some things
of 'ill consequence' had crept in, said the government of the church
was 'the most pious, and the wisest, that any people or kingdom
upon earth hath bine blest withall since the apostles' daies', and
made the strong, but cautious claim that its origins were 'ancient,
even neare to the Apostles' daies'.[58] Sir Henry Slingsby, an
Arminian anticlerical who had voted for Bishops' Exclusion, was a
little cooler but equally emphatic: 'it were not safe to make alteration
from so antient a beginning; we used to say yt custome makes laws,
and our common laws is but antient customs'. He thought 'the
common people judges not with things as they are with reason or
against, but long usage wth ym is instead of all', and feared the
consequences if they should see episcopacy 'so easily subverted'.[59]
Many who were attached to the notion of an ancient constitution
realized, as Charles and Chief Justice Bankes did, that it provided a
better justification for bishops than it did for Parliaments.[60] After
all, Ine's laws, the touchstone for much ancient constitutional
thinking, did begin: 'I, Ine, by the Grace of God, King of the West
Saxons, with the advice and with the instruction of my bishop
Hedde, and my bishop Eorcenwold'.[61] They did not begin with any
reference to the Lords and Commons in Parliament assembled.
There was also a strong feeling that it was beyond the power of
Parliamentary statute to change religion. Robert Holborne, who
had been Hampden's counsel in the Ship Money trial, defended the
right of members to protest at Parliamentary decisions because 'a
Parliament may doe a thing unlawfull, as to change our religion
etc'.[62] He was not the only member of the Long Parliament who

[57] Calderwood, vi. 580.
[58] House of Lords Main Papers, parchment box 7B.
[59] *Diary of Sir Henry Slingsby of Scriven*, pp. 67–8.
[60] *LJ* iv. 142; Dorset RO Bankes of Kingston Lacey MSS, vol. L, p. 13.
[61] *English Historical Documents c.500–1042*, ed. Dorothy Whitelocke
(1955), 364.
[62] *Verney's Notes of the Long Parliament*, ed. John Bruce (Camden Society, 31,
1844), 136.

had not read his Elton. Catholic jibes about faith by statute seem to have gone home.[63]

The strongest Royalist issue in the Commons was the Book of Common Prayer, which was consistently worth some forty or fifty votes more than the bishops. Charles was always ready to put himself at the head of this body of feeling. In December 1640 he enlisted the help of the House of Lords in condemning rioters at Halsted in Essex, who had knocked the Prayer Book, 'established and confirmed by Act of Parliament' out of the hands of the curate, and kicked it up and down the church, calling for 'Scotch blades' to help them. Charles was doubtless disappointed when the Lords decided that 'being poor and silly men', they should be sentenced to nothing worse than a submission.[64] In spite of this typical House of Lords right and left, they had signalled, both to Charles and to the Scots, that they would uphold the Prayer Book by law established. Sir Edmund Moundeford's motion against the Prayer Book at the beginning of the Parliament was shunted aside and ignored.[65] From September to November 1641 there was a series of divisions on the Book of Common Prayer, and Culpepper and the Book's supporters won them all. The first vote against it did not come until February 1642, when many of the Royalist members had ceased to attend. Again, the Book seems to have depended on a belief in preserving what was by law established. Even D'Ewes, who welcomed attacks on the Book once he knew they were safe, expressed great surprise the first time Sir Thomas Barrington and Oliver Cromwell attacked the Prayer Book established by law.[66] Few of its defenders went as far as those who wanted to insert in the Royalist Kentish Petition of March 1642 the phrase that the Book was 'penned by the inspiration of the Holy Ghost', and the phrase was 'upon debate, omitted'.[67] A much commoner feeling was expressed by the crowd at Archcliff Fort, Dover, who greeted the King's proclamation of 10 December 1641 in favour of the Prayer Book with cries of 'God bless his Majesty, we shall have our old religion setled againe'.[68]

In many quarters, the King's ideal of 'decency' in worship, albeit in a very moderate form, seems to have been an object of equal

---

[63] See e.g. Bowyer, p. 52, for Sir Edwin Sandys's complaint that 'the papists would saie, not without shew, that wee professed only a statut religion'.

[64] *LJ* iv. 107, 113; House of Lords Main Papers, 10 Dec. 1641.

[65] D'Ewes (N.), p. 63.

[66] BL Harl. MS 164, fos. 888–90.

[67] *CJ* ii. 502–3.   [68] PRO SP 16/486/72.

attachment. The Commons' order of 8 September 1641, against altars and monuments of superstition, seems to have run into vigorous resistance, and Pym said that in some places attempts to enforce it had led to blows.[69] In a bleached version, the ideal could surface in the most unexpected places: when the Bristol Baptists, on the occasion of their separation, contemplated worshipping in a barn, they found this idea 'could hardly be received. The thing of relative holinesse, and tincture of consecrated places, was not off the people, for they were not as yett prepared, having been soe long nursed up in ignorance and outward forms'.[70] To one whose attachment to outward forms went deeper, the 8 September order could be deeply offensive: Thomas Wiseman Remembrancer of the City said 'the Brownists and other sectaries make such havock in our churches by pulling downe of ancient monuments, glass windows and railes that their madnes is intollerable . . . I think it will bee thought blasphemye shortly to name Jesus Christ, for it is allready forbidden to bow at his name'.[71] It should come as no surprise to learn that Wiseman was a passionate anti-Scot, as were all the people who held that view of the church. If bishops had been preserved, many of them would have agreed to a considerable toning down of Laudian practice, but without bishops, they saw no authority to protect them from the excesses of window-smashing sectarians. These were the people who rallied to the defence of Charles's authority. By following the Scots into the attempt to abolish bishops, Pym and the junto presented Charles with a ready-made party. The Scots had not reformed England, but divided it.

The efforts of the Scots and their English allies to protect themselves against Ireland were even less successful than they were in England. The Scots had not taken kindly to being threatened, during the Bishops' Wars, by an army of Irish Catholics led by the Earl of Antrim, and consequently gave far more support than they would otherwise have been likely to do to the Irish territorial ambitions of the Earl of Argyll. It was also the avowed aim of the Scots and their English allies, in this case both with equal conviction, to eradicate the power of popery in British life. The English Parliament's decision, early in its existence, to cashier all

[69] *CJ* ii. 289.
[70] *Records of a Church of Christ in Bristol*, ed. Roger Hayden (Bristol Record Society; Bristol, 1974), 93.
[71] PRO SP 16/484/68.

the popish officers in the King's army looked like an uncontroversial decision. It caused no protest in England, and the Scots welcomed it as a protection against trigger-happy attempts to break the cease-fire. From an Irish point of view, this insistence that papists could not be loyal might have a very different appearance. Fortunately, we possess a reaction to this decision by an Irish officer in the King's army, who said

the Parliament house are taking an order to cashier all papist officers in the whole army, and among the rest myself. . . . They fall out bitterly against us all, and begin to banish us out of town, and to remove us from court; what will become of us I know not, but we are in an ill taking at this present.

He protested:

Sir, I was never factious in religion, nor shall ever seek the ruin of any because he is not of my opinion.

He spoke too soon: not for the first time, the insistence that religious dissent was disloyal proved a self-fulfilling prophecy, and this officer, John Barry, became within the year a leader of the Irish Rebellion.[72]

Two other British issues played a large part in bringing about the Irish Rebellion. One was the question of the authority of the English Parliament in Ireland, which was of course a question very closely related to the question whether Ireland was safe for Catholics. The conventional opinion in England, and even more the conventional opinion in Ireland, was that the English Parliament had no authority in Ireland. However, the Irish Parliament, using every opportunity which came to hand, had called on the aid of the English Parliament in getting a hearing for the Irish Remonstrance against Strafford.[73] That Remonstrance played a vital part in the junto's strategy, and Pym and Clotworthy made a big contribution to getting it heard. It took the Irish Parliament some while to realize that they had raised a genie they could not control.

Pym for a long while was very cautious in making any claim to authority in Ireland, but it was difficult to impeach a Lord Deputy of Ireland without claiming a jurisdiction over Irish affairs, and the Scots, with a carelessness so consistent that it looks like a case of accidentally on purpose, referred to Ireland as being subject to the

[72] *HMC Egmont*, I. 122.   [73] BL Egerton MS 1048, fo. 13ʳ.

Parliament of England.[74] The lawyers managing the prosecution of Strafford discovered a claim in Coke's report of Calvin's Case that the Parliament of England had power to legislate for Ireland in express words, and found it useful. Viscount Gormanston, one of the senior Irish peers, who was in England as a witness against Strafford, noticed this claim and protested at it.[75] The Irish Privy Council noticed, and objected to attempts to summon the Lord Chancellor and Lord Chief Justice of the Common Pleas, 'persons whose continuall attendance heere is very necessary', to answer questions in England.[76] Some Irish suitors tried to take advantage of the chance to appeal to English jurisdiction, and in June 1641 one Tighe O'Roddy had his appeal referred back to Ireland 'to save time'—pointedly refraining from waiving the claim to jurisdiction.[77] By August 1641 the House of Lords was making a full and explicit claim to authority over Ireland.[78] By 1642 Henry Parker was reacting to an alien jurisdiction in just the same way as the English had done to Scotland in 1604: he claimed that 'England and Ireland are one and the same dominion, there is as true and intimate a union betwixt them as betwixt England and Wales'.[79]

As the anti-popery of the English Parliament grew more intense, Irish anxiety on this issue grew deeper. Roger Moore appears to have seen the danger by February 1641. He told his fellow-conspirators that 'the welfare and maintaining of the Catholic religion, which . . . undoubtedly the Parliament now in England will suppress, doth depend on it: for said he, it is to be feared, and so much I hear from every understanding man, the Parliament intends the utter subversion of our religion'.[80] The charge is one Pym would have found it difficult to deny. Others were slower to take up the issue, but no less strong when they did: Gormanston, appealing to Clanricarde to join the rebellion in January 1642, said 'the Parliament [of England] has wholly assumed the management of the affairs of this kingdom as a right of preheminence due to it.

---

[74] Scottish RO PA 7/2, no 78B; BL Stowe MS 187, fo. 54ᵛ; BL Harl. MS 163, fol. 193ᵇ.
[75] Sir Edward Coke, *Seventh Report*, 17–18; CUL MS Kk vi. 38, fo. 185ᵛ; *History of the Irish Confederation*, ed. J. T. Gilbert, i (Dublin, 1882), 255.
[76] PRO SP 63/258/51 and 68.
[77] *CJ* ii. 187; BL Harl. MS 163, fo. 737ᵃ.
[78] *LJ* iv. 339, 342, and other refs.
[79] Henry Parker, *Observations* (1642), 36.
[80] J. Nalson, *Impartial Collection*, ii (1682), 544.

And what may be expected from such zealous and fiery professors of an adverse religion but the ruine and extirpation of ours?'[81] It is the same voice in which the Scots had protested that the imposition of the Prayer Book meant that they would be no more a kirk or a nation. The Irish rebels recognized the parallel, and one of them, when asked why he had gone into rebellion, replied 'to imitate Scotland, who got a privilege by that course'.[82]

The parallel between the two rebellions was visible to John Warner Bishop of Rochester, who wrote in his diary that the Irish 'as the Scots did, require liberty, religion, laws etc'.[83] Yet though Warner might see the parallel, to men of Pym's stamp, who found it hard to dignify the beliefs of the Irish with the name of 'religion', it was as hard to see the parallel as it was for Charles, who had the same difficulty with the Scots. However close the parallel might be from a multiple kingdom perspective, it was hard to see from a theological one, and in religious terms, what satisfied the Scots must necessarily discontent the Irish.

The other issue which concerned both the Scots and the Irish was the policy of plantation, a security to the Scots and a threat to the Irish. This issue was at stake in the long and tortuous negotiations for the confirmation of the Graces, originally granted in 1626, as part of Charles's war effort, withdrawn at the conclusion of peace, and claimed again in 1640. Throughout most of 1641 there was an Irish committee in London, which was involved both in the prosecution of Strafford, the first victim of British justice, and in negotiations for the renewal of the Graces. If Charles granted the Graces, he would concede security of tenure to Catholic landholders Old English and Irish, and thereby, as both the rebels and the Dublin Council saw it, make Ireland safe for Catholicism. The Graces, in fact, represented a policy diametrically opposed to that which the junto and the Covenanters were pressing for. It was hard to see how Charles could satisfy both, and when he announced the granting of the Graces on 3 April 1641, it was at a time when the negotiations with the Scots and the English Parliament had gone sour. It seems unlikely that this is a coincidence.

For the second time, Charles granted the Graces, and then they were withdrawn before they could be made effective. This apparent breach of faith seems likely to be, for many, an important reason

---

[81] *History of the Irish Confederation*, ed. Gilbert, i. 255.
[82] *LJ* iv. 415.   [83] BL Harl. MS 6424, fo. 99ʳ.

why they supported the rebellion. It is essential to explain why the Graces failed to appear. Once again, the explanation is British, but this time, it is domestic English reasons which seem to have led to their withdrawal. The Irish committee had asked for the Graces to be confirmed by Parliamentary legislation, and under Poynings's Law, this legislation had to be transmitted by the Irish Privy Council for approval by the English Privy Council. That fact provided the necessary opportunity for a determined rearguard action by the Irish Privy Council, which was too much a Protestant body to have ever been in favour of the Graces. They tried many arguments, but the one which ultimately purchased on Charles was that stopping plantation would block by far the most promising opportunity to improve Irish revenue. The Irish Parliament was insisting on the rule of law, and the rule of law, as always, was having the effect of dramatically diminishing royal income. The Irish Privy Council finally played its trump card by insisting, perfectly correctly, that if the Graces were passed, Ireland would need a regular subsidy from the English Exchequer. The summer of 1641, when Charles had lost 60% of his ordinary revenues to English Parliamentary action, was not a time when the English Exchequer could afford to subsidize anything; so it appears, ironically, to have been Pym's success in preventing a regular grant of Tonnage and Poundage in England which contributed the final straw to driving Ireland into rebellion. There can rarely have been a more dramatic example of the law of unintended consequence, otherwise known as Murphy's Law.[84]

The Irish Rebellion, by making the dissolution of the English Parliament impossible, contributed a vital piece to the structure of the Civil War in England, and the Irish Rebellion was not a random event, but a natural consequence of Anglo–Scottish *rapprochement* in religion, helped on by financial breakdown in England. The nearer Charles came to conciliating Pym and the Scots, the greater threat he created to the stability of his rule in Ireland. This point is further emphasized by Pym's handling of the rebellion, which shows exactly the same sublime blindness as Charles's handling of the Covenanters. In fact it is one of the best demonstrations of the influence of religion on politics that, in assessing contributions to Irish affairs, all our political perceptions

---

[84] Conrad Russell, 'British Background to the Irish Rebellion of 1641', *Historical Research*, 61/145 (1988), 166–82, esp. pp. 171–5.

must be reversed. It is Arundel and Cottington who emerge on Irish affairs as the wets, the men who speak of realism and conciliation, and keep the lines of communication open, while it is Holles and Vane who emerge as the hard-line ideologues. Charles now emerges as a reasonably perceptive, if rather weak, politician, while Pym's obstinate insistence that popery should never be tolerated in Ireland, and that the war should be financed by a massive scheme of confiscation, merely had the effect Charles predicted, of making the rebels desperate. Moreover, Pym in Ireland was no more receptive than Charles in Scotland to the argument that what he proposed was impossible. The thought was unacceptable, and in any case irrelevant, since the Irish were, literally, regarded as lesser breeds without the law. The House of Commons resolved, on the news of the rebellion, that 'there is just cause to suspect, that divers of his Majesty's subjects in Ireland have had some hand in the conspiracy and rebellions of the Irish'.[85] The implications of that remark are as breathtakingly insensitive as anything Charles did in Scotland. Where religion changed, political character changed with it. Those who could handle Scotland could not handle Ireland, and vice versa. So long as this was so, England was most unlikely to be able to emerge unscathed from a crisis of multiple kingdoms. Cromwell on the Irish together with Wiseman on the Scots illustrated painfully how such a crisis exposed all the lines of division in the English body politic. For many centuries afterwards, English language has continued to recognize this fact. The word 'Whig' accuses those to whom it is applied of being Scottish Covenanters, while the word 'Tory' accuses those to whom it is applied of being Irish bandits. Every time English parties denounced each other, they commemorated, however unwittingly, the effects of a crisis of multiple kingdoms which at the same time became a crisis of religions. These two created a crisis of authority. The crisis of authority made men fight, and religion endowed them with parties with which to do so.

[85] House of Lords Main Papers, 10 Nov. 1641.

6

The Rule of Law
Whose Slogan?

'WE maintayne that the king is king by an inhaerent birth-right; they say his kingly power is an office upon trust'.[1] These words were written by the Royalist member of Parliament Sir John Strangeways, writing in his commonplace book, probably while in the Tower in 1647. They encapsulate as neatly as one quotation can, a view which has been argued ever since, that the Civil War was fought 'between two clearly formulated ideas of government'.[2] It is to a degree tautological to say that a civil war in which the king is on one side and his enemies on the other must be fought between rival theories of government: if they did not exist, it became urgently necessary to invent them. However, in introducing Strangeways's words into a debate on the causes of the English Civil War, I have broken one of my strictest evidential rules, which is that the cause must precede the effect. Words written in 1647 cannot be any part of the causes of a war which began in 1642. This is done to fasten attention, at the very beginning, on the question whether two rival theories of government were a cause or a consequence of the English Civil War.

If we attempt to argue that rival theories of government were a cause of the Civil War (which Sir John Strangeways did not), we immediately find a large body of evidence in our way, and that body of evidence includes the record of Strangeways's own Parliamentary career. He was not a champion of absolute monarchy or arbitrary government, but a man with as distinguished a record as a champion of the rule of law as any member of the House of Commons. He was a vigorous participant in the impeachment of the Duke of Buckingham in 1626. At the end of the 1626 Parliament, he replied to Dudley Carleton's speech threatening that the King would turn to 'new counsels', by quoting James's famous speech of 1610 in favour

[1] Yale University, Beinecke Library, Osborn Collection, MS b. 304, p. 46.
[2] C. V. Wedgwood, *History and Hope* (1987), 474.

of the rule of law, saying that those kings who did not keep themselves within the bounds of the laws of their kingdoms were perjured, and all those who counselled them otherwise were pests and vipers fit to be cast out. He expressed the rather menacing hope that Charles would inherit his father's virtues, as he had done his crown.[3] He refused the Forced Loan, and in 1628 was a vigorous supporter of the Petition of Right and the Remonstrance.[4] In 1640 he roundly condemned Ship Money because it was contrary to the Petition of Right.[5] His record had earned him the right to write in his commonplace book that 'we of the king's partye do detest monopolyes and shippe moneye and all the grievances of the people as much as any man living: we doe well knowe that our estates, lives and fames are preserved by the lawes, and that the king is bound by the lawes'.[6] The issues on which Strangeways broke company with Pym during 1640–1 were not legal issues: they were the Scottish treaty, Root and Branch, and the Ministers' Remonstrance: he defended bishops on the Caroline ground that 'in matters of ordination they are *jure divino*'. He was quite entitled to argue that it was not delinquency to oppose change in established religion or change of laws without the King's assent.[7] In becoming a Royalist, Strangeways did not contradict any of the arguments he had developed for the rule of law during the 1620s. Moreover, he is one of a considerable number of people who followed a similar course. His career is one which is to Macaulay a stumbling block, and to me a paradigm.

As the spokesmen for Royalism in 1642 were not champions of arbitrary government, but sober defenders of the rule of law, so those who spoke for the Parliamentarians were not, in the main, principled defenders of resistance or champions of an ascending theory of power. If they stood for a rival theory of government, they were extremely reluctant to expose any such theory to the public view. Anyone attempting to explain the English Civil War must come to terms with the extraordinary absence in 1642 of any principled defence of resistance. It was in part because they were so reluctant to defend resistance that Parliamentarians so regularly

[3] CUL MS Dd 12–22, fos. 36–7.
[4] R. P. Cust, *Forced Loan and English Politics 1626–1628* (Oxford, 1987), 189, 355; *1628 Debates*, iv. 146, 154, 157, and other refs.
[5] D'Ewes (N.), p. 63 and 63 n.
[6] Yale University, Beinecke Library, Osborn Collection, MS b. 304, p. 46.
[7] Ibid., p. 4. BL Add. MS 64, 807, fo. 4ᵛ.

insisted that the King had attacked them, and they were fighting only in self-defence—the one ground on which prevailing theory regularly recognized resistance to be lawful.[8] It might be argued that the justification of self-defence constitutes resistance theory. From a practical point of view, this may perhaps be correct, but if so, it is a justification of a very *ad hoc*, limited, and unideological kind. The limitation is visible in the record: 1642 produced no great political manifesto, no Great Charter or Declaration of Rights, and the silence is significant. The Grand Remonstrance, which probably comes nearest to meeting the specification, is a manifesto of politics and religion rather than a landmark in the history of ideas. It seems that the need to sustain this fiction that no resistance was taking place was one of the things which made the outbreak of the Civil War so long delayed: each side was trying to win the propaganda advantage of manœuvring the other side into starting it. It is, of course, possible to argue that appearances are deceptive. The propaganda campaign of 1642, like a general election campaign, was dominated by the need to capture the middle ground, and it is possible to argue that the absence of a defence of resistance need be taken no more seriously than some other assurances given at general elections.

Such an argument would undoubtedly contain some truth. There was only one work defending resistance which passed the press in the month in which the Civil War broke out, and that, significantly, was a reprint of a Scottish tract written by Alexander Henderson in 1639 to defend the First Bishops' War.[9] Yet there undoubtedly were some closet resistance theorists among the Parliamentarians, and careful search may discover hints of their existence, and occasionally something more. The least prudent, and therefore the most explicit, seems to have been Jeremiah Burroughes, one of the Long Parliament Fast preachers, while discussing the Scottish National Covenant in the Earl of Warwick's garden in 1638. Burroughes asked: 'what if the supreme magistrate refuse or neglect that which he ought to doe and is necessarie to be done: may not the people give power to some other to supply his neglect and defect?'

---

[8] Sommerville, p. 15.
[9] *Some Speciall Arguments for the Scottish Subjects Lawfull Defence of their Religion and Liberty, extracted out of the Manuscripts of One of their Cheife Reformers*, BL E. 239(3), dated by Thomason 4 Aug. 1642. I am grateful to Dr Peter Donald for help in identifying this tract.

He said the supreme magistrate's power was originally from the people and asked if the King 'should exercise tyrannie upon his people, and make no conscience of his oath, whether it were not lawfull to refuse obedience unto him, to resist him by force, and to defend our selves and liberties by armes'. This conversation was brought to an end by the Earl of Warwick's steward insisting 'that the point was full of danger',[10] and there is very little similar material. There are occasional hints: Edmund Calamy, preaching at a Long Parliament Fast, made the impeccable point that God took great men from the church when there was most need of them. Three of his examples, Augustine, Ambrose, and Luther, were perfectly safe, but his fourth happened to be Pareus, the Heidelberg resistance theorist whose opinions every Oxford graduate had to forswear as a condition of taking his degree.[11] Sir Henry Ludlow, father of the author of the *Memoirs*, argued in a debate on the Militia Ordinance that, 'the king is derivative from the Parliament and not the Parliament from the king, and if he govern not by Parliament, then he govern by force and abuseth the law'.[12] John Pym on one occasion sketched a doctrine of double covenant with some resemblance to the *Vindiciae Contra Tyrannos*. We might take the risk of adding Henry Marten and William Strode to this list, though their addition would be conjectural.[13] Yet, when all possible research effort has been put into the task, our findings remain a small undercurrent, running against the main flow of Parliamentary thinking. The main stream is much better represented by Roger Hill, member for Bridport, who wrote in June 1642 that the King was coming with an army, and therefore 'we shall not be wanting to defend his matie, our selves and kingdome, against that wicked brood that would destroy both prince and people, and make both a prey unto themselves'.[14] Roger Hill was not resisting the King: he was defending him from himself. Moreover, he was not making a public statement: he was writing to his wife, to whom, one hopes,

[10] William Hunt, *Puritan Moment* (Cambridge, Mass., 1983), 278; Essex RO T/B/211/1/39.

[11] Edmund Calamy, *Englands Looking Glass* (1642), 15.

[12] *PJ* i. 249.

[13] *LJ* iv. 285. I would like to thank my former pupil Mrs Alexandra Boscawen for several valuable discussions of the *Vindiciae* and its possible influence. For Marten, see Gawdy in *PJ* ii. 225, 356–7, 376, and other refs. See also *PJ* ii. 115 for Sir Peter Wentworth.

[14] BL Add. MS 46, 500, fo. 29ʳ. I would like to thank Dr J. S. A. Adamson for drawing my attention to this MS.

he had no need to pretend. In the same vein, the Parliament's
Declaration of 26 May claimed that Hotham's act in closing the
gates of Hull against the King was 'in obedience to his Majesty,
and his authority, and for his service, and the service of the kingdom, for which use only all that interest is that the King hath in
the town'.[15] In the Commons on 28 February 1642 a member
identified only as 'Sir W.' (possibly Sir Walter Earle) used two
emotive images: he 'compared the King to two examples: the first, if
the King should be desperate and would lay violent hands upon
himself; the second, if the King were at sea and a storm should rise
and he would put himself to the helm, and would steer such a course
as would overthrow the ship and drown them all.'[16] To restrain the
King from committing suicide did not appear to him to be morally
resistance. Saye, writing after the event, presented the war as a
defence against a royal *coup d'état*: he said the Parliament 'had a
lawfull and a just cause to tak up arms for their own defence, and
for the defence of the established government of this kingdom,
against force and violence intended against them'.[17] It was because
it justified the plea of self-defence that it was so crucial to
Parliamentarian mythology to portray the attempt on the Five
Members as a planned asault on the whole Parliament, and not just
on some of its members.[18] Such arguments, whether convincing or
not, did at least save the Parliamentarians from having to grapple
with the major theoretical questions whether or for what ends
resistance was lawful.

This was the official Parliamentarian position: when the Marquis
of Hertford was impeached for raising forces for the King, he was
impeached for levying war against King and kingdom.[19] No doubt
for some people this official position was a pose, yet nevertheless it
remains astonishing that it should require a major research effort to
prove that some of those who fought a civil war against the King
believed that resistance was lawful. Even if many of them may in
private have believed in a rival theory of government, their
inability to avow any such fact in public tells us volumes about the
climate of opinion in which they fought. This was a country in
which the doctrine of non-resistance had sunk very deep indeed, and

[15] Rushworth III. i. 584.   [16] *PJ* i. 482.
[17] William Fiennes, Viscount Saye and Sele, *Vindiciae Veritatis* (1654), BL E.
811(2), Epistle.
[18] This point will be developed in Russell, *FBM*.   [19] *LJ* v. 286.

in which the Parliamentary leaders seem to have believed, at the least, that no major party could be collected in the name of any contrary creed. If these men were closet resistance theorists, the trial of the King in 1649 should have given them a belated opportunity to come out into the open, but when they had that opportunity, such men as Saye and Manchester, Burges and Calamy, rejected it with contumely. No member of the leading junto of 1642 supported the regicide in public, and that fact should make us pause before we assume that inside every Parliamentarian there was a Henry Marten struggling to get out. The two sides in 1642 were apparently arguing between rival interpretations of a doctrine of the rule of law whose roots were largely common to both sides, and in this point, appearances are not entirely deceptive.

It is then necessary to explain what a discussion of the rule of law is doing in this book, and which of our initial questions it is designed to help to answer. Belief in the rule of law did not contribute significantly to the division into parties, and, because this negative proposition may create the most surprise, it must claim a very large share of the space. Yet the negative proposition does not mean that the rule of law was irrelevant to the coming of the Civil War: it contributed substantially to the answer to three other questions, why the King lost the Bishops' Wars, why he was unable to dissolve the Long Parliament during the summer of 1641, and to the phenomenon of diminished majesty, which belittled the King to the point where it appeared safe to oppose him. In all these respects, the doctrine of the rule of law contributed to the crisis by weakening and impoverishing the King to an extent which prevented him from riding out a wave of opposition whose strength should have been by no means overwhelming.

The proposition that the rule of law was not a significant part of the ideals dividing the parties is not intended to deny that there were a number of Parliamentarians who saw themselves first and foremost as fighting for the rule of law and for the closely related cause of the survival of Parliaments. Among these people, the names of Saye, Essex, Northumberland, and Selden come to mind. Northumberland, it seems, feared not only the possible extinction of Parliaments, but also the danger that Charles might succeed in reducing them to a rubber stamp: he wrote to Bankes in May 1642 that there was a danger that Parliaments 'shall only be instruments to execute the demands of the King, who were ordained for his greatest and most supreame councel'.[20] The choice of words suggests that for Northumberland it had been Charles's failure to listen to the Short Parliament which had been the traumatic moment, and much other material in Northumberland's papers might support that interpretation. Essex in the summer of 1641 supported the bill for the abolition of Star Chamber, on the ground that they had 'laboured all this Parliament to make themselves freemen and not slaves'.[21]

It is not the object of this argument to play down the sincerity or the importance of these ideals: the argument is that these ideals were not what divided them from any of the prominent leaders of the Royalist party in Parliament, who held them with equal devotion and consistency. On 3 May 1641 the Commons were stunned by the news of Charles's participation in the Army Plot against the Parliament. One member reacted by moving 'for the remonstrance, and the petition of rights to be forthwith read, and then to goe to the Lords, and by that we may try the affection of the kinge, and that if we should be dissolved, that we might be found doeinge the service we were hither sent for'. This member was Sir John Culpepper, the King's leading supporter in the Commons.[22] On 7 December 1640 Edward Hyde complained: 'all our sufferings from the original of Ship Money'.[23] It is not what is in this statement, but what is not in it, which marks Hyde out as a future Royalist. The impeachment of the judges for their Ship Money judgments was largely carried through by the future Royalists Hyde, Falkland, and Waller, and there is no sign in Clarendon's *History* or anywhere else that they ever thought their royalism obliged them to repent of what they had done. Culpepper in November 1640 said that Ship Money

cries aloud, I may say, I hope, without offence: this strikes the first-born of every family, I mean our inheritance: if the law give the King power in any danger of the kingdom, whereof he is judge, to impose what, and when, he pleases, we owe all that is left to the goodness of the King, not of the law: Mr. Speaker, this makes the farmers faint, and the plough to grow heavy.

His attack on monopolies, in the same speech, is too well known to need quoting.[24]

---

[20] G. Bankes, *Corfe Castle* (1853), 122–3.

[21] Bedfordshire RO St John MSS J 1386.

[22] BL Harl. MS 477, fo. 28ʳ.

[23] *Notebook of Sir John Northcote*, ed. A. H. A. Hamilton (1877), p. 38.

[24] Rushworth, III. i. 33. See Russell, *FBM* for a discussion of whether this speech was delivered. It seems to be the balance of probability that it was.

In October 1641, when Hyde argued that 'all particulars weere in a good condition if wee could but preserve them as they weere', he listed the abolition of Star Chamber, the High Commission, and Ship Money as reasons for believing this proposition. D'Ewes correctly identified the point of issue between them by replying: 'I rather thinke the church is yet full of wrinkles amongst us and needes a great deale of Reformation which I hope wee shall shortly see effected'.[25] Edward Bagshaw, unexpectedly classified by Johann Sommerville as holding 'an absolutist attitude to the origins of royal power', began the Long Parliament by moving for it to be made praemunire to break the Statute of Monopolies or the Petition of Right.[26] Similar points can be made about Hopton, Digby, Falkland, or any other prominent Royalist in the Commons. These people were not merely fringe recruits to the Royalist party: for political purposes they were the Royalist party.

The Civil-War Royalists were not lesser breeds without the law, nor even breeds with lesser law: they were not one whit less attached to the principles of the rule of law than their Parliamentary opponents. What divided them from their opponents, then, could be either that they meant something different by the rule of law, or their beliefs on other subjects, or any combination of the two. It seems that both these answers contain large amounts of truth. The purpose of the doctrine of the rule of law is to restrain the arbitrary exercise of power. It seems that only a small number of people in any age are truly and impartially attached to this ideal as an end in itself. For most people, it is necessary to ask whose power, and even more to ask, following Lady Bracknell, 'power to do what?' In 1642, unlike 1628, the Parliament possessed a very large measure of power, and the changes in their attitudes to such things as billeting of soldiers contain a distinct element of the boot on the other foot. When the Parliament put soldiers into Hull in 1642, it proved necessary to billet them. The Royalist member Sir Thomas Bowyer bravely suggested the House should be careful how they did this, for it was against the Petition of Right. Young John Hotham replied from Hull: 'he hoped the house will not stand upon the nicety of law nor lawyers, but that they may be billeted'.[27] They were, and it was left to the King to complain that the decision was

---

[25] D'Ewes (C.), pp. 45–6.
[26] BL Add MS 56, 103 (unfoliated); Sommerville, p. 46. For Hopton, see D'Ewes (N.), p. 467 n.   [27] *PJ* i. 246, 318, 322.

'against law, and express words of the Petition of Right'.[28] When the Commons set out to justify the Militia Ordinance, they found, like Charles I justifying the Forced Loan, that they were reduced to offering a plea of 'urgent and inevitable necessity'.[29] Charles, of course, realized that he had heard these arguments before. He renounced 'the mischief which then grew by arbitrary power, though made plausible to us by the suggestions of necessity and imminent danger: and take heed you fall not into the same error upon the same suggestions'. Making a virtue of his conversion, he promised 'hereafter to keep the rules our self and to our power require the same from all others'.[30] His propaganda deliberately echoed the language of the Petition of Right debates, and when he contemplated the fate of those imprisoned for disobeying Parliamentary ordinances, he repeated Sir Robert Phelips's horror at having to lie in gaol, 'durante beneplacito, remdilesse'.[31]

Yet it would be unfair to all the protagonists to portray this simply as a matter of the boot on the other foot. It is much more constructive to follow up the question 'power to do what?' For Pym, whose attachment to the rule of law, as Jack Hexter rightly remarked, 'had about it a certain quality of intermittency',[32] the rule of law was essentially a shield against the danger of popery. His attachment to the rule of law, as the Grand Remonstrance put it, was in opposition to the 'Jesuited papists, who hate the laws, as the obstacles of that change and subversion of religion which they so much long for'.[33] The imprisonment of unconvicted recusants, for example, did not appear to Pym to be a threat to the rule of law, because it did not threaten the end for which he valued the law. To many Royalists, on the other hand, the rule of law was a protection, either against the illegal enforcement of godly reformation, or simply against vehement partisanship of any sort.

This tendency to rely on the law, and, more specifically, to rely on the law as a bulwark against godly reformation, is a consistent thread in Royalist seditious words. Such words are recorded because they are something for which the Commons had a very careful eye. Christopher Smith vicar of St James, Deeping said it was treason to

---

[28] *CJ* ii. 532. [29] Ibid. 479. [30] *LJ* iv. 687.
[31] Rushworth, III. i. 711.
[32] J. H. Hexter, *Reign of King Pym* (Cambridge, Mass., 1941), 194–5.
[33] S. R. Gardiner, *Constitutional Documents of the Puritan Revolution 1625–1660* (1889; 3rd edn. 1906 repr. Oxford, 1979), 206.

obey an order of the Parliament without the King's hand and seal
thereunto: it emerged that the Parliament had recently issued an
order inserting a lecturer into his pulpit. In June 1641 Mr Allen
Blayne lecturer at St Margaret's, Newington said the Parliament
were men and might err, and had the power to establish but not
to make laws. He refused to take the Parliamentary Protestation,
but said he had another, warranted by the Thirty-Nine Articles,
for justifying the ceremonies now used. Mr Ravenscroft, a
Huntingdonshire JP, horrified Cromwell and Walton by refusing
to take the Protestation on the ground that the House of Commons
without a law could not bind the consciences of men. Robert Smyth
of Bromsgrove prided himself on saving his church windows from
destruction, and added that now the King had proclaimed that an
ordinance of Parliament was not binding without the royal assent,
he cared not a fart for the Parliament's orders. In February 1642
John Browning parson of Much Easton (Essex), who was correctly
identified by D'Ewes as 'a notable Arminian and alter-adorer', made
the similar point that the canons and the (etcetera?) oath were as
good as the Protestation, and added for good measure that Five
Members were justly accused.[34]

ʹThere was nothing new about this use of the ideal of the rule of
law: it can be seen fully fledged in the questions Richard Bancroft
had asked of a Scottish correspondent about the proceedings of
Scottish Presbyteries:

if one, for example, sall be compleaned of for adultery . . . and doe deny
the same, by what course of law doe they proceed against him? Whether
doe they examine · witnesses upon their oathes against the supposed
offender, or whether do they inflict their censure upon a bare relatioun,
without the oath of suche as be accusers? . . . If anye man can suppose
himself to be injured by anie presbyterial consistorie whether he may
appeale, and whither?[35]

For Bancroft's heirs, such as George Digby, the rule of law was
essential as a protection against the threat of a Presbyterian pope in
every parish. For many Royalist members, the rule of law was
especially valuable as a protection against attempts by the two
Houses, or even worse, by the Commons alone, to legislate by

[34] *CJ* ii. 577, 667; *PJ* ii. 337; BL Harl. MS 163, fo. 708ᵇ; *PJ* i. 257; *CJ* ii.
530; *PJ* i. 241; Tyacke, pp 190–3; above, p. 99.
[35] Calderwood, v. 78–9.

ordinance without the King's consent. Sir Edward Dering, in his
speech of 21 October 1641, said that men 'sent us hither as their
trustees, to make and unmake laws: they know they did not send
us hither to rule and govern them by arbitrary, revocable and
disputable orders; especially in religion. No time is fit for that, and
this time as unfit as any: I desire to be instructed herein'.[36] Sir
Roger Twysden, a Kentish JP and antiquarian who had proved his
attachment to the rule of law over Ship Money, made the same
objection to the ordinance for disarming of recusants: 'if a justice of
the peace should take away the goods of any man not prohibited by
law the keeping of armour, whether [he conceived] that ordinance
of the Lords and Commons would save him harmless?'[37] More
generally, Royalists might rely on the rule of law for protection
against partisan justice of any sort. In July 1642 the Lord Mayor
read the King's proclamation for the Commission of Array, and was
promptly impeached because he had done so

in contempt and malice against the Parliament, and the proceedings
thereof; and contrary to his oath, and the faith and trust reposed in him;
and with an intent, purpose and resolution . . . to bring in an arbitrary and
tyrannical government, contrary to the laws and statutes of this realm, and
the settled government established in the same kingdom; and with an intent
and endeavour to levy war against the Parliament.[38]

Challoner Chute, the Lord Mayor's counsel, observed that 'the
adverbs make it not a crime, if it be not so in itself'.[39] This remark,
like the defence of Norwich cathedral, is somewhere near the
epitome of Royalism. For many people, their perceptions of where
and by whom the rule of law was threatened were a function of their
commitments in matters of religion. One of Charles's declarations
made the point in a wicked parable. He asked his subjects to
imagine that

the papists in Ireland in truth were, or by act or accident had made
themselves the major part of both Houses of Parliament there, and had
pretended the trust in that declaration from the kingdom of Ireland, and
thereupon had voted their religion and liberty to be in danger of
extirpation from a malignant party of Protestants and Puritans; and
therefore that they should put themselves into a posture of defence, that the

[36] Rushworth, III. i. 392.
[37] Anthony Fletcher, *Outbreak of the English Civil War* (1981), 77.
[38] *ST* iv. 160–1.　　　　　　　　　　　　[39] *LJ* v. 248.

forts and militia of that kingdom were to be put into the hands of such persons as they could confide in . . . if that rebellion had been plotted with this formality, and those circumstances declared to be legal . . . whether . . . they would believe it the more justifiable.[40]

I know of no Parliamentarian who was so unwise as to answer this question.

By the summer of 1642 the key point Parliamentarians were trying to establish was that the King had no negative voice: they invoked 'the obligation that lieth upon the kings of this realm, to pass such bills as are offered to them by both houses of Parliament, in the name of and for the good of the whole kingdom whereunto they stand engaged, both in conscience and justice, to give their royal assent'.[41] In other words, kings were bound not to enforce anything to which their subjects could not consent. It was possible to invoke rule-of-law language to sustain this point, but it did not in fact rest on any sustainable precedent in English law. At least one prominent Parliamentarian was reduced to admitting in public that his case was unsustainable in terms of the rule of law: Lord Brooke in December 1642 said that

they who thinke that humane laws can binde the conscience, and will examine the oathes they have taken according to the interpretations of men, will in time fall from us: but such who religiouslie consider that such morall precepts are fitter for heathens then for Christianes, and that we ought to lead our lives according to the rule of God's word: and that the laws of the land (being but mans invention) must not check God's children in doing the work of their heavenlie father, will not faint in their dutie.[42]

Nothing could illustrate better why so many Royalists were so profoundly attached to the doctrine of the rule of law.

Nor was this any new attachment: it was entirely consistent with the records of those members who had survived from the 1620s. Both sides in 1642 wanted to appropriate the Petition of Right to their cause, but it seems, on the record of those members who survived from 1628 to 1642, that neither side had a better claim to do so than the other. The Civil War was not fought on the legal issues of the 1620s, and men's attitudes to those issues are no predictor of their allegiance. If we look for members who took an active part in supporting the Petition of Right when it was passed,

---

[40] Rushworth, III. i. 592.   [41] Ibid. 580.
[42] *Two Speeches* (1642), BL E. 84(35), pp. 6–7.

and were alive and free to take a side in the Civil War, we come up with fifteen names, who divide as eight Parliamentarians and seven Royalists. The Parliamentarians are Earle, Hakewill, Pym, Rudyerd, Selden, Strode, Saye, and Warwick, and the Royalists Ball, Coryton, Glanvill, Kirton, Littleton, Seymour, and Strangeways. It is true that Littleton was a very reluctant Royalist, but it seems that Hakewill was an equally reluctant Parliamentarian: his Parliamentarianism seems to have consisted of little more than an old man's decision to remain in London during the war. He was not a member of the Long Parliament, and his only public contributions to the crisis between 1640 and 1642 were to act as counsel for Strafford and for the Kentish petitioners of March 1642, neither of them the act of a Parliamentarian partisan.[43] I have refrained from including Sir Thomas Wentworth and William Noy, both prominent supporters of the Petition of Right, since though we may suspect that both of them would have been Royalists had they lived to 1642, we cannot know it. Other Royalists had equally strong records as opponents of arbitrary government. Sir John Bankes, Chief Justice of the Common Pleas in 1642, was one. In 1626 he said, speaking in the Commons, that 'we have not our privileges by graunt from ye k, but as ancient as is our commonwealth are our privileges, and due by prescription 36 H. Dyer'. In 1628, opposing the King's case on martial law, he said, in a possibly deliberate pun: 'subjects have their rights, and kings their prerogative. Yet the ocean hath banks, and the common law limits prerogative'. For good measure, he added: 'the courts of common law, especially the King's Bench, is the supreme law'. At the end of the 1628 Parliament, he reported the remonstrance on Tonnage and Poundage from committee. It is difficult to regard Bankes's royalism as mere time-serving, since in May 1642 he risked 'the king's indignation in a high measure' for refusing to condemn the Militia Ordinance as illegal. In Bankes's early career, it is his admiration for Lancelot Andrewes, and not a normal attitude to the rule of law, which marks him as a future Royalist.[44] Few people had made more nuisance of themselves in the parliaments of the

---

[43] *LJ* iv. 104, v. 62. I am grateful to Dr J. S. A. Adamson for discussion of the career of William Hakewill.

[44] CUL MS 12–20, fo. 67; *1628 Debates*, ii. 484, iv. 415; Bankes, *Corfe Castle*, pp. 134–6; Dorset RO Bankes of Kingston Lacey MSS, Gospel Commentaries, unfoliated.

1620s than William Mallory. We cannot be sure whether it was Mallory or his son who moved in December 1641 that Sir Arthur Haselrig's militia bill should be burnt in Palace Yard. The voice sounds like the authentic voice of old Mallory, and the fact that William Strode, another veteran of the twenties, attempted to excuse him gives the same impression. Mallory, as well as being an enemy of arbitrary government, was probably a church papist, and therefore, for practical purposes, incapable of being a Parliamentarian.[45] Anyone who still thinks a Catholic cannot be a good constitutionalist should be sentenced, as a penance, to read right through the Irish *Commons' Journals* for 1641. If we look back into the 1620s to see what differentiates a future Royalist from a future Parliamentarian, it is not a difference between a greater and a lesser attachment to the rule of law. The future Parliamentarian shows in Sir Robert Harley's demand for the destruction of the idolatrous monument of Cheapside Cross, or in the complaint of John Hampden, otherwise a very rare speaker in the 1620s, that the Duke would alter religion by trusting papists.[46]

If we cannot see Royalists and Parliamentarians as divided by rival constitutional theories either in the Long Parliament or in their previous careers in the 1620s, it is not necessary to my purposes to go back to James's reign and refute the view that it shows a long-standing dispute between two rival constitutional theories. Even if this view were correct, it would not tell us very much about the causes of the Civil War, since the issues and the people of the Civil War, so clearly did not divide along any of the lines familiar in the 1620s. However, since this old view has recently been so vigorously revived by Johann Sommerville, it is perhaps necessary to the credibility, even if not to the logical coherence, of my case to say something about it. Dr Sommerville has recently argued that 'ideologies which played a vital role on the eve of the Civil War had roots that went back at least to 1603. To this extent the Civil War did have long-term origins'.[47] If this were taken to mean only that people trying to justify what they had done

---

[45] D'Ewes (C.), pp. 246–7; Conrad Russell, 'Examination of Mr. Mallory After the Parliament of 1621', *BIHR* 50 (1977), 125–32. M. F. Keeler, *Long Parliament* (Philadelphia, 1954), 265–6. On the parallel case of Sir Marmaduke Langdale, see J. T. Cliffe, *Yorkshire Gentry* (1969), 293, 311, 313, 315, 318–20, 346.

[46] Russell, *PEP*, p. 277; *1628 Debates*, iv. 121–2, 131.

[47] Sommerville, p. 5.

in 1642 drew on weapons already to hand, the proposition would be tautological. In fact, Dr Sommerville means a good deal more than this. He distinguishes two widely divergent lines of political thought, one of which he calls 'the theory of royal absolutism, or, to give it its traditional title, the divine right of kings'. The other he identifies as involving the view that originally 'power was resident in the community'.[48] He thus sees (among other ideas) two mutually exclusive theories of authority, resembling those normally known to us as ascending and descending theories of power, already locked in conflict by 1603. His work therefore tends to suggest that these divergent theories had something to do with the causes of the Civil War.

My central objection to this view is that, *pace* Walter Ullmann, I do not think that ascending and descending theories of power are mutually exclusive. To take an example familiar to every Tudor and Stuart gentleman, one cannot apply such a distinction to the divine right of husbands. That the office enjoyed divine right was clear enough, and yet it was properly regarded as an elective office: it was certainly not a hereditary one. Dr Sommerville would evade this paradox by invoking what he describes as 'designation theory', whereby the wife, or the people, were to designate the person who should enjoy the power, and God would then confer the authority.[49] It is, no doubt, possible to distinguish in this manner, yet it is hard to believe that many husbands continued for long to believe that their authority was entirely independent of their wives' consent, especially when they were holding an office to which all sorts of lawyers, common, canon, or civil, agreed that no man could enjoy a valid title unless he could prove consent. For Dr Sommerville, the question of the wife's consent is irrelevant to the source of the husband's authority, since the husband's authority is derived *immediately* from God. This question encapsulates many of our disagreements: Dr Sommerville is concerned with the idea that authority is derived *immediately* from God, and with the possibility that the immediacy of the derivation may rule out any possibility of human limitation. To me, it appears a normal proposition that power was derived from God, and an equally normal one that God works through second causes, so divine and human origins of power appear to me not to be mutually exclusive, and divine right appears

[48] Ibid. 9, 62.   [49] Ibid. 22.

to me to be perfectly capable of being combined with legal limitation. I will therefore not presume any statement of divine right to imply absence of limitation on the King's power unless it says so in express words. By a curious coincidence, our disagreements, and especially that about the use of the word 'immediately', reproduce a conversation on 5 August 1638, in the Earl of Warwick's garden, between John Michaelson vicar of Chelmsford and Jeremiah Burroughes, a deprived minister and future preacher to the Long Parliament, who was temporarily acting as chaplain to the Countess of Warwick. Michaelson is telling the story:

'I answered . . . that the powers that be are ordained by God Romans 13.1 not be the people.' To which he ansrit: 'so has every Justice of Peace his power from God.' My reply wes: 'but in a different manner. The supreame magistrate had his immediatlie from God, and all other inferior magistrates theirs mediatlie by the supreame magistrate.' That distinction he seemed exceedinglie to dislike, as appeared by his doubling of the phrase, with a kind of indignation: 'what? immediatlie from God? Immediatelie from God?' Hes the supreame magistrate his power immediatlie from God? Does God say from heaven that King Charles shall be King of England or Scotland?' 'yes', said I, 'for pointeing him out the right here of his father, appointes him to be King: for the crounes of England and Scotland, like other inheritances, falls naturallie and be divine right to the next here.'[50]

Michaelson, in his final point, was faithfully following James VI and I. Yet James is not an unambiguous witness on this issue, and it is possible that Burroughes, in claiming divine right for JPs, was equally following James, who told his judges and JPs: 'that the thrones you sit on, are God's, and neither yours nor mine'.[51] The passage is relevant to the current debate, since it seems to show that James, who was well aware that he appointed judges and JPs, believed that divine right was not necessarily derived *immediately* from God. This makes the more sense of the fact that James was capable of mentioning divine right in the same breath as election. He thought all kings enjoyed divine right, while also believing that 'some had their beginning by conquest, and some by election of the people'.[52] James clearly believed that his own divine right was

[50] Essex RO T/B/211/1/39. In 1641, Michaelson acted as an informant to Strangeways on the organization of crowds. Bodl MS Rawl.D 932, f 57ʳ.
[51] *CJ* i. 145.
[52] *Political Works of James I*, ed. C. H. MacIlwain (Cambridge, Mass., 1918), 309.

immediately from God, but he did not believe, it seems, that this was the only form of divine right, nor that monarchy was the only form of authority in Scotland or England which enjoyed divine right.

Every authority, however small and however local, enjoyed divine right. Any authority which did not was not duly constituted, and saying it had no divine right was a denial of its legitimacy. The statement that an authority had divine right, however, said nothing about how that divine right was derived. It might come by a descending theory of power, from God down through duly constituted authorities, or it might ascend from the people by election. At least one key local office, that of churchwarden, was supposed to do both at once. The churchwardens, whose role in parish government was vital, were to be chosen by the minister and the parishioners jointly 'if it may be', and if not, they were to choose one each.[53] Parish constables, who were among the 'powers that be' that Romans 13 declared to be ordained by God, might often be elected, without thereby forfeiting either their divine right or their descending authority as the king's man in the parish.[54] It was, indeed, only if ascending and descending theories of power were compatible that the authority of King-in-Parliament was conceptually possible.

In fact, the basic proposition that kings ruled by divine right was a proposition almost universally accepted, not particularly controversial, and utterly uninformative about the extent of the king's powers. Statements of the king's divine right are like penal statutes: they should be construed strictly, and never presumed to imply more than they say in express words. When this rule is applied to James VI and I, what he says in express words usually turns out to be rather little. He was dedicated to the two anti-Melvillian beliefs, that ecclesiastical powers could not depose him, and that no authority existed in his kingdom which did not ultimately proceed from him.[55] Both these beliefs were ones in which he enjoyed the

[53] E. Cardwell, *Synodalia*, i (Oxford, 1842), 296. I am grateful to Ms Julia Merritt for drawing my attention to this passage.

[54] I am grateful to Miss Lynda Price for much help on matters to do with parish constables.

[55] See Jenny Wormald, 'James VI and I, *Basilikon Doron* and *The Trew law of Free Monarchies*: The Scottish Context and the English Translation', in Linda Levy Peck (ed.), *Mental World of the Jacobean Court* (Folger Shakespeare Library, forthcoming). I am grateful to Dr Wormald for allowing me to see this piece before publication.

specific backing of English common and statute law, in particular of the Act in Restraint of Appeals, the Act of Supremacy, and the Statute of Praemunire. So long as James did not see these points as threatened when they were not, there was no necessary reason why he should clash with English Parliaments or with the common law.

The basic proposition of divine right was conceded by Pym, who said to James that 'the image of God's power is expressed in your regal dignity', and by Coke, who described the king as 'God's lieutenant'.[56] It is hard to use a proposition they all three accepted as a way of explaining differences between them. It was also perfectly possible to believe in divine right, and yet to believe at the same time that the law by which, and the political order within which, the king ruled, enjoyed the same right. A believer in divine right could easily argue, like Robert Holborne, that it was not true that 'the frame of the English government stands in the royal power'.[57] It was easy to argue that the political order within which the king ruled, as much as the king himself, enjoyed right immediately from God. John White, speaking in the Long Parliament in November 1640, said that in the first institution of kings God set laws to limit them.[58] This was a line of argument which tended to reduce all human government to the status of local government, and local government, by definition, cannot be absolute.

It is also possible to misinterpret statements on this subject because some of our sources, especially sermons addressed to potentially refractory subjects, may be giving us one barrel of a double-barrelled doctrine. It was a standard homiletic task of preachers to tell people to do their duties, and a sermon setting out the duties of subjects may therefore give a very misleading impression unless it is set beside a sermon from the same author setting out the duty of kings. The same point applied between husbands and wives. William Gouge, in the Epistle to his *Domesticall Duties*, complained that he had been misunderstood by the audience which had heard the sermons delivered, because he had handled wives' duties first:

---

[56] Conrad Russell, 'Parliamentary Career of John Pym 1621–1629', in Peter Clarke, Alan G. R. Smith and Nicholas Tyacke (eds.), *English Commonwealth 1547–1640: Essays presented to Joel Hurstfield* (Leicester, 1979), 154; *1628 Debates*, iii. 272.

[57] *ST*, iii. 971.

[58] *Notebook of Sir John Northcote*, ed. Hamilton, p. 9.

There was taught (as must have been, except the truth should have been betrayed) what a wife, in the uttermost extent of that subjection under which God hath put her, is bound unto, in case her husband will stand upon the uttermost of his authoritye; which was so taken, as if I had taught that a husband might, and ought, to extract the uttermost, and that a wife was bound in that uttermost extent to do all that was delivered as duty, whether the husband exact it or not.

He said that once he came to deliver the husband's duties, a clearer picture emerged. It is possible that, in reading homilies on obedience, we have made the same mistake as William Gouge's parishioners.[59]

In fact, it seems that none of the disputes between James and his Parliaments were about divine right. Where they were about power and authority, they tended to be about powers such as the power to levy impositions, which James claimed by English law, and which had been upheld by the judges in open court. Sir Edward Coke was not synonymous with English law, and many of the disputes of James's reign were between rival interpretations of the common law, sometimes between the interpretation of Coke and that of Lord Chancellor Ellesmere. A king in a strange country who relies on his lord chancellor to tell him what the law is cannot fairly therefore be credited with hostility to the law. In a dispute between rival interpretations of the law, where the essential point at issue is what the law says, it is an unfair piece of question-begging, not to say *petitio principii*, to credit either side with being more in favour of the law than the other. In many of these disputes, both legal traditions went back a very long way, a point which Ellesmere, in Calvin's Case, chose to underline sharply by his effusive praise for one of the judges who had answered Richard II's questions in 1386, and had been impeached in 1388. Not very far between the lines, Ellesmere was saying that judges on the Bench were better interpreters of the law than Parliaments.[60] This is, in all senses of the word, a judicial view, even if not necessarily a Parliamentary one.

It is not easy to distinguish rival extreme views on the king's power by invoking theories about the origins of power which might

---

[59] William Gouge, *Domesticall Duties* (1626), Epistle. I am grateful to the Rev. Dr Daniel Doriani for many valuable discussions of these issues.

[60] L. Knafla, *Law and Politics in Jacobean England* (Cambridge, 1977), 227. In making this point, Ellesmere was contributing to a current dispute with some members of the House of Commons.

often coexist in the same person, and which in any case tell us little or nothing about the extent of the king's powers. It is perhaps better to distinguish extreme views by looking, on one hand, for those who defended resistance, and on the other, for those who believed that the king by himself could make law. This method produces very few extremists, but for that very reason, it appears to be in line with the political facts. It is, of course, hard to put much weight on the silence about resistance, since the idea was taboo, and its expression was likely to lead to prosecution. However, if there had been any number of closet resistance theorists, the Civil War gave them an opportunity to come into the open and it is an opportunity which, on the whole, they did not take.

The belief that the king had the power to make law might lead to trouble while a Parliament was sitting, but it was much the less dangerous view of the two. Dr Sommerville has argued that 'the King's power to make law was a straightforward consequence of absolutist theory'.[61] If so, it is a consequence which is remarkably little in evidence. It is unwise to extrapolate such a view from men's views on the origins of power, as at least one of Dr Sommerville's examples shows. He credits Edward Bagshaw, a lawyer and member of the Long Parliament, with 'an absolutist attitude to the origins of royal power', yet Bagshaw, in the Long Parliament, called for violation of the Petition of Right to be made praemunire.[62] He was clearly no absolutist in practice, and his case helps to cast doubt on whether there is such a thing as an 'absolutist attitude to the origins of royal power'. The purpose of many such ideas, including Bagshaw's, was to exclude the Pope. It is not always wise to draw out of such ideas implications about the powers of Parliaments, which their authors were not discussing. The power to make law is too important a mark of supreme power for it to be wise to credit anyone with attributing it to the king alone, without direct evidence, and direct evidence is very hard to come by. It seems that J. W. Allen was right when he argued that 'there is hardly anywhere to be found any suggestion that the King can make law', and it is a rather poor sort of absolutist who does not believe that the king by himself can make law.[63]

[61] Sommerville, p. 36.   [62] Ibid. 46; Rushworth, III, i. 27.
[63] J. W. Allen, *English Political Thought 1603–1660*, i (1938), 11. J. W. Daly, 'The Idea of Absolute Monarchy in Seventeenth-Century England', *HJ* 21/2 (1978), 227–50.

There are a few possible candidates for such a belief. Dr
Sommerville himself has listed some, of whom all but one are
clergy. Some of these were making, in the passages quoted, general
statements about the limits of obedience, into which statements
about the legislative power can be read with difficulty, if at all.
Others, such as Francis Mason, were explicitly concerned with
ecclesiastical laws. Here, Charles in 1640 and James in 1604 did
explicitly claim power to make canons with the assent of their
clergy, and not of their Parliaments. However, since they believed
this power to be explicitly confirmed by the Henrician Act for the
Submission of the Clergy, the major debate to which it gave rise was
not a debate between absolutists and their opponents, but between
rival interpretations of the law of the land. In this area, as in many
others, Digby, Bagshaw, and other future Royalists sided against
the King, and he was forced to give way before he could collect a
Royalist party. A high proportion of those cited by Dr Sommerville
wrote specifically to please James, and their remarks should be read
accordingly.[64] James's views on this subject were deeply coloured
by his Scottish experience, and his special objection was to
independent clerical legislative power, whether papal or Presbyterian.
It is worth remembering that in this struggle it had been James, not
Melville, who had built up the legislative sovereignty of the
Scottish Parliament in support of his case. It is perhaps as dangerous
to translate statements aimed at Pope or presbyter into criticisms of
Parliaments as it is to translate modern statements about Parliamentary
sovereignty from Westminster to Strasburg. James's opening speech
to the Parliament of 1621 should also be read in this Scottish light.
James was concerned in that speech to deny to Parliaments the
Melvillian claim to a power independent of himself. The claim that
'he is the law-maker and they to advise him in makeinge lawes' does
not claim that he can make laws without their advice, a proposition
he did not assert. In the light of the rest of the speech, it should be
read as a claim, justifiable in English law, that Parliaments exist by
royal authority, and are subject to it.[65]

Other possible examples include a certain Dr David Owen, who,
in the course of an onslaught on Pareus the continental resistance
theorist, quoted with apparent approval from William Barclay that

[64] Sommerville, p. 46.
[65] *Commons' Debates in 1621*, ed. Wallace Notestein, Frances Helen Relf, and
Hartley Simpson (New Haven, Conn., 1935), iv. 3, ii. 4.

'the prince alone may constitute an universall law'.[66] This is a lonely passage in a work of over 100 pages, and it is hard to assert with confidence that this single passage proves that Owen thought the king alone could make law. There are a few others who were more explicit. One was Justice Crawley in the Ship Money trial, who asserted that 'the first regal prerogative is this, that containeth all the rest, that the King may give laws to his subjects.' This is utterly unambiguous, but it is not as typical of the judges who judged for the King in the Ship Money trial as Sir Robert Berkeley's obstinate insistence, in the teeth of the King and the Attorney-General, that the Petition of Right was a statute, and binding.[67] Others who believed the king could make law include Sir Francis Kynaston Gentleman of the Privy Chamber in the 1630s, and William Beale Master of St John's College, Cambridge, and one of Charles's chaplains.[68] The reactions of mainstream Royalists to such people are better illustrated by the words of Sir Thomas Jermyn Comptroller of the Household when instructed to protect Beale from the Short Parliament by claiming privilege for him as a King's servant: 'the King's servant in ordinary if he gett out of the way. All that are of his opinion wishes wee were soe ridd of him'.[69] Jermyn's words cannot be explained by fear of getting into trouble: he was delivering a royal message, and prudence of all sorts dictated that he should make no additions to it. Beale and his like were a small and highly unpopular group, mostly clergy, with whom the bulk of the King's lay supporters emphatically and often rudely disagreed. It is hard to make absolutists out of people who took offence at the suggestion that the King could make law. Royalists are even less persuasive as absolutists than Parliamentarians are as resistance theorists.

---

[66] David Owen, *Anti-Pareus* (repr. York, 1642), 76. The statement by Owen quoted by Sommerville (p. 182) that 'the Parliament in England possesses no power except from the King and under the King', is a plain and factual statement of the position in English law. It is still true today.

[67] *ST* iii. 1083. I am grateful to Miss Penny Watts for drawing my attention to this passage. For Berkeley, ibid. 1107. Berkeley had been a member of the Parliament of 1628.

[68] PRO SP 16/233/52; Esther S. Cope, *Proceedings of the Short Parliament of 1640* (Camden Society⁺, 19, 1977), 185–6.

[69] *Short Parliament (1640) Diary of Sir Thomas Aston*, ed. Judith D. Maltby (Camden Society⁺, 35, 1988), 113. I am very grateful to Dr Maltby for allowing me to see this diary before publication.

The absence of any major dispute about the legislative power is highlighted by the lack of any action, or even any great volume of debate in the Long Parliament about Proclamations. There was, it is true, much dispute about the extent of the king's power to dispense with existing law, but this power, in the form of the power of pardon, still exists. Technically, the power by which the king released priests was the prerogative of mercy, which is not at all the same thing as the power to make new law. Power to pardon the breach of an existing law does not imply the power to punish for what was not previously an offence. It is the latter power which was not a matter of dispute, since the King did not lay claim to it. It was the King's power to raise money, not his power to make law, which came under attack in 1640 and 1641. There is in fact little sign that Charles's proclamations had attempted to make new law, and Professor Barnes is surely right in his argument that most of them were grounded on broad common-law offences such as fraud or nuisance. For example, when the Attorney-General proceeded against the Earl of Bedford for illegal building in Covent Garden contrary to the proclamation, the charge was that his houses were a 'public nuisance', for such practical reasons as that there was no sewer to carry away the water they occasioned.[70] In the whole of Charles's proclamations, almost the only one which appears to me to make new law was one of November 1627, which commanded the use of bits instead of snaffles for horses, and even this proclamation offered a plea of military necessity.[71] It is a weak foundation for an argument that the Civil War was a clash between rival political theories, and it is hard to argue that in any major clash of political theories the issue of who had the power to make law would have been left so severely alone.

How then did belief in the rule of law contribute to the causes of the Civil War? It seems to have done so most significantly by weakening and impoverishing the monarchy, and therefore by contributing to its defeat by the Scots during the Bishops' Wars. Throughout the period, the view that the Crown could do nothing but what it was entitled to do by law enjoyed a popularity which was

---

[70] T. G. Barnes, 'Prerogative and Environmental Control of London Building', *California Law Review*, 58 (1970), 1350, 1353, 1355–62; Esther S. Cope, 'Sir Edward Coke and Proclamations 1610', *American Journal of Legal History*, 15 (1971), 215–21; Alnwick Castle MSS Y III box 2, envelope 4.

[71] *Stuart Royal Proclamations*, ii, ed. James F. Larkin (Oxford 1983), 170.

frequently embarrassing. In 1627, when counsel opened the case for the Five Knights who had refused the Forced Loan, they were greeted with 'wonderful applause even of shouting and clapping of hands, which is unusual in that place'.[72] Ten years later, when Oliver St John opened the case for Hampden in the Ship Money trial, 'he was much applauded and hummed by the bystanders though my Lord Finch signified his displeasure for it'. Finch's displeasure seems to have achieved little, since two days later the crowd did it again.[73] It is hard to believe that such emotions contributed nothing to the difficulty of collecting Ship Money in 1640, and the difficulty in collecting Ship Money undoubtedly contributed to England's ill success in the Second Bishops' War. Not many were as bold as the constable of South Newington, Oxfordshire, who said no Ship Money had been or could be gathered in their parish until the sheriff made known to them a law or statute binding them to pay it.[74] When rating objections were so easy, and so comparatively acceptable, there was no need to utter the forbidden fundamental objections. When, for example, Walter Long the veteran of the tumult in the House of 1629, complained of his local constable for unequally assessing him for Ship Money, it would be straining credulity to ask us to believe that he was unaware of or uninterested in the major legal objections to the levy.[75] In May 1638 copies of Justice Croke's Ship Money judgment were being sold in London for 10s. each, a startlingly high price for what were presumably manuscript copies. The drop in Ship Money yields which was happening at this time had many causes, but it is not unlikely that the arguments contained in this judgment were among them.[76] It seems that the long list of supposedly arbitrary actions for which Charles had been blamed since 1625 had left behind a considerable weight of anger, and that that anger was a barrier to co-operation with the King against the Scots, even for people like Seymour and Hopton, who had no sympathy with the Scottish cause. This anger found direct expression in 1632, when a peculiarly accident-prone messenger of the Chamber was staying at an inn in Trowbridge, and spent the evening reminiscing about his

---

[72] Cust, *Forced Loan*, p. 237.   [73] *HMC 9th Rep.*, II. 496.

[74] *CSPD 1635–6*, vol. cccxviii, no. 75.

[75] *CSPD 1639*, vol. ccccxxii, no. 45.

[76] Ann Hughes, *Politics, Society and Civil War in Warwickshire 1620–1660* (Cambridge, 1987), 89.

exploits, after the 1629 Parliament, in arresting that dangerous desperado Walter Long. As he left the next morning, he had a chamber-pot emptied over him, and discovered, too late to keep his mouth shut, that the inn was kept by two of Walter Long's cousins.[77] In 1642 Long, Strode, and Holles seem to have constituted a sort of Martyrs' Corner in the House of Commons.

In the Short Parliament, Pym seems to have deliberately channelled this anger over legal issues into courses which would interfere with the war effort. On 2 May he said that

since the King did require an answere hee thought most fitt to give a resolute one the taking away of shippmoney hee said were not enough for (hee said) wee might bee as much opprest by millitary charges as with shipp money hee would therefore have it published that no charges should bee laid upon the people without their consent in Parliament.

Charles's anger at the attack on military charges marks his recognition of the threat to the war effort, and in August 1640, when the Yorkshire gentry protested about billeting, the Privy Council replied that

they assume the billetting of soldiers to be contrary to the ancient lawes of this kingdome and to the Petition of Right: whereas neither his Matie. nor wee ourselves have seene or read any such law to prohibit it. Nor was it ever in the thought of his Maty. to devest the Crown of that necessary power, without wch expedient, it is impossible for armies to march.[78]

The proposition that *inter leges silent arma* seems to be as true in 1640 as it had been in 1628, and anger at Charles's record of lack of respect for the law made a significant contribution to English failure in the Second Bishops' War, and perhaps in the First also.

This anger seems to have been particularly important in the failure of the Short Parliament, a failure which played a vital part, not only in weakening the English war effort, but in encouraging the Scots to take the risk of direct intervention in English affairs. If the King had approached the Second Bishops' War with the support of a Parliament behind him, he would have been much more likely to win, and even if he had not won, the effects of defeat might have been much less disastrous than in the event they proved. The paradigm figure of the Short Parliament was not Pym, who was often working against the grain of the House, but Sir Francis

[77] *CSPD 1631–3*, vol. ccxv, no. 26.
[78] Cope, p. 190; PRO SP 16/464/17.

Seymour, who would have liked to reach a deal with the King
whereby the King gave up Ship Money and other illegal measures
in return for support against the Scots. The failure of Charles and
Seymour in the Short Parliament to reach the working understanding
they reached a year later is crucial to the failure of the Parliament.
Seymour was certainly held back in any attempt to come to terms
with Charles by the depth of his anger at those 'who have betrayed
the King to himselfe, and soe committed worse treason than those
who betray him to others, who tell him his prerogative is above
all laws, and that his subjects are but slaves to the distruccion
of property', his anger at the judges for imprisoning members of
Parliament for what they had done in the House, and his anger at
the long absence of Parliaments.[79]

Early in 1641 Charles realized that if he were ever to get the
Scots out of England, he would have to make common cause with
his fellow anti-Scots, Seymour, Strangeways, Kirton, and the like.
He realized that, in order to do this, he would have to satisfy their
basically legal concerns. It seems to have been this awareness which
forced him into the vital concession he offered in his speech to the
Lords of 23 January 1641: 'what parts of my revenue that shall be
found illegal or grievous to the public, I shall willingly lay down,
relying entirely upon the affections of my people'.[80] Without this
concession, and the Triennial Act which came with it, Charles
would not have had a Royalist party. These concessions are ones
Charles stuck to, and it was because, in the end, they chose to
believe in them that men like Hyde, Falkland, Culpepper, Bristol,
Digby, Waller, Hopton, Seymour, Kirton, and Strangeways rallied
to the King. This concession, then, served its purpose, but having
made it, Charles was boxed in by it. He had no option but to agree,
for example, when the Parliament passed a Tonnage and Poundage
Act which reversed the judgment in Bate's Case, and reasserted the
principle that the king could enjoy no customs revenue without
Parliamentary consent. With Tonnage and Poundage coming in
grants of Damocles, for a few weeks at a time, monopolies swept
away, and the Star Chamber abolished, Charles was made as
dependent as a beggar on financial support from the Parliament, and
that was something Pym was in no hurry to provide. Charles was in
no position to resist this turning of the financial screw, not only

---

[79] Cope, pp. 140–3.   [80] *LJ* iv. 140–3.

because of his promise, but because of his difficulty in causing people to believe in it. Charles in the capacity of champion of the rule of law did not immediately carry conviction, since he had a very great deal to live down. For that reason, he enjoyed less ability to react angrily to what was done to him than a more trusted king might have done. He could not, for example, collect Tonnage and Poundage without consent without reminding such men as Seymour and Kirton of a vast body of old anger which he desperately needed them to put behind them if he was to have any hope of retaining a party. Having committed himself to these people, Charles was, to a degree, their political prisoner. This is an important part of the reasons why Charles was unable to dissolve the Long Parliament during the summer of 1641, and thereby an important part of the causes of the Civil War.

Belief in the rule of law, and other ideas attendant on it, also played a large part in constructing a body of ideas which made it possible for the Parliamentarians to defy the King's personal authority. There had, for a long time, been a notion of loyalty being owed to the Crown, or to the State. There was nothing necessarily subversive about such a notion, and in 1588, when Recorder Fleetwood and Solicitor-General Egerton talked of 'popish traitors' against 'her Majesty and the State',[81] they meant nothing to which the most devout monarchist could take exception. In Ireland, the phrase 'letters of the state' was a convenient shorthand to indicate letters emanating from the Dublin Council but not from the King.[82] When Robert Cecil wanted to refer to the government of Edward VI, he called it 'the state'. On the other hand, the notion possessed equivocal possibilities of which Shakespeare was surely aware when he had Macbeth, fresh from his first encounter with the witches, professing his loyalty to Duncan's 'throne and state'.[83] Such notions of loyalty were publicized because they formed the staple argument of the losing side in Calvin's Case in 1608, in which the judges had to decide whether allegiance was owed to James VI and I, who was one king, or to the English and Scottish states and laws, which were several. As misfortune would have it, this was also one of the earliest cases which began the growth of Parliamentary

[81] PRO SP 12/212/70.
[82] *Proceedings in Parliament 1610*, ed. Elizabeth Read Foster, ii (New Haven, Conn., 1966), 26; *CSP Ire. 1603–6*, ccxv 63.
[83] *Macbeth* I. iv. 28.

distrust of the judges, and the arguments of the losing side in Calvin's Case did not go away. Ellesmere roundly condemned any notion of impersonal allegiance: 'this is a dangerous distinction betweene the king and the crowne; it reacheth too farre. I wish every good subject to beware of it: It was never taught either but . . . by traitors, as Spencers bill in Ed. 2 time . . . or by treasonable Papists . . . or by seditious sectaries and Puritans'.[84] It seems that exhorting people to beware of this doctrine had the same effect as a notice telling people to keep off the grass, and a very large proportion of the Parliamentary arguments in 1642 seem to have been drawn from those of the losing side in Calvin's Case. The Parliamentarians of 1642 merged the old notion of an impersonal allegiance with a rivalry with the judges which had been growing ever since Bate's Case and Calvin's Case, and consequently portrayed themselves as the King's supreme court, whose judgment was the King's whether he liked it or not. They explained, in their Declaration of 19 May 1642, that

the king judgeth not of matters of law, but by his courts, and his courts, though sitting by his authority, expect not his assent in matters of law, nor any other courts, for they cannot judge in that case, because they are inferiour: no appeal, lying to them from Parliament, the judgement whereof is in the eye of the law the king's judgement in his highest court, though the king in his person be neither present nor assenting thereunto.[85]

This doctrine enabled them to claim, ingeniously, to override the King, but to do so in his name and in virtue of his authority. The doctrine was ingenious, but it was not foolproof; the King's proclamation of 18 June 1642, probably written by Chief Justice Bankes, distinguished neatly between the true and the false: 'these persons have gone about subtilly to distinguish betwixt our person and our authority, as if, because our authority may be where our person is not, that therefore our person may be where our authority is not'.[86] On another occasion, he complained that 'it is too great and palpable a scorn to persuade them to take up arms against our person, under colour of being loving subjects to our office, and to destroy us, that they may preserve the King'.[87]

---

[84] Knafla, *Law and Politics*, pp. 244–5; Sir Edward Coke, *Seventh Report*, 10–11.
[85] Rushworth III. i. 698.
[86] *Proclamations*, ed. Larkin, ii. 773.
[87] *Exact Collection of Remonstrances*, BL E. 241(1), p. 378.

During 1642 argument increasingly came to concentrate on how far the authority of the Crown could be separated from the King's person, rather than on the extent of the authority of the royal office. On 19 May 1642, in a declaration mainly written by Pym, the Houses argued that the King should be treated as if he were a minor, in captivity or insane. D'Ewes disingenuously supported this line of argument by pointing out that Richard I had never consented to the levy for his ransom.[88] Oliver St John, in a set of legal notes probably taken during the 1630s, was following the same line of separating authority from the King's person when he noted that the Parliament of 1258 had 'erected' the authority of twelve peers. From a man who was probably joint author of the Petition of the Twelve Peers in August 1640, this comment compels attention.[89] However, the main line of precedents in the minds of the Parliamentary leaders were possibly those created by the insanity of Henry VI. This thrust of argument, tending towards the appointment of an afforced Council and a Protector, rather than towards permanent Parliamentary authority, was underlined by the earnestness of the attempt to appoint a *Custos Regni* or High Steward when the King left for Scotland in August 1641. This officer, as Strode and others outlined his powers, would have been a fully-fledged viceroy, and the Earl of Pembroke, the preferred candidate for the position, was probably quite ready to play the part.[90] Behind this line of thinking, and even more behind the Nineteen Propositions, was the whole conciliar tradition of English constitutionalism. This ran back through the Lords Appellant under Richard II and the Lords Ordainers under Edward II, to Simon de Montfort under Henry III. There is very little sign here of any fully-fledged Whig commitment to Parliamentary sovereignty, but rather an improvising readiness, as occasion demanded, to draw on whatever proved useful in a long-established English tradition. It is a tradition from which the Parliamentarians might have taken warning, for on all these occasions, the King had taken a dim view of these attempts to deprive him of any personal part in the process of government, and had succeeded either in fighting back against his imposed Councillors, or, in Richard II's case, in defeating them piecemeal. Charles's protest that he was 'no ideot, nor infant,

---

[88] Ibid. 208–9; *PJ* ii. 41–2.   [89] BL Add. MS 25, 266, fo. 113ʳ.
[90] The point will be developed further in Russell, *FBM* and in forthcoming publications by Dr Adamson.

uncapable of understanding to command'[91] was one many of his royal ancestors would instinctively have understood. Yet this very same familiarity about the Parliamentary arguments, and even more the makeshift and almost ramshackle manner in which they were put together to meet circumstances as they arose, tend to suggest that the body of ideas about how the country should be governed were not really the central element in the cause for which they fought: they were, like their medieval predecessors, *ad hoc* ideas constructed out of any materials ready to hand, to serve the immediate purpose of clipping the wings of a king with whom they simply could not cope.

[91] *Proclamations*, ed. Larkin, ii. 773.

7

The Poverty of the Crown
and the Weakness of the King

'AND for my particular I may say thus much that if sitting so near the storm and seeing it coming in the air, I should have suffered it to break and bemoaned myself in a private corner without resorting to the natural place for remedy, I were not worthy to carry this staff in my hand'.[1] These words were not spoken by Lord Treasurer Juxon about the Second Bishops' War, though we might have had a higher opinion of Juxon if they had been: they were spoken by Robert Cecil, Earl of Salisbury, in his opening speech to the Parliament of 1610. Many, indeed most, of the storm clouds which met in 1642 were ones Robert Cecil could not have seen coming, but in this speech, he saw and plotted with exemplary accuracy one of the storm-tracks which met in the hurricane of 1642: the failure of the King's finances.

In an undated letter probably written about Christmas 1642, Wat Montague, the Queen's Catholic courtier, undertook the task of explaining the English Civil War to Cardinal Mazarin. He began his account by saying that 'the present rebellion of England began by the belief the factious in Parliament had in the feebleness of the King'. He explained that members of Parliament had 'comforted' the people by relieving them of the taxes the King had established, and so had become masters of their affections and their spirits. They thus hoped, he said, to compel the King to submit by the necessity in which he found himself.[2] It was in response to this sort of pressure that Charles resolved not 'to be starved or brought out of any more flowers of his crowne',[3] and turned to war almost literally in order

---

[1] *Proceedings in Parliament 1610*, ed. Elizabeth Read Foster, ii (New Haven, Conn., 1966), 17–18. For a very similar form of words, see *Collection of Several Speeches . . . of the Late Lord Treasurer Cecil*, ed. Pauline Croft, *Camden Miscellany* (Camden Society⁴, 34, 1987), 287. In this version, which was addressed to James, Cecil omitted his reference to the Parliament as the natural place for remedy.

[2] PRO 31/3/73, fo. 91ʳ⁻ᵛ.

[3] PRO PC 2/53, p. 200.

to be able to put bread in his mouth. The sort of pressure Charles was put under in 1641–2 is the sort to which only a king esteemed weak could have been subjected: not even the most rabid Presbyterian would have thought it worth telling Queen Elizabeth she could not have Tonnage and Poundage until she agreed to abolish bishops. The weakness to which the Crown was reduced in 1641 was military as well as financial: it resulted in large measure from a military defeat at the hands of a normally inferior enemy, and it was a vital part of the opportunity for the Militia Ordinance that there had been no unquestionably legal method of raising troops ever since the lapsing of the Marian militia statute in 1604. Why the House of Commons let the King go all the way through the wars of the 1620s with no unquestionably legal method of raising troops for war is a question which demands more thought than it has yet received, but the fact that they did so was a necessary condition of the passage of the Militia Ordinance in 1642. The failure of royal power is as vital a part of the coming of civil war as any revolutionary passion. People do not, it is true, attack a king simply because his power has failed, but equally they do not normally attempt to coerce a king obviously powerful enough to snap his fingers at them.

The King's financial and military weakness appears to have contributed to his failure to negotiate in 1642: war presented him with a chance of appealing for contributions, while peace was simply more than he could afford. A document submitted to Edward Nicholas on 28 December 1641 lists the effects of the Long Parliament on Charles's revenues: £407,225 per annum was being held in suspense under the Bill of Tonnage and Poundage, and sources worth £120,955, mostly made up of monopolies and the like, were expected to fail altogether. This left Charles with a gross income of £334,480 per annum, which was short by £285,340 of the sums he needed to meet his ordinary standing charges. It is these figures which make it a plausible view that Charles could not afford peace.[4]

Apart from the absence of negotiation, the other questions this financial and military weakness can contribute to answering are why the King lost the Bishops' Wars, why he could not dissolve the Long Parliament, and the phenomenon of diminished majesty. Money

    [4] Conrad Russell, 'Charles I's Financial Estimates for 1642', *BIHR* 58/137 (1985), 109–20.

contributed more to defeat in the Second than in the First Bishops' War. One of the ways this weakness seems to have operated is through the collapse of the arrangements for supplying arms. On 18 August 1640, ten days before the battle of Newburn, young Francis Windebank reported to his father the Secretary that his troops had no arms, and said that if they had arms, they would be ready to go on 'as speedily as may be'.[5] The next day, Ashburnham told Nicholas that more than one third of the army was still unarmed, while Strafford said he had heard from Sir Jacob Astley that a fourth part of the army was left behind without arms.[6] The lack of arms clearly contributed to the lack of fighting spirit among the English troops, and the lack of arms is very largely a result of lack of money, and of the late arrival of money. It also measures a lack of capacity in the English armaments industry, which had been run down by a long period of peace. In 1633 John Browne the gunfounder recalled that under James, the musket-makers, finding that their services were not in great demand, had emigrated *en bloc* to the Netherlands. The result, he said, was that since then the King had had to buy a much greater proportion of his arms from abroad.[7] The armourers told the Council in 1640 that they could make arms for 700 foot a month, if they made no horse arms.[8] At that rate, supplying arms for 30,000 foot would have taken three-and-a-half years, which was rather longer than was available. Arms could be, and were, bought on the continent, but at the height of the Thirty Years' War, many arms suppliers seem to have had commitments to customers more regular than the King of England, and much of what was bought turned out, when inspected by Mr Thatcher the King's Pike-Maker, to be insufficient.

If the lack of money contributed to the defeat at Newburn, it contributed even more heavily to the inability to continue the war after Newburn. The King seems at first to have believed that because he still had a larger army available than the Scots did, he could fight on. The financial information which reached the King and Vane during the days after Newburn seems to have been what persuaded him otherwise. An estimate showed that to keep the army together for another twenty-eight days, they needed £29,623. 16s., plus another £1,200 for contingencies, while another report showed

---

[5] PRO SP 16/464/26. [6] Ibid. 16/464/44; Hamilton MSS 1229.

[7] *CSPD 1633–4*, vol. cclvi, no. 32.

[8] *CSPD 1639–40*, vol. ccccxlii, no. 56.

that on 4 September there was £1,037 left in the Exchequer. The Customs were anticipated for four years, impositions for two or three, and the Wards for two. All those willing to lend to the King without a Parliament had already lent all or more than all they possessed. Revenues were falling off, and the sheriff of Northamptonshire reported that with Ship Money he had reached the point where severity would be self-defeating.[9] By the time the Great Council of Peers met, four weeks after Newburn, Charles could ask it nothing more far-reaching than how to keep the army on foot until a Parliament could meet.[10] Charles's poverty put him at the mercy of the Long Parliament.

From the beginning of the Long Parliament, Charles desperately needed a new financial settlement, and it was doubtful whether his authority could be recovered without one. By an interesting paradox, it seems that future Parliamentarians were often more eager to supply him with one than future Royalists. Enthusiasts for further reformation, such as Pym or Alexander Rigby, might want it badly enough to be prepared to pay for it, and even to propose settling a 'constant revenue' on the King.[11] By contrast, people like Hyde, Kirton, and Strangeways had no such incentive to vote large sums of money. When Sir John Culpepper made heroic efforts to secure a grant of Tonnage and Poundage without a reciprocal concession on Root and Branch, these people did not stir a finger to help him. Hyde even disputed that a new financial settlement was needed, arguing absurdly that the amount spent in the past two years was enough to conquer Germany.[12] These people no doubt did not kill the King, but they certainly did not strive officiously to keep him alive: the ideal of legality and low taxation, for which they stood, was one which led inexorably to the impoverishment of the monarchy. Their silence on revenue issues through the summer of 1641 was one of the important reasons why Charles could not dissolve the Parliament.

Lack of money also contributed to diminished majesty, because, in all the senses of that word, it had diminished the King's credit. In the First Bishops' War, when the King summoned the peers to York

[9] PRO SP 16/468/127, 469/72, 469/50, and 445/54.

[10] Ibid. 16/468/23.

[11] PRO 30/53/12, fo. 11ᵛ; *Short Parliament (1640) Diary of Sir Thomas Aston,* ed. Judith D. Maltby (Camden Society⁴, 35, 1988), 11; *HMC 14th Rep.,* IV. 60.

[12] *Notebook of Sir John Northcote,* ed. A. H. A. Hamilton (1877), 59.

at their own expense, he got some angry replies. Lord Herbert of
Cherbury said that the King still owed him £2,500 for his
ambassador's expenses from 1624, his expenses for writing the
history of the Rhé expedition, and his research expenses for the
History of Henry VIII, and therefore he could not bring the sort of
attendance he desired, but he would come. Lord Maynard said he
had served the King twenty-eight years, at his continual yearly
charge, and the King had had nearly £900 from him in three years,
for which he was paying interest. He said his fortune was far less
than might be thought, but he would come from devotion to the
King's service. From two Arminian peers, these replies should have
been taken as a warning, but from the version Edward Nicholas sent
to the King, all the criticism had been edited out.[13]

In 1642, when the King needed to raise an army in England, this
resentment at his failure to pay his bills became an important
political force. When the King left London for Windsor after his
failure to arrest the Five Members, very few people attended him,
but those who did included unpaid veterans of Rhé and Cadiz
asking for payment of their debts.[14] The Earl of Leicester and Lord
Feilding both failed to rally to Charles, and both expressed
indignation about unpaid ambassadors' expenses. In neither case is
this a sufficient explanation of their failure to become Royalists, but
their resentment certainly helped to make their failure to obey
easier. The payment of £1,500 to Lord Feilding on 18 August 1642,
as part of his expenses as Ambassador to Venice, might be seen as a
case of 'too little too late', but it could equally well strengthen the
case for seeing Feilding as having more serious motives. After the
Incident, his loyalty to his brother-in-law Hamilton may well have
influenced him against the King.[15] Sir John Meldrum is known to
historians of the 1620s as the patentee of Dungeness lighthouse, and
an object of Parliamentary complaint, but in 1642 he helped Sir
John Hotham to hold Hull against the King. His main reason seems
to have been that as a Scot, he had been passionately opposed to the
Bishops' Wars, but he also told the King he had been left with 'a

[13] PRO SP 16/412/77 and 88; 413/117.
[14] PRO 30/5/6, pp. 460–1. I am grateful to Dr J. S. A. Adamson for this
reference.
[15] *LJ* iv. 724, 679; Warwicks. RO Feilding of Newnham Paddox MSS C.
1/17, 20, 103; PRO E 403/2814, fo. 40ʳ; J. Godwin, 'Steps of Descent', *BIHR*
60/141 (1987), 109–15. Mr Godwin and I have reached closely similar conclusions by very different routes.

deep ingagement in 2,000l. debt, after the spending of thirty six years of time in your Majesty's father's and your own service'.[16] He was telling Charles the Crown was not worth serving. Charles seems to have taken the point, and through the spring and summer of 1642, when money was at its shortest, there are a succession of orders for paying old debts, such as £100 to Anne Mynne, widow of the King's harbinger, for entertaining ambassadors in 1625–6, due by a Privy Seal of October 1629, and £50 to Barbara Wood and others in part payment of a debt of £2,003 for the wardrobes of James I and Prince Henry.[17] These orders suggest that among the difficulties besetting Charles, he had come to give the diminution of his credit a very high priority.

There is no news in stressing the financial difficulties of the early Stuarts. It is conventional to blame the Stuarts themselves for their financial misfortunes, and their reigns, especially that of James, give plenty of material to justify blaming them. However, to say that the Stuarts mishandled their financial system is not to say that it would have worked if they had handled it well, and it is the central contention of this chapter that the Stuarts inherited a financial system which was already close to the point of breakdown. In any country which believes in taxation by consent, the financial and political systems must be very closely related, and the English political system, although it still enjoyed almost universal support and affection, was becoming obsolete because it was no longer capable of successfully financing war. The system the Stuarts inherited was, in essentials, that of the fourteenth century: Dr Harriss is right in arguing that by 1369 'the institutions by which England was to be governed and administered until the Civil War had been brought into existence'.[18] What we are witnessing is the painful death of that system.

Nothing better underlines how thoroughly it needed replacing than a study of the measures which ultimately superseded it. In Dr Chandaman's study of the English public revenue from 1660 to 1688, all the sources of finance available to James I except Tonnage and Poundage are lumped together in the chapter on the 'small

[16] Rushworth, III. i. 628. On Meldrum's Dungeness lighthouse patent, see Conrad Russell, *Origins of the English Civil War* (1973), 15–16.

[17] PRO E, 403/2814, fos. 9ʳ, 28ʳ, 28ᵛ, 38ᵛ and other refs.

[18] G. L. Harriss, *King, Parliament, and Public Finance in Medieval England to 1369* (Oxford, 1975), p. viii.

branches' of the revenue.[19] James I's legal sources of revenue suffered very heavily from the fact that, even after Robert Cecil's best efforts, they were not buoyant, and did not increase with inflation or economic growth. By the reign of Charles II, most of them were used for patronage rather than for revenue raising. The staples of the new financial system of the eighteenth century, the excise, the Land Tax, and the Bank of England, were all new, and all demanded a fundamental change in the relationship between the Crown and its Parliaments. In the early seventeenth century, that change, or any other possible change, had been resisted with equal intensity both by Parliaments and by the Crown, and as a result, they were condemned to run a broken-down system, like a fifth-hand Mini, until it was ready for the scrap-heap. It was by no means unusual in suffering a collision on the way there.

Because it depended on sources of revenue of limited buoyancy, the old system had always been periodically in need of repair. For many statesmen, the classic precedent of successful repair was the early part of the Hundred Years' War, ending in the grant of Tonnage and Poundage. To those who were aware of these precedents, there were a set of almost ritual moves. The Crown threatened, if it were not helped, to extend its prerogative in unpleasant and provocative ways. The Commons threatened to attack ministers, and demanded restrictions on waste and corruption. In the end, in return for large grants, they might hope for equally large concessions. These had included, in Edward III's case, sharply increased control of local government by their own kind in the form of Justices of the Peace.[20] The other method favoured by precedent was the one used by Henry VIII, who, in Robert Cecil's phrase, 'raised to himself in effect another Crown in point of revenue by the fall of abbeys'.[21] The problem we have to solve for the early seventeenth century is why neither of these methods of repair proved effective.

Pym and Bedford in 1641 hoped they might use Henry VIII's method, by confiscating the lands of bishops and of deans and chapters, but apart from the fact that such a solution was unacceptable to Charles I, who said he would rather starve than take

---

[19] C. G. Chandaman, *English Public Revenue 1660–1688* (Oxford, 1975), 110–37.

[20] Harriss, *Finance in Medieval England*, pp. 403–10.

[21] *Proceedings in Parliament 1610*, ed. Foster, ii, 21.

any more from the church,[22] there was simply not enough left. Bishops' lands were worth only some £26,000 a year,[23] which would have been no more than a drop in the ocean, and even the addition of deans' and chapters' lands was not going to make it enough. The church was a non-recurring windfall. The question, then, is why the English achieved neither the solution used under Edward III, involving a grant of a major new source of revenue by a Parliament, nor the solution which appeared to be emerging across the Channel, whereby estates either disappeared, as in Savoy, or survived at the price of rubber-stamping what was wanted, as in Naples. Perhaps one reason for the delay was that England was normally insulated by the Channel from the consequences of military defeat. The English achieved no major land victory overseas between Agincourt and Blenheim, except the Battle of the Dunes in 1658, which was fought under a different financial and military system. Any continental state with such a military record would have been forced to reform its system: England was not forced to do so until defeated on a frontier which refuted the proposition that England is an island.

That acute financial difficulty arrived too early to be created by the Stuarts can be seen by looking at some of the figures Robert Cecil noted down on the first day of James's reign, and subsequently repeated to the Parliament of 1610. Between 1594 and 1602 he calculated that the war in Ireland had cost £1,924,000, the Low Countries £534,470, and aid to the King of France £292,480. Towards this sum, Parliamentary subsidies had contributed £1,562,224, leaving a shortfall of some £1,296,000.[24] This was a very incomplete enumeration of war costs: it left out all the cost of naval operations, for example, yet these figures alone seem to show that the Crown had incurred a bigger debt than it could easily clear, on an annual revenue which in 1602 amounted to £357,617.[25] These shortfalls had been met by a mixture of land sales, borrowing

---

[22] PRO SP 16/476/19.
[23] BL Harl. MS 2071, fo. 148ᵛ, gives a figure of £21,000 for 1600, excluding York, Bangor, and St Asaph. I am grateful to Dr K. C. Fincham for the reference and for advice on episcopal revenues.
[24] *HMC Salis.* XV. 1–2. I am grateful to Dr Richard Stewart for this reference. Also *Proceedings in Parliament 1610*, ed. Foster, ii. 19–20. The latter reference conflates two sets of figures, since when Cecil drew up the first, he did not have all the costs available.
[25] National Library of Wales, Wynnstay MSS L. 450.

at interest, and simple failure to pay bills, of which two diminished future income, and the third diminished political credit. As Robert Cecil later told James, 'it is not a thing that all men know, that the late time had much to do to save itself from the dangerous effect of want, even whilst the late Queen of happy memory lived'.[26] Nevertheless, it is true.

The fall in the yield of the Parliamentary subsidy, the greatest threat to the survival of Parliaments in England, had been going on most of the way through the second half of the sixteenth century, but the steepest fall is during the Elizabethan war with Spain.[27] The subsidy debate of 1593 seems to indicate that the gulf between the largest sum politically acceptable and the smallest sum administratively viable, the bane of subsidy debates under the Stuarts, had already appeared before Elizabeth died. Sir Walter Mildmay, in his subsidy speech of 1584, was surely right in his diagnosis of the problem:

one, the costliness of the warres and the great increase of prices of all thinges in this age: farre surmounting the times before. And the other the easines of the taxation of the subsidies which how favorably thei be handled in all places no man here can be ignorante.[28]

In 1593 Sir John Fortescue pointed out that the subsidies were worth less than half of what they were worth under Henry VIII, and also that the men rated at £3 in goods made up more than half the payers. He was hinting that more accurate assessment of the gentry was needed. It was a hint which fell on deaf ears: even gentlemen who were eager to prosecute the war and anxious about the burden on the poor shared in the adamantine resistance of Tudor and Stuart gentlemen to accurate valuation of their estates. Sir Walter Raleigh suggested that this was because accurate valuation would destroy the credit of gentlemen who were living on the belief that they were worth more than they were. Francis Bacon preferred the pious phrase: 'and in histories yt is to be observed that of all nations the English care not to be subject, base and taxable'.[29] Yet from the cynical and the sententious, the underlying purpose was the same: not even for the sake of national survival would English gentlemen

---

[26] 'Collection of Several Speeches', ed. Croft, p. 285.

[27] See among much else PRO SP 12/224/76.

[28] Northants RO Fitzwilliam of Milton MSS, vol. 2, fo. 31.

[29] BL Cotton MS Titus F ii, fos. 29–30, 49^r, 50^r, 51^r. I am grateful to Dr David Dean for lending me a transcript of this diary.

consent to be accurately valued for taxation. It was a message which did not change. In 1606 Yelverton opposed a proposal to compound for purveyance, saying the composition payment could not be charged on lands without a general survey:

and I must tell you it is the develles walk to treade over England and Wales, and full it is of danger to have it knowen what land the realme containeth: and how much every man hath in possession; againe, you must in this case erect new offices and officers for the collecting of this money so rated on the landes, and new fees appointed to the officers of the Exchequer for doing their dutyes in enterances, giving tallyes *et huiusmodi*.[30]

It was an old and familiar voice: Yelverton here spoke as the heir of the Anglo-Saxon Chronicler.[31] Edward Alford in 1621 asserted the key principle which kept subsidy assessments down: 'the assessing to be as was usual, by neighbours'. In 1628 the draft of the subsidy bill directed that men should be assessed 'at the best value'. The Commons deleted these words, and inserted instead 'after the usual manner'.[32]

Below the level of the gentry, underassessment also happened, though probably on a less dramatic scale. Few of Pym's Somerset tenants at Wollavington were assessed on any scale approaching their real wealth, and Agnes Andrewes alias Pym, who was the widow of Pym's uncle William when it suited her, only appears in one subsidy roll out of three.[33] James Hayward, a rapidly rising yeoman who had paid an entry fine of £460 in 1619 for a three-life lease at a rent of 29s. 6d., was assessed for subsidy in 1640 at £4. 16s. in goods.[34] It seems to have often been possible to escape paying the subsidy altogether, and many Sussex hundreds, which were not suffering a decline in population, nevertheless showed a sharp decline in the number of taxpayers. A clause designed to reverse this trend in the Subsidy Act of 1624 suggests that it was a general one.[35] The subsidy was not alone in being resented, and musters and militia charges met a resentment which even national emergency did not remove. The day before the Armada was sighted

[30] Eric Lindquist, 'Failure of the Great Contract', *Journal of Modern History* (1985), 645 and n.; Bowyer, p. 75.
[31] Entry for 1085.
[32] Russell, *PEP*, p. 90 and n.; *1628 Debates*, iv. 15.
[33] PRO E. 179/172/390 and 171/349; BL Add. rolls 28, 275.
[34] Somerset RO DD/BW/Pym MSS no. 151; BL Add. Rolls 28, 275.
[35] Anthony Fletcher, *A County Community in Peace and War: Sussex 1625–1660* (1975), 360–4; *Statutes of the Realm*, 21 *Jac. I c. 33*, clause xiv.

off the Lizard, Burghley wrote to Walsingham about resentment at
the 'unsupportable charges' of musters, and said that 'I se a generall
murmur of people, and malcontented people will increas yt to ye
comfort of ye enemy'. In Somerset, Deputy Lieutenants were
encountering lawyers who claimed their commissions were not
legally valid.[36] This cannot be blamed on Stuart misgovernment.

James, then, inherited the throne at a moment when people
expected relief from a severe burden of war taxation: in Robert
Cecil's words, 'your Majesty may therefore please to remember first
that you found a people worn with great and heavy burthens . . .
which in matter of payment continues yet not a little burdenous to
those that expected ease'. James, whose inability to manage money
was notorious both in Scotland and in England, was not the ideal
king to inherit the throne in this situation. It used to be argued that
Robert Cecil did not attempt to check James's extravagance, but the
letters recently published by Dr Croft finally and conclusively prove
the contrary.[37] It was Robert Cecil who told James that

all other charges and expenses may in some sort be timely foreseen and
provided for, saving that expense aforesaid which follows your majesty's
princely desire to give and your troubles to deny, which is past my
reckoning, for certainly, Sir, though the liberality and goodness that lieth
in you are virtues, worthy of you as you are a great king, yet they are
somewhat improper for this kingdom, which beng compared with other
monarchies may certainly be counted potent, but not opulent.[38]

Two lists in State Papers, which may be the source of Cecil's
comments, show expenditure of £42,904 under the heading of
'extraordinaries accrued and paid since 1 May 1608'. A few of
these, such as £1,310 for coat and conduct money for soldiers sent
into Ireland, are genuine emergency expenses. The vast majority,
however, is made up of such items as £1,000 to the Earl of Home
and £1,000 to Sir Charles Cornwallis 'of free gift'. These do
illustrate James's 'princely desire to give and your trouble to deny',
and very little else.[39] In the 1606 subsidy debate, an obscure

---

[36] PRO SP 12/212/63 and 230/26.
[37] 'Collection of Several Speeches', ed. Croft, p 289. Robert Cecil stressed
whichever part of the problem his hearers were able to correct. To the Commons,
he stressed shortage of income, and to James he stressed excess of expenditure. To
understand Robert Cecil's analysis of the problem, it is necessary to take both halves
of his analysis together.
[38] Ibid. 284.   [39] PRO SP 14/40/43 and 4

member translated this into the even blunter proposition that they were asked to fill the King's coffers 'but if the bottomes be out then can they not be filled'.[40] James, then, was one reason why people were able to avoid admitting any need to solve the King's financial difficulties: the temptation to blame him was so easy as to be irresistible.

Robert Cecil under James tried to meet these expenses by making efforts to increase ordinary revenue which his father had not made under Elizabeth. After doing a vast amount of work for disproportionately limited returns, he was forced to the conclusion that most of the King's revenues cost more labour to improve than he could easily supply. They did not naturally grow with inflation, and this fact was not easily changed. This was partly because they were made up of so many small items, each of which would need to be laboriously and separately improved, and partly because attempts to secure the King's rights involved reproving the negligence of people it was unwise to offend. On the manor of Falmer (Sussex), a large number of copyholders of inheritance owed between them £33, 14 cocks, 3 ewes and 80 eggs. The mind boggles at the thought of collecting and transporting 80 eggs, and at the problem of auditing them. It boggles even more at the problem of ending such fixed copyhold tenures by individual agreement with each tenant, and ratifying the whole by a private Act of Parliament. Stewards of Crown manors were also supposed to pay over to the Crown fines for new leases, and the profits of manorial courts, but only the steward himself normally knew what these sums were. A laborious investigation came up with a list of 51 stewards of Crown manors who had made no certificate of these sums to the Lord Treasurer's Remembrancer, and the list turned out to include Sir Edward Phelips Speaker of the House of Commons, and the late Lord Treasurer, the Earl of Dorset. It suggested no method of checking the truthfulness of those who had returned certificates.[41] It is doubtful whether much money was recovered in this way. In the Crown woods, the task was even more laborious: in the New Forest, the King's woodward, appropriately called William Christmas, turned out to be giving away the King's trees to a man who owned a brick kiln. The Crown then attempted to count the King's trees, and to carve the King's arms on the bark of each tree. It ended up listing

[40] Bowyer, p. 77.   [41] PRO SP 14/40/37 and 34.

the *individual* oaks in the New Forest for which the task had been done. It is no wonder that Cecil's biographer complained that 'his lordship . . . thought himself in a wood indeed'.[42]

When, as was very often the case, the Crown's revenue depended on valuations by neighbours, it was a simple matter to keep the charge down simply by not increasing valuations in line with inflation. Lawrence Squibb Teller of the Exchequer believed in 1641 that recusants' estates were consistently returned at 10% of their real value, so an estate worth £100 per annum was returned at £10, and the King got for his forfeited two thirds £6. 13s. 4d.[43] The Court of Wards under Charles I achieved its remarkable increase in revenue by turning this principle into a rule of thumb, and valuing every estate at ten times the sum it was returned at.[44] For subsidies, Robert Cecil believed the correcting multiplier should be doubled, and that men did not pay a twentieth of their real worth.[45]

In 1641, when the Long Parliament experimented with a graduated Poll Tax, the desire to keep assessments down overrode even snobbery. There was one rate for Esquires, and a lower one for plain gentlemen, and it was reported that many 'reputed Esquires' shrank their title to plain 'gent.' in order to save themselves £5.[46] The same problem affected valuations for customs, which were carried out in periodic Books of Rates. Hand-knitted stockings were valued at £1. 6s. 8d. the pair in 1582, and were still valued at the same sum in 1619, when their selling price had increased to between £2 and £4.[47]

Yet the customs presented far less difficulty in the way of raising revenue than anything else, since their yield did tend to increase with the volume of trade, and the issuing of new Books of Rates did present an opportunity (however hard it might be to take it fully) to update valuations in line with inflation. When a list was drawn up, in or about 1608, of increases in annual revenues since 1603, the

[42] PRO E. 178/3097, parts 4, 10, 11, 12, 19, and 21. J. Gutch, *Collectanea Curiosa*, i (1781), 123.

[43] *CSPD 1641–3*, vol. cccclxxxv, no. 104.

[44] Ibid., vol. cccclxxvii, no. 70. For a case-study of some of the ways in which undervaluation could be achieved, see Conrad Russell, 'Wardship of John Pym', *EHR* 84/331 (1969), 303–17.

[45] *Proceedings in Parliament 1610*, ed. Foster, i. 81.

[46] PRO SP 16/482/110.

[47] Pauline Croft, 'Rise of the English Stocking Export Trade', *Textile History*, 18/1 (1987), 4.

list was overwhelmingly dominated by the customs, which accounted for £110,000 out of total increases worth £130,000 per annum. Of this grand total for customs increases, nearly half was contributed by the new impositions raised in the wake of Bate's Case.[48] This pattern, both the general dominance of the customs and the specific dominance of impositions, was steadily accentuated right up to 1641. This meant that the most buoyant source of revenue the King had was one which, though it had been upheld by the judges in open court, was persistently regarded as illegal by Parliaments from 1610 right through to the establishment of Parliamentary control over it in 1641.[49] This did not help when, as in 1610 and 1641, kings came to Parliaments and pleaded the case for extra endowment because they did not have enough.

It did not help either that requests for exceptional endowment for the monarchy were being made in what were unusually hard economic times. In terms of food prices and of wage rates, the 1590s were exceptionally bad times to ask for multiple subsidies. We have, it is true, been taught to think of 1597 as only a 'two-star crisis', but the fact that it proved no worse is perhaps in part a measure of how bad people expected it to be, and therefore of the effort that was put into organizing relief.[50] The fact remains that the 1590s as a whole were hard times: Abbot, preaching in 1596, said: 'one year there hath been hunger, the second year there was dearth and a third, which is this year, there is great cleannesse of teeth'.[51] Times did not get much easier: neither the depression of the early 1620s nor the plague of 1625 provided ideal circumstances for voting heavy taxes, and Parliamentary historians ought not to forget that Wrigley and Schofield's list of crisis mortality months includes March 1610, May 1614, and April and May 1640. Economic hardship seems to have been capable of changing standards of sexual behaviour, and *a fortiori* is likely to have affected attitudes to taxation.[52] It is true that not all remarks

    [48] PRO SP 14/40/46.
    [49] Russell, 'Charles I's Financial Estimates for 1642', p. 116. By 1641 customs and impositions were yielding £407,225 per annum, as against £334,480 for all other clearly legal sources of revenue.
    [50] This is my deduction from Michael Power, 'London and the Control of "Crisis" of the 1590s', *History*, 70/230 (1985), 371–85, esp. pp. 381–4.
    [51] Andrew B. Appleby, *Famine in Tudor and Stuart England* (Stanford, 1978), 141.
    [52] E. A. Wrigley and R. S. Schofield, *Population History of England 1541–1871* (Cambridge, Mass., 1981), 338–9. Ingram, *Church Courts*, 276–7 and other refs.

members of the Commons made about the burdens on the taxpayers need to be taken at face value, but there are surely some which should be. These should include the suggestions of Sir Thomas Cecil and Sir Walter Raleigh in 1593 that they should spare those under £10 or under £3 in the subsidy books. They should include Sir Francis Hastings's misgivings about the burden on the people in 1604, since he moved for a subsidy in spite of them, and only expressed the misgivings in private. They should include, since he spoke against his own interest, Robert Cecil's reminder of the dangers of the poll tax. Above all, they should include Kirton's expression in 1628 of the member of Parliament's ultimate nightmare: 'they will not pay in the country, what we give'.[53] It is worth looking for a parallel to the early fourteenth century, the last time the population had approached subsistence level, and there Dr Harriss found that the Commons took a very similar attitude *until* population pressure was eased by the Black Death.[54] We should also remember that, in looking at national taxation, we are looking at the tip of a fiscal iceberg: the reigns of Elizabeth and James were reigns of proliferation of rates: militia rates, powder rates, coat and conduct money, plague rates, poor rates, highway rates, bridge rates, paving rates, water rates, maimed soldiers' rates, and rates for bastards and houses of correction. These rates did not benefit from any generally agreed method of assessment. Nationally England was a lightly taxed country, but locally it may have been another story. In some counties, at least, a light assessment for subsidy was vital because it carried a light assessment for all these other rates. An anonymous member of the Parliament of 1593 pointed this out: 'according to a man's valuation in the subsedye they are at all other charges as to warres and in tyme of muster with horse and armour and the charge maketh men unwilling to be raised in the subsedye'.[55] It was a difficulty particularly apparent in wartime, and one whose consequences were particularly serious in wartime.

Another reason for resistance to taxation was the sense of resentment sometimes felt against courtiers or officials, either for corruptly financing themselves out of public money, or for raising money by extortion from subjects. This is often thought of as a

[53] BL Cotton MS Titus F. ii. fo. 49ᵛ; *Letters of Sir Francis Hastings*, ed. M. Claire Cross (Somerset Record Society, 69, Frome, 1969), 85–6; *CJ* i. 995; *Proceedings in Parliament 1610*, ed. Foster, ii. 25; Russell, *PEP*, p. 21.
[54] Harriss, *Finance in Medieval England*, pp. 333–4.
[55] BL Cotton MS Titus F. ii, fo. 52.

Stuart phenomenon, is associated with the impeachment of Buckingham, and is taken back, at furthest, to the monopolies debate of
1601. In fact, like most other things that were wrong in finance, it
went back well into the reign of Elizabeth. In the subsidy debate of
1571 Robert Bell

> sayd that a subsedie was by every subject to be yeilded, but for that the
> people were robbed (by two meanes) it would hardly bee levied: namely by
> lycences and the abuses of promooters, for which if remedie were
> provided, then would the subsedie be payd willingly, which hee proved,
> for that by lycenses a fewe were enriched and the multitude impoverished.
> Addinge that if a newe burden should be layd on the backs of the comons,
> and noe redress of the common evilles, then there might happely ensue that
> they woulde lay downe the burden in the middest of the way, and turn to
> the contrary of their duties.[56]

The abuses Bell mentioned are ones which belong to the family of
grievances commonly known under the heading of 'monopolies'.
Many of these are widely and deservedly known as abuses, yet they
are also evidence of something more specific than that original sin
was known in the sixteenth century. These things were, in essence,
part of a trend to the privatization of law enforcement.[57] Such tasks
as the supervision of licensing of inns or alehouses, or control of the
manufacture of gold and silver thread, could be delegated, by a
grant of monopoly, to a private individual, who would then recoup
himself out of the fines levied for the offence in question. From the
Crown's point of view, the system had two major advantages: it
made enforcement possible in areas where the Crown was unable or
unwilling to do it, and it made it possible for the Crown to deal with
public servants it could not afford to pay adequately by, in effect,
contracting out to them the task of raising their own incomes at the
expense of the public. The public, however, seem to have remained
unconvinced that such payments were in the public interest,
especially when monopolists 'compounded' with them, or, in other
words, took a private payment to free them from the threat of legal
proceedings. It was a procedure perilously close to blackmail. They
might also use the law for their own profit, to maximize the chance
of convicting offenders whose fines they would then receive. In the
end, since the State cannot avoid being held responsible for law
enforcement, much of the unpopularity rubbed off on the Crown.[58]

---

[56] Hartley, i. 202.
[57] I am grateful to Dr D. L. Thomas for this point.
[58] Russell, *PEP*, pp. 66, 102.

For a while, officials and monopolists acted as a lightning-conductor, but attempts to tighten up on corruption did not remove the problems of public servants whose salaries, and whose numbers, had often not increased since the reign of Henry VIII, though prices, and often their workload, had increased many times over. The link between a clampdown on corruption and a claim for increased salaries was made almost explicit by the Comptroller and Surveyor of the Navy in 1640, in an early example of a pay claim based on inflation. They said their fees had remained the same as they were in the reign of Henry VIII, 'att what time one pound would have gone further than three now in regard of the great increase of price upon all manner of provision'. They said that 'the like number of officers was employed then as now when the business of the navye was not a 6th part of whatt it is now'. They admitted that the perquisites of which they had been deprived by the Jacobean navy were 'unwarrantable', but still felt the need to show 'what our predecessors had what we doe now enioy'.[59] It is worth listening to one public servant's version of his own story. In or about 1588 a certain Mr Middlemore (whose office is not recorded) said he had served the Queen 'in this place' for twenty years without fee or wages, and had sold land worth £3,500. Even if it is taken with a pinch of salt, the story of the Crown's attempts to pay him indirectly is a chapter of accidents which tells us volumes about Tudor and Stuart finance, for even if we are to suppose that none of his story is true, there is nothing in it which could not have been true. First, he was given a grant of concealed Crown lands, an unpopular and highly litigious, but sometimes highly successful, way of raising money. He lost it. He was then given the supervision of licences and forfeitures for not bringing in bowstaves, another piece of private-enterprise law enforcement. This cost him £20 a year for attendance and for employment of ten staff, but the Queen stayed it, presumably because it was complained of. Then he was given a licence to export peas and beans, a privilege which he would normally have sold on the open market to someone able to take advantage of it, but the price rose above the limit within which export was permitted, and it proved valueless. He failed to obtain a lease in reversion of Crown lands, which would have made him money because the existing tenants would have had to buy him out

---

[59] Alnwick Castle MSS, vol. 15 (BL Microfilm 286), fos. 155–9.

in order to retain their lands. He finally obtained the searchership of London, a customs office whose legitimate profits were extremely small. At the end of the story he was still, in effect, unrewarded for his service.[60] While the system (if the word is permissible) of paying Crown servants was no more reliable than this, the shortfalls which appeared in the Crown's official balance sheets were no more than the tip of the iceberg of the Crown's financial difficulties.

All this information ought to be borne in mind when assessing the Stuarts' difficulties in getting adequate supply out of their Parliaments. There are not many Whiggish cases of supply witheld in order to achieve redress of grievances. The attempt was made on four occasions between 1604 and 1640: 1614, 1626, 1628, and the Short Parliament, producing three failures and one apparent success. An equally common pattern is that of 1593, 1606, 1624, and 1625, when the dispute was over the question whether the Crown was asking for too much, rather than whether supply should be granted at all. In 1606, for example, Sir Edward Montague was attempting a careful and characteristic balancing act when he said that one subsidy and two fifteenths was too little for the Crown, and three subsidies and six fifteenths too much for the country, and therefore proposed that they should vote two subsidies and four fifteenths. It was the Crown's attempt to obtain a third subsidy which caused the dispute, and which, in the event, was carried by the nail-biting majority of one vote.[61] In 1624, again, James asked for, and needed, six subsidies and twelve fifteenths, and succeeded in getting only half that sum, after Sir George More, Donne's father-in-law, had proposed to follow the King 'afar off, as Peter Christ'.[62] There was a perpetual hankering for other remedies: Laurence Hyde in 1606 and Sir Francis Seymour in 1625 turned to the traditional remedy of an Act of Resumption,[63] while in 1626 Sir Dudley Digges, saying that a subsidy burdened poor men, came up with a proposal for a West India Company which was in effect a

[60] PRO SP 12/228/1. On some of the methods of rewarding crown servants of which Mr Middlemore had tried to take advantage, see C. J. Kitching, 'Quest for Concealed Crown Lands in the Reign of Elizabeth I', *TRHS*[5], 24 (1974), 63–78; A. Hassell Smith, *County and Court: Government and Politics in Elizabethan Norfolk* (Oxford, 1974), 234–7; and D. L. Thomas, 'Leases in Reversion on the Crown's Lands 1558–1603', *Economic History Review*[2], 30 (1977), 67–72.

[61] Bowyer, pp. 31, 84.

[62] Russell, *PEP*, p. 188.

[63] Bowyer, p. 63; *Debates in the House of Commons in 1625*, ed. S. R. Gardiner (Camden Society, NS 6/1873), 111.

proposal for the privatization of war.[64] The Long Parliament tried a similar scheme in 1642, in their proposals for the Irish Adventurers, who were to finance the war in return for promises of confiscated land. Unfortunately, they found in the process that they had privatized the power of war and peace in Ireland, where the Crown has not yet fully recovered it. A great deal of the trouble seems to have come from plain incomprehension of the sums needed, illustrated in frequent errors in the number of noughts in reports of financial statements.[65] In 1625, after Sir John Coke had offered a perfectly reasonable financial statement, Sir John Eliot commented in his memoirs that 'the immense calculations and accomptes, and the far-fetched and impertinent relations; the positions and conclusions that were laid, all held artificiall and prestigious'[66]—prestigious being here used in its original and correct sense, of juggling or deceitful. If this was to be members' reaction to perfectly honest and helpful figures, life was becoming very difficult for the Crown. In March 1641, when a new financial settlement was on the agenda, D'Ewes expressed surprise that any more money should be wanted for the navy:

and now when his majestie hath not onlie received this subsidie of Tonnage and Poundage without law, but hath alsoe received vast sums in another illegall way (I meant shipp-monie) and hath advanced his customes to an higher rate than ever anie of his roial progenitors enioied, wee may well wonder that the Fleete should be now unprovided for.

Such sentiments rested on ignorance, but they were a significant obstacle to the conclusion of a settlement, and therefore indirectly a cause of war.[67]

The Crown's difficulties were compounded by the tendency of Parliaments, when called, to ask for concessions in return for their subsidies, since these concessions almost always cost money, and so diminished the net value of their grants still further. The temporal grievances of 1610, for example, were endorsed, when received, as being 'those that only towched matters by which the k. made profit'.[68] The extreme case was the Addled Parliament of 1614, in which the Commons wanted James to give up impositions, worth £70,000 per annum, in return for a grant which would probably

---

[64] CUL MS 12–20, fo. 45.   [65] See e.g. Bowyer, p. 43.

[66] Sir John Eliot, *Negotium Posterorum*, ed. A. B. Grosart, i (1881), 117.

[67] D'Ewes (N.), p. 500.   [68] *CSPD 1603–10*, vol. lvi, no. 18.

have been £140,000, or two subsidies. They were asking James to sell impositions at two years' purchase. This was a bad bargain for the Crown, and was rightly turned down. In the Short Parliament of 1640, when the political, as distinct from the financial, case for a successful Parliament was exceptionally strong, the Crown offered a bargain which was not much better: it offered to give up Ship Money, worth almost £200,000 per annum, for twelve subsidies, worth, at most, £840,000—an offer to sell Ship Money at just over four years' purchase. Many of the Commons, such as Sir Francis Seymour, refused this offer on the unrealistic ground that the bargain was not good enough. He said that 'without betraying the trust of the country hee could not doe it. He wished therefore an humble Remonstrance to the King of the impossibilitie of it for his parte hee could not'.[69] Among successful Parliaments, that of 1624, in which the King gave up, or appeared to give up, monopolies, informers, and the hunt for concealed Crown lands, seems to have started a murmuring campaign that subsidies were not worth their price. Sir Francis Nethersole said the Commons' bills were 'some of them of such importance, as those of monopolies, concealments, that here wise men estimate that the subject hath more of the king in them, and the pardon, than the subsidies come to'. It is not certain that this was good financial arithmetic, but it was a case against Parliaments which did not go away. Laud, discussing the question whether to call a Parliament in 1628, said the habit of Parliaments was 'to sell subsidies, and not to give them', and cited the example of 1624: 'the last Parliament of King James, they gave three subsidies, and had that of the King that was worth eight, if not ten, to be bought and sold'.[70] Laud's figures were out, among other reasons, because he omitted to mention the fifteenths which came with the subsidies, which added some £140,000 to the value of the grant, but it was intelligible that he should love Parliaments no more than they loved him. This line of argument continued to appeal to his co-religionists, and William Beale, in 1635, defended it with a less injudicious piece of arithmetic: 'the Parliament gives the King a subsidy or two, and takes away two or three'.[71] It was not entirely self-evident that this line of argument was unsound, and the Crown was bound to be tempted by it when it was finding Parliaments an

[69] Cope, p. 195.
[70] Russell, *PEP*, pp. 52–3 and n.
[71] Cope, p. 186.

exceptional nuisance. Shortage of money was thus a direct cause of constitutional difficulties.

The Crown never seems to have reached a final decision about whether it was more impossible to finance itself with Parliaments or without Parliaments. One rare occasion when the issue was discussed and recorded was the Council committee in December 1639 which decided to call the Short Parliament. It was an agreed basis for discussion that a million pounds were needed within the year. Northumberland, one of the chief advocates of a Parliament, had to admit that 'to persuade a Parliament to furnish the King presently with so much, was conceived a very unlikely thing.' Writing privately to his brother-in-law, he admitted it would not happen 'unless the Parliament be more liberall in their supplies to the Kinge, than they have ever beene since my time'.[72] On the other hand, those who proposed excises and such things were met with so many 'weighty objections' that they hastily retreated and agreed to a Parliament, even though even its warmest advocates did not pretend that there was any possibility of it voting enough.

Under these circumstances, the King was under a constant temptation to arbitrary government, whenever he could overcome the 'weighty objections' which usually centred on the problem of collection through a gentry-dominated system of local government. This temptation goes back to the failure of the Great Contract in 1610. Before the Contract, Salisbury had pinned his faith to a Parliamentary solution, to which he had not realized impositions were an obstacle, writing to the King 'showing as well by arguments as precedents that his Majesty's estate cannot be supported in any proportion, without levies from his people'. After the Parliament, he could only ask to be handled graciously, 'though I be not able to recover your estate out of the hands of those great wants to which your Parliament hath now abandoned you'.[73] It was only in form that this was a milder complaint than James's, that there was 'no more trust to be laid upon this rotten reed of Egypt'.[74] Even some people in the Commons seem to have realized that they had delivered a sword into the hands of their enemies. Richard Martin, in a remarkable speech, said that lay Councillors, who had

[72] KAO De L'Isle and Dudley MSS C 85/4; Alnwick Castle MSS, vol. 15 (BL Microfilm 285), fo. 28ᵛ.
[73] 'Collection of Several Speeches', ed. Croft, pp. 280, 313.
[74] *HMC Salis.* XXI. 266.

possessions and posterities, would not attempt to extend the prerogative beyond the bounds, but feared that 'the king's wants may drive him to extremities', and that this would present the clergy with a situation where 'the highway to get into a double benefice or to a higher dignity is to tread upon the neck of the common law'.[75] To Arminian clergy, engaged in a perpetual struggle to prove that they were more the King's friends than their critics were, this was a heaven-sent opportunity. Howson had already been in trouble in 1604 for speaking words of 'scandal and scorn' of the House of Commons,[76] and Richard Neile in 1614 was to follow in his footsteps. From John Howson to William Beale, a high proportion of supposed 'absolutist' utterances should be explained in this way.

The fact that Parliaments continued when the Crown found that they were no longer fulfilling the function for which they were created should alone be enough to acquit the Crown of any deliberate and conscious absolutist programme, since the practical case against holding Parliaments was becoming very strong indeed.

James, as might have been expected, nevertheless succeeded in keeping his options open, and the issue of Parliaments' survival did not come to a head until the 1620s, when the country was again contemplating war. James's estimate in 1624 that he needed a million pounds was realistic, and the gross amount he got was £353,000. This might have been manageable, if it had not been accompanied by the sort of pressure which came from any Parliament, to refrain from raising other revenues which were illegal. The two things together surely condemned the King to break the law or to lose the war, which is one reason why James avoided real war for the remainder of his lifetime. In 1625 the grant of two subsidies, worth approximately £140,000, was nothing like enough to support the war many members purported to be demanding. When Sir John Eliot began to look around for scapegoats for the failure of the Cadiz expedition, he should have begun with himself. In 1626 the Commons refused supply in the middle of a war Charles believed they had themselves asked for. It is no wonder that Charles began to doubt their loyalty: he was perfectly entitled to protest that they were 'enforcing us to new courses for the necessary defence of ourself and people'.[77] If heads of state, in any age, are

---

[75] *Proceedings in Parliament 1610*, ed. Foster, ii. 327–9.
[76] *CJ* i. 235.		[77] Richard Cust, *Forced Loan* (Oxford, 1987), 33.

forced to choose between ruling illegally and not defending their countries, they will rule illegally. In the Short Parliament, again, the attempt at bargaining failed because the Commons would not pay the price of power. It was the same problem as it had been in 1593: the gulf between the maximum politically possible and the minimum administratively viable had not been closed. In England, as in almost every country in Europe, the costs of war had risen so high that they were beyond the limits of consent.

The mention of Ship Money highlights once again the way changes in the organization of war could upset a political system. 1588, the last English naval success of any substance, had also been almost the last appearance of private enterprise naval war, by something resembling the system of indentured retainers. It was also one of the last appearances I know of an attempt to finance war by ransoms.[78] By 1634 this system was out of date, and only regular king's ships could keep up with the growing French and Dutch fleets. Yet the law still allowed the King to conscript private ships, but did not allow him to raise money to fit out his own. It allowed him to do what he did not need to do, but did not allow him to do what he did need to do. This is why, throughout the Ship Money trial, the King had to pretend that he was conscripting ships, and not raising a tax.[79] The problem of Ship Money was a problem of failure to bring the law up to date, and bringing the law up to date was one of the things kings were supposed to have Parliaments for. In their willingness to encourage wars, and their entire unwillingness to face the consequences, many of them deserve to be known as Parliaments in the manger. That they came so close to extinction was in large measure their own doing. That they nevertheless survived was in large measure the King's doing.

The links which lead from financial breakdown to civil war are in all cases indirect: it is not necessary to suppose that any number of people fought the King simply because he was running out of money. Yet the breakdown of a financial system tends to generate a large amount of anger in all participants, and that anger is directly visible, not least in Charles I himself. The lack of money thus

[78] *CSPD 1581–90*, vol. ccxv, no. 60, vol. ccxvi, nos. 9, 10. For a later attempt, which proved abortive, see PRO SP 16/74/10. I am grateful to Andrew Thrush for this reference.
[79] Conrad Russell, 'Ship Money Judgements of Bramston and Davenport', *EHR* 77/303 (1962) 312–18.

contributed considerably to the atmosphere of ill-will and distrust, as well as contributing significantly to many of our list of questions. There does not seem to be sufficient reason to suppose that financial breakdown by itself was ever likely to lead to civil war, but it did make it very much more likely that the upheaval precipitated by the Scottish invasion of 1640 would do so.

8

The Man Charles Stuart

'YOU can not believe the alteration in the opinion of the world touching his Majesty'.[1] This comment, by the Earl of Kellie to the Earl of Mar, marks the end of the 'honeymoon period' at the beginning of Charles's reign, and it is dated 26 July 1625, when Charles had only been four months on the throne. It marks a remarkably swift general recognition, during Charles's first year, that as a king he was not a success, and that judgement is one which has never been reversed. Yet, whenever we attempt to analyse *why* Charles as king was not a success, this general agreement instantly evaporates, and attempts to explain an agreed judgement rapidly degenerate into adjectival incoherence.

Our problem is partly the result of the fact that we are dealing with a dimension which cannot be recorded on paper. The reasons why people in politics do or do not annoy each other are often ones which cannot be recaptured in the paper reports of their speeches. We may read the most perfect report of a speech, yet if we do not know that this speech was delivered with the head in the brief, never looking at the audience, that one was delivered with waves of anger which the audience reciprocated, or the other was read in a flat and inaudible monotone, we will not know why they created the reaction they did. That some part of Charles's ability to create the wrong reaction resided in these unrecordable personalities seems to be a strong balance of probability, and into this area we will not penetrate. In analysing the written record, we are aiming, at best, to recover a small part of his ability to rub people up the wrong way. If we recover that small part, we will be examining it for clues to the rest, but clues are the best we will be able to get.

The existence of an unsuccessful king on the throne is perhaps the only thing which is capable of contributing to the answers to all the initial list of questions which this book has set out to ask about the causes of the English Civil War. Above all, there is no difficulty in

[1] Russell, *PEP*, p. 240 n.

invoking Charles's character and policy as one of the causes of the
Bishops' Wars. The decision to impose the Scottish Prayer Book,
from which all the British troubles began, was so entirely Charles's
decision, and followed so naturally from his settled convictions
about the nature of authority, of Britain, and of the church, that to
deny his responsibility would amount to a wholescale rejection of the
evidence. If he shares responsibility with others, such as Laud
or Wedderburn Bishop of Dunblane, these are people whom he
appointed, with whom he shared a common outlook, and whom it
seems he appointed because they shared a common outlook.
It is even clearer, if we follow the winding stair of Charles's
correspondence with Hamilton between the imposition of the
Prayer Book and the outbreak of war that the policy which led from
one to the other was almost exclusively the King's personal
responsibility. Scottish policy was something on which the English
Privy Council could not advise. The Scottish Privy Council, save
for occasional individual visits to London, remained in Edinburgh,
and were only too aware of their lack of influence. Some Scottish
bishops could (and did) urge Charles forward, but their influence
was diminished after 1638. Hamilton was almost alone in being
consistently able to advise the King, and no one who has read his
advice in full is likely to believe that the resultant policy was his.
Nor is anyone who looks at the comparatively quiet stream of
Scottish records for the main part of the 1630s likely to doubt that it
was in the King's power, if he had chosen, to refrain from imposing
the Scottish Prayer Book, and so to avoid detonating the mine whose
explosions reverberated for the rest of his life.

In answering our second question, why the English lost the
Bishops' Wars, Charles's responsibility is less central. His report
that '*I* estimate' the cost of the First Bishops' War at £200,000[2] is,
no doubt, a piece of lazy and egocentric over-confidence, yet it is
hard to imagine any policies Charles could have followed which
would have led to a secure success in the Bishops' Wars. Either
better handling of the Short Parliament, or refraining from calling
it at all, could easily have given him a better chance of success.
So, perhaps, might a decision to fight at Berwick in 1639, when his
army was still in pay. Yet, whatever allowance is made for these
miscalculations, the run-down of England's military power had

[2] Hamilton MSS 10,490.

causes which were too deep in the structure of English society and government to be blamed entirely on one king. Where Charles can perhaps be held responsible is in failure to allow adequately for a difficulty of which he had already been warned.[3]

Our third question, why there was no settlement between the King and the Long Parliament, is the one for which Charles has most traditionally carried the blame. Here, his contribution was doubtless unhelpful, but he can only be blamed for preventing a settlement if there was in fact one available to be reached. Even so, the change of religious inflexibility lies no more clearly against Charles than it does against Pym; both of them stood for causes to which there was very widespread public hostility, and neither could wholly give way to the other without building up a party of the discontented larger than it was safe to leave behind. Yet the heaviest responsibility for preventing a settlement rests on the Scots, without whom there would have been no chance to negotiate for one in the first place. Charles's understanding of the depth of hostility to Scotticizing discipline was both one of his skills and one of his strengths. Charles did not manage the settlement negotiations particularly well, but he deserves only one share among many in the responsibility for their future.

He was rather more responsible for the failure to prorogue the Long Parliament at the end of the summer of 1641. The Act requiring the Parliament's consent to a dissolution or a prorogation was the result of his own unwisdom in undertaking the Army Plot to save Strafford, and his failure to return from Scotland before the outbreak of the Irish rebellion led to his missing the six-week window of opportunity for a prorogation between the Scottish treaty and the outbreak of the Irish Rebellion. That delay was the result, in part, of his determination to save Montrose and Traquair. His determination to save his servants may do him credit, but his servants never seem to have been much the better for it.

In the gathering of parties, Charles' contribution is considerable. Both in Scotland and in England, he showed (with occasional intermissions) a skill in nursing and strengthening 'my partie'[4] which he never showed in the task of leading a whole country. Here, the fact that his ideological position was considerably off-centre is undoubtedly relevant. Had he had the task of being a party

<hr/>

[3] Ibid. 327.1.   [4] Ibid. 10,527.

leader in a modern polity, he would not have been a great success, but his failure would have been a great deal less dramatic than in the event it was. In the failure to negotiate during the spring of 1642, his contribution was of course central. The need to negotiate with the Parliament, like the need to negotiate with the Covenanters and the need to make peace after the Civil War, hit Charles in his area of deepest weakness, the need to do business with those whose loyalty he did not trust.[5] In the process of failing to do business, he generated, as he often did, a considerable body of anger which helped to fuel the fires of the other side.

In trying to understand Charles, then, we may hope to shed some light on all our initial list of questions, but most of all on the question why there were Bishops' Wars, and why negotiation in England failed. That failure, among much else, indicated a deep loss of confidence in the man on the throne. For that, Charles must take a large share of the responsibility, even if not quite as big a share as S. R. Gardiner would have given him.

In April 1642 Charles summoned his household officers to attend him at York for St George's Feast. Essex and Holland, Lord Chamberlain and Groom of the Stool, refused to go, and therefore were dismissed from their offices. In reply, the House of Lords voted 'that what person soever shall accept of either of these offices, thus taken away, until satisfaction be given to both Houses of Parliament, shall be accounted to do an ignoble act, and to offer an affront to the Parliament, and thereby render himself unworthy of any place of honour or trust in the commonwealth'.[6] In other words, the Lords declared these two offices black. In this highly unusual act, they contradicted the main line of baronial policy ever since 1258, which had always centred on the conviction that the way to deal with an untrustworthy king was to place trustworthy men in the key offices about him. In this very remarkable act, the House of Lords, by implication, drew attention to a number of propositions about Charles, all of which deserve attention, and some of which are very contrary to the mythology which has been handed down from that day to this.

---

[5] On Charles's concern from early in his reign about his subjects' loyalty, see R. P. Cust, 'Charles I and a Draft Declaration for the 1628 Parliament', *Historical Research* vol. 63, no. 151 (1990) 143–161. I am grateful to Dr Cust, both for allowing me to use the article in typescript, and for many helpful conversations.

[6] *LJ* iv. 719.

In the first place, the House of Lords drew attention to the fact that Charles was not, as we often like to think, surrounded only by yes-men. The mere fact of having a Lord Chamberlain and Groom of the Stool who were capable of refusing to attend his person should alone be proof of that, and moreover, it was not their first offence. Both of them had been invited to leave London with Charles in January 1642, and had refused to do so.[7] In spite of this refusal, they were still in office to be dismissed four months later. This dissent, moreover, was not an isolated example: when Charles issued a Proclamation for the arrest of the Five Members, the Lord Keeper refused to put the Seal to it,[8] and when the Civil War broke out, some quarter of the Councillors who had been in office in October 1640 fought for the Parliament. The loyalty of the remainder was by no means always enthusiastic.

Not only did Charles tolerate some dissent about him; he often allowed it to be expressed with considerable freedom.[9] In June 1639 in the camp at Berwick, Bristol, who can hardly have been confident that he was *persona grata* with the King, spoke publicly of the ground of the quarrel and for a Parliament, and told the King that most of the Lords in the camp, both Councillors and others, were resolved to petition the King for a Parliament.[10] The King's reply to this plain speaking was not to dismiss Bristol from his presence: it was to take him aside for an hour's private conversation, at the end of which the preparations for the Pacification of Berwick were in train. In this, one may suspect that Bristol was acting as front man for Holland, who had restored him to favour in 1637, and was at the time acting as mediator for the Covenanters.[11] Whoever was responsible, the incident clearly shows that Councillors could not only speak freely to Charles, but could even persuade him to do what he would not otherwise have done. This was not the first time such a thing had happened: Richard Cust has described an occasion when Manchester and Conway, apparently on their own authority, decided to alter a royal letter commanding the pressing of loan

---

[7] *CJ* ii. 525 and other refs.

[8] *Stuart Royal Proclamations*, ii, ed. James F. Larkin (Oxford, 1983), 757 and other refs.

[9] On this see Cust, 'Charles I and a Draft Declaration'.

[10] PRO SP 16/423/67.

[11] Plas Newydd MSS box XII; [JRL], Crawford MSS 14/3/35. I am grateful to the Marquess of Anglesey and the Earl of Crawford and Balcarres for permission to quote from their family papers. The Crawford MSS are now in the NLS.

refusers. He has also shown that the decision to call the Parliament of 1628 was taken, in the face of considerable resistance, after an all-night sitting of the Privy Council.[12] Not even the Civil War freed Charles from dissident Councillors: in January 1646 he complained to Henrietta Maria that 'there is none doth assist me heartily in my steady resolutions but Sir Edw. Nicholas and Ashburnham: all the rest are very inclinable to most flexible counsels, yet grumbling when they are not employed, and when they are, do rather hinder than further business'.[13] By October, writing to Culpepper and Jermyn, who were the main objects of these criticisms, he was calling them 'those who either takes courage and morall honesty for conscience, or those who were never rightly grounded in religion according to the church of England'.[14]

By 1646, when most proceedings had to be on paper because of Charles's physical isolation, this disrespect between the King and his Councillors appears on paper often enough for us to be sure it was mutual. Will Murray, writing to Lanerick in September 1646, said the King's plan to go to London 'will in my judgement be his certaine ruine', 'but he is in this not to be *overruled*'. He said that Essex's death was a great blow for the King's affairs, 'though ase yet he cannot be made understand it'.[15] Lanerick himself, Secretary for Scotland, said that he had 'dayly assaulted him for changing his deepest resolution',[16] and Sir Robert Moray, reported to Hamilton that the King 'hath never made right use of any opportunity', and, recounting the disaster facing the King's affairs, said 'not one serious thought of it from the king, but this is not newes to you'.[17] These passages surely go to show that the trouble was not, as Parliamentary mythology had it, that Charles did not have a free-spoken Council, but that he was unable to establish a good working relationship with them when he had them.

This is the same conclusion we should draw from the remarkable, and unique, spectacle of a Groom of the Stool going into rebellion. A king whose Groom of the Stool rebelled was one of whom no one could honestly say that 'as his Council was about him, so he was led'. Holland's action marks a final recognition that access did not confer

[12] R. P. Cust, 'Charles I, The Privy Council and The Forced Loan', *Journal of British Studies*, 24 (1985), 227; id., *Forced Loan* (Oxford, 1987), 83.

[13] *Charles I in 1646*, ed. J. Bruce (Camden Society, 63, 1856), 11–12.

[14] *Clar. SP* ii. 270.

[15] Hamilton MSS 1939: my italics.

[16] Ibid. 2024.   [17] Ibid. 2053, 2071, see also 2070.

influence, and with that recognition, all the normal rules of court politics were suspended. In any normal world, people spend much of their time wanting to change things, and under a monarchy they normally pursue this ambition by the pursuit of place about the king. A king about whom people no longer wanted place was a king who had lost the greatest part of his dominion.

What did Charles do, or refrain from doing, which produced such an upheaval in the normal rules of politics? The fact that he lost has made it easy to abuse him, and indeed often easier than to understand him, and many charges have been made against him which do not seem to be fully sustained. Some judgements simply represent the value-system of the winners. For example, his scheme to get help from Ireland in 1645–6 in return for toleration of Catholicism was described by Bruce in the moral phrase 'this most foolish and wicked business'.[18] If this phrase is just, it is no more just than it would be if used about the attempts of Fiennes and others to procure a similar invasion by the Scots in 1640, and they had done it first.

Similarly, the perennial charge of bad faith seems to me to be no more justified against Charles than it is against most politicians with long careers. Indeed, had he been more prepared to act in bad faith, he would have been less open than he was to the potentially divergent charge of inflexibility. In October 1646 he explained to Culpepper and Jermyn that a war fought with the Scots as his allies would not lead to the recovery of his rights, 'except I should resolve to violat my faith (to which I am sure none of you will councell me)'.[19] That was, in fact, what Culpepper and Jermyn were hoping the King would do, but they could not bring themselves to tell him so. In November 1642 Henrietta Maria complained of his promise to observe everything which had passed in the Long Parliament, 'but it is a thing done'.[20] Between the two of them, it was clearly assumed that if Charles had given his word, it was to be kept. Charles was not above equivocation, and, as he once said, 'it may be I give them leave to hope for more than I intended',[21] but the degree of deception involved here is no more than is normal in the statements of governments of all persuasions. If Charles deceived

---

[18] *Charles I in 1646*, ed. Bruce, p. xiii.   [19] *Clar. SP* ii. 274.
[20] *Letters of Queen Henrietta Maria*, ed. Mary Anne Everett Green (1857), 142–3.
[21] *Charles I in 1646*, ed. Bruce, p. 11.

his subjects more deeply than this, it was because they allowed themselves to be deceived and into believing that when he used phrases like 'innovation', 'true religion', and 'just grievances', he meant by them what they would have meant themselves.

Nor does Charles seem, within his own political terms of reference, to have been stupid. His analyses of situations are often shrewd, and sometimes show understanding of points others had not taken. His analysis of why he was entitled to expect supply from his first two Parliaments is a powerful one, and deserves more answer than it has been normally given either then or now:

When his Majestie, by the death of his deare and royall father, of ever blessed memory, first came to the Crown, hee found himselfe ingaged in a warre with a potent enemy . . . and invited thereunto, and encouraged therein, by the humble advice of both the Houses of Parliament, and by their large promises and protestations to his late Majestie, to give him full and reall assistance in these enterprises, which were of so great importance to this realme, and to the generall peace and safetie of all his friends and allies.[22]

His comments on Ship Money, after the dissolution of the Short Parliament, also deserve more attention than they have usually been given:

All his aime was but to live like their king, able to defend himself and them, to be usefull to his friends and considerable to his enemies, to maintain the soveraigntie of the seas, and so make the kingdom flourish in trade and commerce. The ordinary revenue now taken by the Crown could not serve the turn, and therefore that it must be by shipping money or some other way.

He said he was willing to let them settle it how they would, 'so the thing were done, which so much imported the honour and safety of the kingdom'.[23] Even in 1646 he was able to retort the charge of impracticality on Sir Robert Moray, who made it so forcibly against him:

And when I shew him that it is against my conscience, and besides that, though it were not, yet it could not be effected, the Independant being as

[22] *Declaration of the True Causes which moved his Majestie to Assemble, and after inforced him to Dissolve, the Two Last Meetings in Parliament* (1626), 4–5; see also pp. 14–16 and *passim*. The point is paraphrased in May 1628: see Cust, 'Charles I and a Draft Declaration'.

[23] *His Majesties Declaration* (1640), BL E. 203(1), pp. 13–14.

great an enemy to the Presbyterian as Episcopall government, and even all the English Presbyterians will never admit of the Scots' way, his answer is still, that the Scotts will go no less.[24]

This one was surely Charles's point.

Two reasons for his confidence in his intransigence after the Civil War are worth mentioning, since they both represented shrewd political judgements, though ones which ultimately proved to be incorrect. In January 1646 he told Henrietta Maria that one of his securities was that 'this Parliament without doubt determines with my life', in which he was undoubtedly legally right.[25] In December 1646 Jermyn and Culpepper told him that Mazarin would declare for him if there was a general peace, and though Charles never shared their confidence in Mazarin, he was entitled to hope, both that the Peace of Westphalia would come sooner than it did, and that the Parliament would dare take fewer liberties in a time of European peace. He perhaps went beyond the evidence in December 1646, when he told Sir Robert Moray that the plenipotentiaries of France, Spain, and Holland had agreed at Münster that he should be restored to his throne.[26]

One reason for the intransigence of Charles and Henrietta Maria which is not generally appreciated, and which makes their position appear less irrational than it is often taken to be, is the resolute refusal of Pym and his fellow-Parliamentarians to allow Henrietta Maria her Mass, or the services of any priest whatsoever.[27] It was that insistence which made Henrietta Maria, whose conscience and honour equally forbade her to do what was required, fear for her life if she remained in England under Parliamentary rule.[28] Under these circumstances it was natural that Henrietta Maria should never be quite free from the fear that she, like Strafford, might be sacrificed to the peace of the kingdom—itself a reason why the King could never cease to stress his guilt for the death of Strafford. It was a subject on which Henrietta Maria could not rest: she wrote to him in September 1642 'to remind you of what you promised me at Dover, and have since often written to me, that you would never

---

[24] *Charles I in 1646*, ed. Bruce, p. 4.   [25] Ibid. 7.
. [26] *Clar. SP* ii. 302; Hamilton MSS 2074.
[27] Gardiner, *Constitutional Documents of the Puritan Revolution* (repr. Oxford, 1979), 164. For a full discussion of this issue, see Russell, *FBM* (forthcoming), and ch. 3 above.
[28] *Letters of Queen Henrietta Maria*, ed. Green, pp. 96, 117, 329, and other refs.

consent to an accommodation without my knowledge and through me . . . If you do not take care of those who suffer for you, you are lost'.[29] In the light of known Parliamentary sentiments about popery, it is hard to say her fears were unreasonable, and they did not make Charles's life easy.

If Charles did listen to critical counsel, was not stupid, and was not more deceitful than most rulers, where was his failure? It seems that it lies in the number of occasions on which his Council half-persuaded him, and found that the half-persuasion was worse than none. In 1638 and 1646, the two years in which Charles regularly took counsel by letter, he was open to counsel about means, but never open to any counsel about his 'grounds': the ultimate objectives of his policy. On both occasions, it was the grounds themselves with which Councillors profoundly disagreed but advice to that effect was taboo. Councillors, like true seasoned politicians, of course tried to provide their master with a way of saving his face with honour, by suggesting expedients which were in fact incompatible with his grounds, in the hope that Charles would recognize the fact without needing to say so.[30] In fact, what happened on each occasion was that Charles, who knew he was supposed to be flexible, accepted the expedients, while still clinging to the grounds which were incompatible with them. On three major occasions when Charles's Councillors persuaded him to do what he would not otherwise have done, the summons of the Parliament of 1628, the Pacification of Berwick, and the summons of the Short Parliament, Charles was in fact following two incompatible policies. This misled people very severely, and the fact that they were misled made them accuse the King of duplicity. In fact, the King, with a residual honesty, always warned anyone who was listening that there was no real change in his policy, and those who were deceived were deceived voluntarily.[31]

Immediately after the decision to call the Parliament of 1628, the decision for a Ship Money levy, and its use as a loyalty test, showed that Charles was still fixed on the questions he would have to stop asking in order to hold a successful Parliament.[32] The Councillors,

---

[29] *Letters of Queen Henrietta Maria*, ed. Green, pp. 118–19.

[30] See e.g. Hamilton MSS 718, Traquair to Hamilton (July 1638).

[31] See Russell, *PEP*, p. 383 on the King's second answer to the Petition of Right. L. J. Reeve has said 'Charles could not be trusted to keep his word as others understood it': *Charles I and the Road to Personal Rule* (Cambridge, 1989), 173.

[32] Cust, *Forced Loan*, p. 83.

The Man Charles Stuart 195

in stopping the levy, probably supposed that they had weaned
Charles away from this outlook, but when Charles came to give his
opening speech to the Parliament, he made it quite clear that
'tedious consultations' were not to be regarded as in order, and that
their only alternatives were to vote supply, or to let him raise it
without them.[33] This truly was a vision of what the French
ambassador once called a 'parlement à sa mode'. The French
Ambassador said that Charles intended to confine the Short
Parliament to discussing Scottish affairs, 'et par ce moyen de se
rendre absolu en ce pays'.[34] It emerges very clearly from this
remark that the ambassador was crediting Charles with a temperamental, not a constitutional, arbitrariness. He was not accused of
intending to do without Parliaments, but of forcing them to adopt
his perspective and his point of view as a condition of doing business
with him. Tunnel vision surely goes farther than constitutional
theory towards explaining such a position. It was also an alarming
example of a tunnel vision which was very characteristic of Charles.
His concerns were perfectly proper ones, but he never sufficiently
absorbed that anyone else had any different ones, and therefore
interpreted Parliamentary reactions as meaning what they would
have meant if members had shared his concerns. He said the voting
of supply was delayed because members were 'diverted by a
multitude of questions', raised 'by some turbulent and ill-affected
spirits (to mask and disguise their wicked intentions, dangerous to
that state)'.[35] He would, no doubt, have been quite entitled to be
angry with the Parliament of 1628 for not sharing his concerns, but
the ability to interpret their actions as meaning what they would
have meant if they had shared them simply prevented him from
ever engaging with a complex set of problems. Similarly, when the
Councillors persuaded Charles to the Pacification of Berwick, they
persuaded him to do something which only made sense if he
intended to abandon Scottish episcopacy. Hamilton, a true politician,
seems to have thought that this was Charles's intention, and feared
that he would save his face by letting him (Hamilton) do the deed,
and disowning him when it was done.[36] In fact, Charles had not
been persuaded to agree to the abolition of Scottish episcopacy, and

[33] *1628 Debates*, ii. 2–3. See also Cust, 'Charles I and a Draft Declaration'
(forthcoming).
[34] PRO 31/3/71, fo. 154.   [35] Rushworth, i, app. 1.
[36] Hamilton MSS 948. This letter is not easy to interpret.

in agreeing to the Pacification of Berwick had embarked on a half-policy which was bound to fail. In this way, the union of Charles and his moderate Councillors produced policies worse than would have been followed by either in isolation.

It is not easy to establish how Charles came by this tunnel vision. In 1624, when he was functioning successfully in Parliament as Prince of Wales, Chamberlain allowed himself to show rather more surprise than was flattering, commenting that he was doing so well that he was thought to have concealed himself before.[37] It is not very useful to pursue Charles into that concealment: the sources are few, scattered, and sometimes mutually contradictory. The only clear and significant point is their fewness. In 1621 Charles had been heir to the throne for nine years, and an heir to the throne who can keep out of the news for nine years must either have something, or, more likely, not have something. It seems likely that those early years left him with a want of confidence in his political abilities, but why or how this came about, or whether it was a cause or a consequence of his famous stutter, I will not venture to speculate.

Charles, like Pym, suffered a good deal from a religious position which was off-centre, and a great many of his errors arose from simple incomprehension of ideological positions remote from his own. That is a failing which is not peculiar to Charles, but nevertheless one from which he suffered severely. After the Short Parliament, he offered to give directions to the archbishops and bishops 'that no innovations in matter of religion should creep in'.[38] This phrase, remarkable though it may seem, was the origin of the canons of 1640.[39] After the session of 1629 he made a similar promise that 'neither shall we ever give way to the authorizing of any thing, whereby any innovation may steal or creep into the church; but to preserve the unity of doctrine and discipline established in the time of Queen Elizabeth, whereby the church of England hath stood and flourished ever since'.[40] He never seems to have understood that his critics believed he was using such declarations to justify exactly the opposite, any more than they ever seem to have comprehended that he meant exactly what he said.

---

[37] PRO SP 14/161/4 (20 March 1623/4).

[38] *His Majesties Declaration* (1640), p. 18.

[39] The question of Charles and innovation is more fully discussed in Russell, *FBM*.

[40] Rushworth, i, app., p. 4.

Charles's vision of the church of England, when it was ultimately made articulate in 1646, was extreme enough to startle even some of his most committed supporters. It was, as might have been expected, one in which theology and ecclesiology were inextricably linked in a style reminiscent of Richard Montague:

the reformation of the Church of England hath no relation to the reformation of any church, and albeit she is unwilling to censure any of her neighbours, yet none of her true children who rightly understand themselves, can with a safe conscience so far communicate with any of the Calvinists as to receive the sacrament of the eucharist with them, there being none of the reformed churches abroad (except the Lutherans) that can justify the succession of their priests, which if this could not undoubtedly do, she should have one son less for me.

Next, I believe that bishops are *jure divino*, because I find as much authority for them as for some articles of the creed; and for the Presbyterian government I hold it absolutely unlawful, one chief (among many) argument being that it never came into any country but by rebellion.[41]

He told Jermyn, Culpepper, and Ashburnham that without bishops, 'we should have neither lawfull priests, nor sacraments duly administered', and insisted that 'the presbiterian tenents and government are more erronious than the church of Rome'.[42] These views appeared startling, not only to the other side, but even to Jermyn and Culpepper, who replied with pardonable exaggeration:

but if by conscience [it] is intended to assert that episcopacy is *jure divino exclusive*, whereby no Protestant (or rather Christian) church can be acknowledged for such without a bishop, we must therein crave leave wholly to differ. And if it be an error, we are in good company; ther not

---

[41] *Charles I in 1646*, ed. Bruce, pp. 26–7. For similar views expressed before the Civil War, see Richard Montague, *Originum Ecclesiasticarum*, ii (1640), 463–5. I am grateful to Dr Anthony Milton for this reference. On the early history of Charles's religious convictions, see Tyacke, pp. 113–14. It does not appear to be possible to discover the origins of his convictions: I am grateful to Dr Tyacke for many interesting discussions of this topic. The contrast with the Calvinism of Elizabeth of Bohemia makes it difficult to regard his views as the only logical result of an upbringing in James's court.

[42] *Clar. SP* ii. 243, 247. Whether these were views Charles had held since the beginning of his reign, or developments from views he had held since the beginning of his reign, is not clear, but there is no inconsistency between this and the less full records of his early views.

being (as we have cause to believe) six persons of the Protestant religion of the other opinion.[43]

This came rather nearer than courtesy permitted to repeating the Parliamentary charge of popery against Charles, and moved Charles in return to accuse them of being 'never rightly grounded in religion according to the church of England'.[44] Even Hyde, drawing up his will in 1647, was careful not to commit himself to Charles's view: having praised episcopacy highly, he scrupulously added that 'I am not sure that it is so essential to the soul's health, that no other way may be complied with'.[45] A view of religion which caused such trouble and surprise among the inner ring of his own supporters clearly caused him political difficulty, not only because, as he often complained, he was being asked to change his religion, but because, in trying to understand his opponents, he was seeing the view from a long way away.

It is more serious that, in committing himself to the political process, Charles never accepted the view that it was the art of the possible. In 1646 he maintained that 'the prudential part of any consideration will never be found opposite to the conscientious'.[46] By itself, this is merely the same conviction as Gladstone's 'what is morally wrong can never be politically right', but Charles never had Gladstone's care to keep the ace of trumps up his sleeve, nor even Cromwell's to keep his powder dry. Charles's political method consisted simply of discovering what his conscience demanded, and asserting it: he never accepted that the political process demanded bargaining and concession up to the very outer limits of that demand. In his Declaration after the Short Parliament, he complained that ill-affected subjects had introduced a course of 'bargaining and contracting' with the King, repugnant to the duty of subjects.[47] He does not seem to have understood that, in renouncing such a process, he was renouncing precisely that which kept subjects well-affected, and rejecting one of the disciplines to which all power, even the most arbitrary, remains subject.

[43] *Clar. SP* ii. 263. Jermyn and Culpepper's 'six' could easily be doubled, or perhaps trebled, but their exaggeration was a pardonable one.
[44] Ibid. 270.
[45] Ibid. 359. See also ibid. 317 for Hyde's attempt to resolve Edward Nicholas's 'scruples' about communicating with the French Huguenots: 'our religion is too much one, to be divided in communion'.
[46] Ibid. 260.
[47] *His Majesties Declaration* (1640), p. 52.

These priorities could make life rather difficult for Charles's servants. When Hamilton returned to England for consultation in September 1638, he explained to the King what it was necessary to do to gain a 'considerable pairtye' for the Glasgow Assembly, but 'his answer was, that the remedy was worse than the disease, and to those things he nather would not could condiscend, yet willing he was to yield to any thinge that might give his *good* subjects satisfactione, that he never intended nor wold intende innovatione in religione nor lawes'. Traquair, the recipient of this letter, was of all men peculiarly well qualified to read the frustration between the lines.[48]

By 1646 Charles seems to have understood that the role of martyr was the only one compatible with these political priorities: he wrote to Jermyn, Culpepper, and Ashburnham:

I conjure you by your unspotted faithfulness, by all that you love, by all that is good, that no threatnings, no aprehensions of danger to my person, make you stire on jot from any foundation, in relation to that authority the Prince of Wales is born to. I have alreddy cast up what I am lyke to suffer: which I shall meete (by the grace of God) with that constancy that befits me. Only, I desire that consolation, that asseurance from you, as I may justly hope that my cause shall not end with my misfortunes, by asseuring me that misplaced pittie to me doe not prejudice my sone's right.[49]

The policy was of course successful, and it would be possible to justify it as a peculiarly macabre piece of *realpolitik*, had the course of Charles's life suggested that he was capable of any alternative.

Jermyn and Culpepper, in reply, certainly thought they were dealing with a rejection of the political process: they told him he was not obliged to perish with the bishops merely out of pity, 'and certainly you have nothing els left to assist them with'. They said his arguments showed which he should prefer if he had a free choice, but 'alas you are far from it'. As they said 'the question in short is, whether you will chuse to be a king of presbitery or no king, and yet presbitery or perfect independency to be'.[50] Perhaps the most revealing of Charles's correspondents were Bishops Juxon and Duppa, whom he had consulted about how far he could make concessions with a good conscience. Their replies sound remarkably like a conscientious defence of the political profession: they explained to the King that he was 'destitute of all means

---

[48] Hamilton MSS 719: my italics.
[49] *Clar. SP* ii. 243.   [50] Ibid. 263.

compulsory', and therefore entitled to proceed 'by the best ways and means you have now left you', and specifically, to 'permit that which you cannot hinder if you would'.[51] Charles's indifference to this beautifully crafted advice raises the problem of how we identify the point where conscience, fear, and self-will meet.

At least, in this rejection of the political process, Charles was making a conscious and explicit choice. The position he took on this occasion was defensible on political grounds, and was defended by Hyde on the ground that 'it is ill logic to infer, that because you cannot have it cheaper, therefore you must give whatsoever is asked'.[52] The same cannot be said for the frequent occasions on which Charles attempted to do the impossible: these were simple and plain failures to size up the political facts. One of the most extreme of these was the time in 1639 when he learnt that a Scottish Covenanter had spied out the fortifications of Berwick, and commanded Traquair, who had no army, to fetch him out of Scotland, and to deliver him to England for trial.[53] Traquair seems never to have answered this letter, perhaps because words failed him. For a long time, Charles showed a similar obstinacy in insisting on dimensions for the *Sovereign of the Seas* which meant that she could not use any English harbour, and, as Trinity House put it, 'the wild sea must be her port'.[54] It was in this vein that he insisted on more powder for the first Ship Money fleet than the whole country possessed,[55] and believed in 1641 that he could enjoy the services of Pym as Chancellor of the Exchequer and Juxon as Archbishop.[56] It was this habit which forced the Earl of Nithsdale, of all unlikely critics, to explain what bad politics it was to say 'never' and then have to retreat afterwards.[57] The only way Charles showed any sign of learning this lesson was in refraining from retreating afterwards.

A similar lack of political perception led him into a consistent misunderstanding of his opponents' motives, and especially into a failure to understand the genuineness of their religious convictions. Without understanding these, he was always making plans based on the wrong facts. In 1629 he commented on his religious critics that

[51] *Clar. SP* ii. 267–8.   [52] Ibid. 237.

[53] *CSPD 1639–40*, vol. ccccxxxvi, no. 41.

[54] *CSPD 1634–5*, vol. cclxxiii, no. 25.

[55] *CSPD 1635*, vol. cclxxvi, no. 73.

[56] *HMC De L'Isle and Dudley*, vi. 637.

[57] Hamilton MSS 883.

'the true care of the church never came into their hearts',[58] a statement which is saved from plain falsity by the careful use of the qualifying adjective, a linguistic habit highly characteristic of Charles. In October 1638, when he insisted that in Scotland 'the pretext of religion is (I dare say) fully satisfied',[59] he simply did not realize what he was up against. In 1646, when he said that 'I have proposed the business of Ireland to stay their stomachs, instead of the church's patrimony, which I am confident is their great case of conscience, on which they so much insist, whatever they pretend',[60] he was simply planning on the wrong facts. However, this is an error which was far from peculiar to Charles. Indeed, it is merely the mirror image of the error Pym made about him, in believing that he was willing to trade his vision of the church for a regular annual revenue. This was not a fault of the man Charles Stuart, but a fault of deep religious division.

The area of Charles's deepest inflexibility was not that of mere religion; it was the area where religion and his authority met. His definition of the Royal Supremacy was one which made this area unusually large. That definition, which went back to Edward Foxe rather than to Christopher St German, was one which placed great emphasis on the principle that clerical affairs were under clerical control.[61] It then vested that control in the bishops, whose appointment was one of the 'essentials of monarchy'.[62] This is a view which clearly goes back to his 1626 Proclamation, which was issued by the advice of his 'reverend bishops', instead of by the advice of the Privy Council,[63] and it underlay the ferocity of his rejection of the Scottish National Covenant. It was because it deprived him of the sole control of church affairs symbolized in the imposition of the Prayer Book by Proclamation that he believed that 'not only now my crowne, but my reputation, for ever, lyes at the stake', and that 'so long as this covenant is in force (whither it be with or without an explanation) I have no more power in Scotland than as a Duke of Venice, which I will rather dye, than suffer'.[64]

[58] Rushworth, i, app. p. 6.   [59] Hamilton MSS 10,508.
[60] *Charles I in 1646*, ed. Bruce, p. 4.
[61] Alistair Fox and John Guy, *Reassessing the Henrician Age* (Oxford, 1986), 170–3, and other refs.
[62] *Clar. SP* ii. 277–8.
[63] *Stuart Royal Proclamations*, ii, ed. Larkin, 91. I am grateful to Dr Tyacke for drawing my attention to the wording of this proclamation.
[64] Hamilton MSS 10,484 and 10,492.

He explained these convictions more fully in 1646, when he began to appreciate that even his nearest and dearest did not fully understand them: 'the difference in point of church government is not that which the Scots look more at, although they make it their great pretence, but it is that taking away of the church's dependence from the Crown, for their chief meaning is to make it independent from any civil authority'. The English objective was different, though equally damaging: it was that 'under the pretence of a through reformation (as they call it) they intend to take away all the ecclesiastical power of government from the crown, and place it in the two houses of Parliament'.[65] This was an accurate perception of their aims, and it was an area in which Culpepper, for example, came closer to Pym than he did to Charles.[66] Charles clung so hard to these powers for the same reason for which his opponents were so determined to take them away: because his religious views were so remote from those of the majority of his subjects.

With this conception of his authority, Charles held to a strong rejection of the notion of conditional loyalty, and it was this which lay behind his passionate rejection of the Covenant. As Hamilton, speaking for once in his master's voice, put it, 'this covenant of theirs is intended to linke this wicked people together, as they meane never to obey any of your maties commands, nor of your successors, but such as shall be pleasing to themselves'.[67] Here, of course, Charles had a point: in a situation when religious divisions were so deep, conditional loyalty was a manifestly unsafe foundation for government. It was Charles's misfortune that, in any normal human affairs, conditional loyalty is the only loyalty there is, and if conditional loyalty is disloyal, then loyalty does not exist anywhere.

Richard Cust has recently demonstrated that this obsessive concern about his subjects' loyalty goes right back to the first years of the reign, and that the question of future Parliaments was dominated by the King's conviction that 'a meeting of Parliament should be earned through a demonstration of loyalty'.[68] This conviction should be seen as the result of a mistaken definition of loyalty. It is an arbitrary conviction, but it appears to me, though not to Dr Cust, to be a temperamental, rather than a constitutional,

---

[65] *Charles I in 1646*, ed. Bruce, pp. 41–2, 71.

[66] Rushworth, III. i. 33.   [67] Hamilton MSS 10,507.

[68] Cust, 'Charles I, The Privy Council', pp. 211, 219, and *passim*; id., *Forced Loan*, pp. 325–8; id., 'Charles I and a Draft Declaration', *passim*.

arbitrariness. It certainly led him to dislike Parliaments, but it seems to have been his conception of their personal motives, more than of their constitutional functions, which he so much disliked. In 1634, when Wentworth was about to summon an Irish Parliament, Charles warned him 'as for that hidra, take good heed; for you know, that here I have found it as well cunning, as malitious'.[69] What this sentence does not say needs as much attention as what it does. Charles as a politician suffered from tunnel vision, and tunnel vision and Parliamentary debate do not easily go together.

This difficulty applied to conciliar debate as well as to Parliamentary debate, since Charles's notions of loyalty gravely restricted the area in which he would accept counsel. Early in the Council debates on the Forced Loan, Charles required an acknowledgement that 'the question was of obeying the King, not of counselling',[70] and in 1635 Laud said that he dared speak no more to the King on the dominion of the seas.[71] If ever there was a time when a King needed counsel on the major political choices facing him, it was the Short Parliament, but Finch, opening it, indicated plainly that such counsel was not required: 'his majesties kingly resolutions are seated in the arke of his sacred brest: and it were a presumption of too high a nature for any Uzzah uncal'd to towch it'.[72] In 1646, having told Jermyn, Culpepper, and Ashburnham what his policy was on all the big questions before him, he then asked for counsel on the one specific point of whether it was better to be a prisoner in his dominions, or at liberty elsewhere.[73] He then told them, he required to be 'heereafter assisted (but no more trobled) by you in matter of religion'.[74] It seems he wanted not only a *Parlement à sa mode*, but a Privy Council *à sa mode*.

It should in fairness be said that the assassination of Buckingham, and the obvious lack of grief with which it was greeted, left Charles with some excuse for doubting his subjects' loyalty. After the Duke's death, he remained shut up in his room for two days without admitting anyone, and when he emerged, he had to face the risk that riot might disrupt the Duke's funeral. This did not encourage him to love his people. At crucial moments in his life, such as the decision to execute Strafford and the decision to leave London in 1642, physical fear for his wife and children was the key force

---

[69] Knowler, i. 233.   [70] Cust, *The Forced Loan*, p. 82.
[71] *CSPD 1636–7*, vol. ccxlviii, no. 62.   [72] Cope, p. 116.
[73] *Clar. SP* ii. 247–8.   [74] Ibid. 260–1.

which drove him to do what he did, and it is hard to say the reaction was irrational.[75] Yet, in the light of Richard Cust's work, it must be said the attempt to use the death of Buckingham as an explanatory device falls on the chronology: Charles's obsessive anxiety about his subjects' loyalty clearly pre-dates the death of Buckingham, and cannot be explained by it.

What does appear from the very beginning of the reign, and perhaps does more to explain Charles's fear about loyalty, is a constant nagging doubt about his status and capacity. As early as February 1626, when the Earl of Mar opposed a plan to raise 2,000 soldiers from Scotland because of the country's poverty, Charles exclaimed that the Scottish Council had disobeyed him, 'and ye durst not have doun so to my father'.[76] The first year of a new reign is much too early to talk in this style, unless it is to be made a self-fulfilling prophecy. This slighted note is one which grew more common in Charles's utterances as his reign progressed, and however much it may raise sympathy on a human level, on a political one, it merely signalled that he was down enough to be kicked. In Edinburgh in 1641 it was reported that 'glad he is when he sies any man that he thinkis loves him yit'.[77] In March 1642 he protested 'in our understanding, (of which God hath surely given us some use)', and complained that 'he hath reason to take himself somewhat neglected'.[78] In May 1642 he complained that 'we are the only person in England, against whom treason cannot be committed'.[79] When we try to exaplain the phenomenon of diminished majesty, the King's relentless determination to draw attention to its diminution is one of the things which should go into the explanation. This 'lost child' note grew stronger as his reign progressed, and in 1646 he wrote to Hamilton that 'I see that all men have not foresook reason; or at all least, I am some tymes in the right'.[80] A few weeks later he told Jermyn and Culpepper: 'I fynd not by our letters that any thing is much considered that I wryte in comparison of other information and intelligence. Nay, I cannot see that I am belived concerning myselfe'.[81] With this cast of mind, it is likely that Charles had more than a symbolic meaning when in

---

[75] *CSP Ven. 1628–9*, p. 283; *Charles I in 1646*, ed. Bruce, p. 19; *ECR* BL E. 243(1), p. 537.

[76] *HMC Mar and Kellie*, I. 145–6.

[77] Bodl. MS Carte 1, fo. 460ᵛ.

[78] BL E. 241(1), pp. 126, 469.

[79] *LJ* v. 52.

[80] Hamilton MSS 171.

[81] *Clar. SP* ii. 314.

November 1641 he left the Scottish Privy Council with the final message: 'to remember his birthday'.[82]

It seems likely that this sense of personal inadequacy underlay many of Charles's less fortunate political characteristics. It may help, for example, to explain his readiness to stake his authority where more prudent kings might have kept it in reserve, as in his insistence in February 1638 that he had seen the whole of the Scottish service book before publication.[83] Authority seems to have been something of which he felt very much in need. It perhaps helps to explain the apparently vindictive assertion of his authority over trifles, as in the Proclamation described by Conway as a 'proclamation for the hanging of greyhounds',[84] because they had disturbed his sport. It may help to explain the possibly mildly paranoid, and certainly premature, imputations of disloyalty to his opponents, as in his description in 1640 of the Parliaments of the 1620s, in which he said that 'in stead of dutifull expressions towards his person and government, they vented their own malice and disaffections to the state, and by their subtle and malignant courses, endeavoured nothing more then to bring into contempt and disorder all government and magistracy'.[85] This antedates the earliest Parliamentary use of the word 'malignant' by a very long time. It may well be that it was Charles's persistent conviction that his reputation was at stake which, in the course of the reverses to which all politicians are subject, did more to diminish it than all other forces put together.

It may be that it is this same sense of his lack of capacity which made Charles, in negotiation, cling to his grounds with the determination of a drowning man. His reluctance to enter into free negotiation may well have been partly because he did not believe that enjoyed a long enough spoon to sup with the devils by whom he believed himself to be surrounded. This is a suspicion I share with Henrietta Maria, who in October 1646 told him, in tones more appropriate to a son than to a husband, 'take care not to agree to the propositions they make, before you are aware of what you are doing,

[82] *RPCS* vii. 482–3. The celebration of course contained enough official symbolism to make it unnecessary to perceive this personal note, yet at this time, and from this man, it is hard to believe it was absent.

[83] *Large Declarations*, 19 Feb. 1638 (1639), 48; and Reeve, *Charles I and the Road to Personal Rule*, 173–9.

[84] *Proclamations*, ed. Larkin, 597 n.

[85] *His Majesties Declaration* (1640), p. 3.

and be well resolved thereupon, however they may promise you'.[86]
It is perhaps not fanciful to see the same anxieties behind Charles's
own description of how he set about negotiation. Reproached by
Jermyn, Culpepper, and Ashburnham on the ground that his
propositions consisted entirely of negatives, he replied:

Albeit it be true that most of my arguments runnes upon negatifs, yet I
deny it to be contrary to my method in discussing affaires of this nature.
For I always did and doe thinke it the best way, when necessity brings
consultations of chusing the least ill, that what is not to be done, should be
first resolved; because heereby the degrees of inconveniencys (in my
judgement) are easiliest deserned, and men ar not so reddily stolen into
errors. But cheefly at this tyme, I thought it of absolut necessity to fix my
negatives; easily foreseeing how I was to put too it by unhard of unlawfull
violence'.[87]

As a method, this is likely to achieve its declared objective. It is not
likely to reveal the unexpected common ground which can make the
most unpromising negotiation come alive and while it may have
preserved Charles from being 'stolen into errors', it did not lead to
the constructive embracing of opportunities.

   This picture of Charles has the advantage of going some way to
reconcile the politicians' inflexible image of him with Henrietta
Maria's picture, which could easily have been signed 'Lady
Macbeth'. In March 1642 she told him that 'want of perseverance
in your designs hath ruined you'.[88] In May she told him to
'remember your own maxims, that it is better to follow out a bad
resolution, than to change it so often', and even told him that 'you
are beginning again your old game of yielding everything'.[89] It is
only if we suppose, as we have some reason to do, that Charles
himself did not trust his capacity to negotiate with seasoned
politicians, and that he had persuaded Henrietta Maria to take him
at his own low valuation, that her picture can be reconciled at all
with the one we have come to find so familiar.

   Charles's low valuation of his powers as a negotiator was probably
justified, and justified by the fact that he tended to have a somewhat
two-dimensional view of other people, and therefore to lack skill
in predicting their reactions. Henrietta Maria, whose perceptions

<hr/>

[86] *Letters of Queen Henrietta Maria*, ed. Green, p. 327.
[87] *Clar. SP* ii. 273.
[88] *Letters of Queen Henrietta Maria*, ed. Green, p. 55.
[89] Ibid. 65, 68.

were of course sharper on her own side of the religious fence, saw
this most clearly in Charles's treatment of Ireland: 'if you do agree
upon strictness against Catholics, it would discourage them to serve
you. And if afterwards there should be no peace, you could never
expect succours either from Ireland or any other Catholic prince,
for they would believe you would abandon them after you had
served yourself'. In the end, she exclaimed: 'I am astonished the
Irish do not give themselves to some foreign king; you will force
them to it at last, seeing themselves offered in sacrifice'.[90]

The charge of insensitivity to Ireland is one which could be made
against most Englishmen: it is no way peculiar to Charles. Yet
Charles's ability to be blind to ordinary human reactions which did
not happen to be within the limits of his current concerns reached a
great deal closer to home than Ireland. In 1633 Cottington replied
to Wentworth's condolences on his wife's death in childbed:

I was going with my poor sad family to Hanworth, but by Secretary
Windebank I received a commandment from the King not to absent myself
from this town, but to attend his service; yet in a whole week, he never sent
to take notice of my loss. You will give me leave to say no more, for indeed
I cannot.[91]

That Charles I, whatever his virtues, was unfit to be a king seems
clear enough, but this statement by itself does not answer the
question how far he can be held responsible for the causes of the
Civil War. Historians, still busy emancipating themselves from
Thomas Carlyle, are remarkably resistant to the notion that any one
man (or woman) can be held responsible for a major series of
events. The reasons for this reluctance command respect, since in
almost any society, there are long-term changes in progress which
no single individual can create, or reverse. It is, however, worth
remark that practising politicians are a great deal less reluctant to
hold a single individual responsible for major events. Historians
may, if they choose, suppose that the politicians suffer from the
illusion of Dudley Digges's fly on the wheel, believing that they
raise the dust.[92] Yet there is also force in the politicians' perception
that a very great deal of the anger generated, or avoided, in the
course of normal political friction is the result of the personal
relations between the parties concerned. Above all, politicians

[90] Ibid. 279, 336.   [91] Knowler, i. 214.
[92] PRO SP 16/19/107.

expect, where they cannot persuade, to have been listened to and understood. It is that sense of being heard which provides the hope which is the necessary illusion of their craft. It is of precisely that hope that Charles tried to ensure that the politicians with whom he dealt were consistently deprived. It was for them, an experience one would expect to bring them to the point where frustration borders on fury. A man who has reduced his politicians to this state does not then find it easy to draw on them for an exceptional fund of good will when events turn against him. One of the most conspicuous facts of 1642 is the lack of any warmth or enthusiasm for the King among most of those who had the experience of daily doing business with him.

It seems fair to regard Charles I as a necessary condition of the Civil War. Without his decision to impose the Scottish Prayer Book, the whole train of events which led to the Civil War we know could not have been set in motion. A king without Charles's unusual ecclesiology would not have felt under nearly as much pressure to take that decision as Charles did. A king with a less clericalist view of the chain of command in the church would, in contemplating the imposition of the Book, have taken more advice from the Scottish Council, and less from the Scottish bishops, than Charles did. Indeed, under a different king, many of these men would not have been bishops. The fury felt by Traquair and Roxburgh at this resolute dependence on clerical advice is alone enough to give it significance, and they were shrewd enough politicians to suggest to us that their frustration in fact marks a real political problem. A king less indifferent to evidence would have been a great deal readier for the uproar the Book in the event created, and might, in Machiavellian style, have been prepared with rather more force to quell a disturbance he would have foreseen. One may perhaps excuse Charles for imposing the Book, but it is much harder to excuse him for his surprise at the reaction he provoked, and even more for his inability to accept that he had provoked such a reaction when the fact was plain to almost everyone else.

In the course of the political storm the Scottish crisis created, it did not make life easier to have a king on the throne who did not believe in the political process. Charles's inability to read the political map meant, if nothing worse, that every decision was reached too late, and every attempt to calm feelings was made when they were already too aroused to be soothed. For example, the offer to trade Ship Money for twelve subsidies in the Short Parliament did not succeed when it was made on 4 May, but might well have succeeded if made during the third week of April. Even in 1640 Charles still enjoyed a fund of political good will, but found it hard to cash it.

In 1641 Charles dissipated a large part of that good will by his participation in the Army Plot.[93] That plot, by introducing the threat of physical force into the daily atmosphere in London, did a great deal to sour the atmosphere, and, as the *Lords' Journals* for the two weeks after the plot very clearly record, went a long way towards convincing sober and responsible politicians that Charles was not fit to be trusted with power. More specifically, it began the process of convincing them that Charles was not fit to be trusted with military power. It went a long way to strengthen the conviction to which senior ministers are liable enough at normal times, that they could have done the job better, and even more, made it respectable to give way to that conviction. This impatient conviction of Charles's incapacity made a very large contribution to the attempt to take power away from him, and, in effect, to put the Crown into commission. The extent to which senior political figures like the Lord Keeper and the Lord Admiral were prepared to go along with such moves made an important contribution to the breaking of a taboo on major challenges to the King's personal authority. The sense of Charles's incapacity, then, went a very long way towards transforming a political crisis into a power struggle. When Charles himself became the issue, that issue was one it was impossible to resolve by negotiation.

Yet a comparison between 1642 and the relevant precedents suggests that we cannot explain the Civil War by saying Charles was incompetent. If that were all, either the English would have overcome their squeamishness about resistance and deposed him, or Charles would have ended up so destitute of a party that no war was possible. The comparison with Edward II, Richard II, and Henry VI highlights Charles's strengths, not his weaknesses. Perhaps only Henry III among English kings was incompetent enough to be reduced as low as Charles was in 1641, while yet being clever enough to raise a party to fight back. Perhaps the real lesson of 1642 was that Charles was incompetent, but not quite incompetent enough to leave the kingdom free from civil war.

[93] Conrad Russell, 'First Army Plot of 1641', *TRHS*[5] 38 (1988), 85–106.

It is here important that the depth of Charles's ideological
commitment gave him skills as a party leader which matched his
weaknesses as a national leader. Only in the Army Plot and the
attempt on the Five Members did these skills entirely desert him.
So long as he remembered the depth of most English gentlemen's
devotion to the law, Charles was able to benefit from a widespread
dislike, which he understood far better than many of his moderate
Councillors, of 'further reformation' and enforced godliness. To say
this is to say that Charles enjoyed an advantage over Edward II,
Richard II, and Henry VI because he ruled over a deeply divided
society. It is also to reiterate, yet again, that the Reformation, and
the religious division which followed from it, had undercut the
structure of authority in England. Religious division made the Civil
War partly because it was the force to which Charles was most
willing and able to appeal in his attempts to create a party. The
terms of Charles's initial agreement with Hyde, for example, were
that Hyde should defend the church until Charles could go to
Scotland and conclude the treaty, and Charles should defend it
thereafter.[94] One of Charles's enduring assets was that his
ideological conviction gave him an instinctive understanding of the
fears of such men as Hyde, Nicholas, Strangeways, and Wiseman,
and it was that instinctive understanding, plus the very lack of
flexibility which made him so poor a national leader, which made
him into a party leader whose faithful knew he would stand by
them. It also enabled him to raise up, as party leaders tend to do, an
opposition leader in his own image: Pym, like Charles, was a man
of inflexible ideological conviction, off-centre, though less extremely so
than Charles, and a proponent of policies which, quite as much as
Charles's, were regarded with fear and hatred on the opposite side of
the political fence. Above all, both of them were men whose politics
were dominated by fear, and men with the limited flexibility that
domination entails. Over and over again, through the months from
November 1641 to August 1642, it was apparent that these two men
needed each other to validate their demonologies. This raises the
question whether, if someone other than Charles had been on
the throne, someone more flexible than Pym would have come to
the fore at Westminster. Pym's very limited success in Parliament
under James suggests that the answer to this question may well be

---

[94] Edward, Earl of Clarendon, *Life*, i (Oxford, 1857), 77.

'yes'.[95] It is one of the functions of a good party leader to flush out opposition, and this Charles certainly did. In the process, he amply demonstrated the truth of Argyll's conviction that 'it can never be for his mats. honor nor saftie to make himself head of ane pairtye'.[96] Charles's strengths, as well as his weaknesses, then, made a major contribution to the coming of civil war.

In addition to being the major cause of the Bishops' Wars, Charles contributed greatly to the division of England into parties, helped as much as he could to ensure that there would be no negotiation in the summer of 1642, and, by severely diminishing the respect in which he was held, contributed greatly to the problem of diminished majesty. These are contributions big enough for any one man, but they do not make Charles the sole cause of the Civil War. He did not create the British problem, though he failed to handle it with the care that was needed. He did not create religious division, though he exploited and exacerbated it with all the strength at his command. He did not create his financial problems, though, by his indifference to them when his conscience was at stake, he made it possible for his Parliamentary opponents to gain a financial stranglehold on him during the summer of 1641. In 1641, as in 1646, he suffered heavily from being surrounded by men given to 'most flexible counsels'. The English in 1641 were deeply divided, but few of them wanted to push those divisions to the point of war: the pull of good neighbourliness, and the resultant urge to compromise, were very strong indeed. Perhaps from no position below that of king could this urge have been overcome. Charles's determination to prevent compromise shines through almost every line he wrote, and, in the end, he had his way. It is perhaps instructive to imagine what might have happened had it been Charles, and not Bedford, who died of smallpox in May 1641. The question is of course hypothetical, and attempts to answer it must savour of personal bias, but for myself, with Charles dead, I find civil war without him almost impossible to imagine.

---

[95] Conrad Russell, 'Parliamentary Career of John Pym 1621–1629', in Peter Clarke, Alan G. R. Smith, and Nicholas Tyacke (eds.), *Tudor Commonwealth: Essays Presented to Joel Hurstfield* (Leicester, 1979).
[96] Hamilton MSS 1749.

9

Conclusion

THE search for the causes of the English Civil War has taken us into a very disparate series of times and places, from the Guildhall buttery in January 1642 to Moreton Corbet (Shropshire) in the 1560s, from the militia in Somerset under Elizabeth I to the Synod of Linlithgow in Scotland under James VI. It is time to ask what all these threads had in common, and how they came to form cords stretching to the King's raising of the standard at Nottingham in August 1642. The first chapter of this book argued that it was hard to see what all these things had in common, save only the fact that Charles I had to deal with them. Is this a case where it is a sufficient explanation to blame the man at the top?

Charles's failings as a ruler are an important, and indeed a necessary, part of the story. If Charles's sister Elizabeth had succeeded James, the Civil War as we know it would have been an impossibility. If a civil war had happened under Elizabeth of Bohemia, at least the sides would have been reversed. If Charles, instead of Bedford, had died of the smallpox in May 1641, it is hard to imagine anything worse than a confused regency resulting. Charles's frequent habit of saying he would rather die than do what necessity required of him was one which, at the last, made it necessary to take him at his word, to which it should be said that he proved true. His allergy to the hotter forms of Calvinism often made it impossible for him to understand what he was dealing with, and so led him to political calculations based on false premisses. However, if Charles's failings had been the whole of the story, we would be explaining a deposition and not a civil war. No amount of listing Charles's failings will easily explain why he found a party to fight for him.

The first chapter argued that the Civil War should be ascribed to a conjunction of seven events and non-events, why there were Bishops' Wars, why England lost them, why there was no political settlement in England, why the Long Parliament was not dissolved in 1641, why England divided into parties, why there was no serious negotiation to avoid war, and why respect for majesty came to be so deeply diminished. It is now time to face the question, on which the first chapter preserved an echoing silence, how far this conjunction was fortuitous. It clearly contains a fortuitous element; if the Irish Rebellion had been postponed three weeks, it would not have kept the Long Parliament in being, and there would have been no Parliament to participate in a civil war.

Yet, though the fortuitous element cannot be ruled out, the conjunction was not entirely fortuitous. It was the result of three long-term causes of instability, all of them well established before Charles came to the throne, and all of them ones which can be observed to have troubled European, as well as British, monarchies. There is nothing peculiarly British (still less English) about any of them: they were not even exceptionally acute in England. What is peculiar to the two cases of England and the Netherlands is that all of them came to a head at the same time. These three long-term causes were the problem of multiple kingdoms, the problem of religious division, and the breakdown of a financial and political system in the face of inflation and the rising cost of war.

The problem of multiple kingdoms was always a likely cause of instability from 1603 onwards. The temptation to press for greater harmonization was always there, and was always likely to produce serious troubles. In 1603 England encountered what Britain is to encounter in 1992, the shock of subjection to a supra-national authority. That shock was the less, but also the less adequately dealt with, because the English always tried to pretend it was not there, and wished to treat both James and Charles as if they were only kings of a single nation-state called England. Since this was patently not the case, and the kings could not help knowing it, the English were always likely to misread royal actions, and in particular to press their kings to do things which, in British terms, they could not do. When, as in 1637, a British king fell victim to a similar misapprehension, and attempted to govern all Britain as king of England, he found this was something he could not do.

As our perspective lengthens, it is possible to wonder whether this problem is entirely in the past. We may wonder whether the Act of Union of 1707 was an interval, rather than a solution, to the problem, and how much of the success of 1707 was due to the fact that it was followed by two centuries of economic growth. England's basic error in 1603 was the failure to absorb that what had taken place was the union of two sovereign, and therefore legally equal, states. Not even James could really turn Scotland into 'North Britain'. It was a state with institutions, law, and culture of its own, and one determined to insist that any resulting relationship must be a legally equal partnership. This is a message the English have not yet entirely absorbed. They are still apt to insist (wrongly) that Britain has a single history and a single culture, and that insistence still provokes Scottish protests. Lord Morton of Shuna, speaking in the House of Lords in 1988, said:

Perhaps I may speak for a moment as a part of an ethnic minority. The difficulty is that the English have always said: 'as long as you join our culture, that is fine. However, don't bring your culture to us. We shall be totally tolerant if you will try as hard as you can to become good English people.[1]

The English attitude of which he complains is very old: it is surely the same as the proposal of Justice Warburton, under James VI and I, that Scotland should become 'parcel' of England. It is that attitude which provoked the 'Scottish imperial' demands which wrecked the peace of England in 1641. In 1988, when an opinion poll shows 35% of Scots in favour of full independence,[2] and the security of the Ulster plantation is still in daily doubt, can we yet say that the British problem has safely receded into history?

It is fortunately easier to say so with the problem of religious division, since it was a problem which derived its explosive force from the belief that religion ought to be enforced. It was a problem of a society which had carried on the assumptions appropriate to a society with a single church into one which had many churches. The process of adjustment to a society with many faiths is one whose resolution is still in the future, but it is one which almost ceased to be fraught with physical danger with the passage of the Toleration Act of 1689.[3] In the century after the Reformation, this adjustment

---

[1] *House of Lords Official Report*, 21 June 1988, cols. 681–6. I am grateful to Lord Morton of Shuna for permission to quote from his speech.
[2] *The Times*, 1 May 1988.
[3] This is not intended to imply that religious passion ceased to be dangerous after 1715: the assaults on Dissenting Meeting Houses in Manchester in 1715, among much else, prove the contrary. Yet though religious passion retained its capacity to threaten individuals, and its power as a cement of party, with the end of regular State enforcement it lost its power to create civil war. I am grateful to Dr Paul Monod, Dr Jan Albers, and Dr Kathleen Wilson for many discussions of

was a cause of instability in every country where it happened, and was avoided only in countries where persecution was too successful to allow it to arise. In this, England was by no means peculiar. The fact that England was so incompletely and ambiguously reformed was not necessarily a disadvantage, but what it bought was time and not improvement. If the problem had been postponed another thirty or forty years, it might perhaps have been enough to allow temperatures to cool, but August 1640, when the Scottish army, by entering England, merged the religious problem with the British problem, was too early for it to have cooled enough. One might say of the English Calvinists what Machiavelli said of the Pope in Italy: they were too weak to unite the country, but too strong to allow anyone else to do so. When the Scots entered England, they were able to join forces with a large group of people who preferred Scottish religion to what was coming to be taken for their own.

The strains caused for monarchies by the combination of inflation with the massive increases in the cost of war known collectively as 'the military revolution' is also a European theme. The financial difficulties faced, after the conclusion of the long wars of the 1590s, by James VI and I, Philip III of Spain, and Henri IV of France have too much in common to be entirely coincidental. The changes following the regular use of gunpowder, especially the trend to larger-scale fortifications and to larger armies, much increased the economic drain of war. The resulting financial pressures put strain on the principle of consent to taxation everywhere in Europe, and perhaps only the Netherlands, with the advantage of a visible enemy at the gate, were able to combine consent with the levying of taxes on the scale needed. England, because the principle of consent to taxation was so particularly well entrenched, was perhaps put under more constitutional strain by this process than some other powers. Yet kings' impatience with legal forms which restricted their capacity to wage war is not confined to England. Philip IV and the Conde Duque of Olivares, facing the constitutions of Catalonia, felt all the same frustrations as Charles I.[+] The similarity of their remarks on 'necessity', and the rights it gave to a monarch, perhaps suggests that they were facing a common problem, and that the

these questions. These words were written before the publication of Mr Salman Rushdie's *Satanic Verses*. It remains to be discovered how far the resulting disturbance will supersede what is written here.

[+] J. H. Elliot, *Revolt of the Catalans* (Cambridge, 1963), *passim*.

pressure on constitutional forms in both countries did not result from a theoretical drive to 'absolutism', but from the simple fact that legal forms no longer permitted the king to carry on the necessary business. Philip IV after 1640 would have understood Robert Cecil's remark in 1610: 'when a king extendeth his uttermost authority, he loseth his power'.[5]

No one, or even two, of these forces was in the event enough: it took the conjunction of all three to drive England into civil war. To ask whether any one or two of them could have created civil war is to ask a question which is unanswerable because hypothetical. Yet it is a fact that no one or two of them did create civil war, and they had a long time in which to do it if they were capable of it. Both the religious and the financial problem had been plainly visible by the 1550s, and they had not created civil war in ninety years since then. England in 1637 was, no doubt, a country with plenty of discontents, some of them potentially serious, but it was also still a very stable and peaceful one, and one which does not show many visible signs of being on the edge of a major upheaval. It tells us something about England in the 1630s that the Barringtons were invited to settle at Watertown, Massachusetts, but it also tells us something that the author of the invitation felt it necessary, as an inducement, to stress the excellence of the hunting, the hawking, the fowling, and the fishing.[6] The one fact, perhaps, should be given as much significance as the other.

Only a clairvoyant could assert dogmatically that England could not have had a civil war without a Scottish invasion, but it remains fair to say that in 1637 civil war was not visibly imminent. Moreover, it seems that in the religious issue, the only one likely to be able to divide the English into two warring parties, time was on the whole on the side of peace. Religious division slowly lost its terrors by growing familiarity, and every decade in which it did not produce the Babylonish confusion threatened by the 'Homily of Obedience' made the old terrors less easy to sustain. Moreover, on the Parliamentary side, the men who made the Civil War were an ageing generation, whose strength would have been very sharply diminished by another fifteen years of peace. There is perhaps some

[5] *Proceedings in Parliament 1610*, ed. Elizabeth Read Foster, i (New Haven, Conn., 1966), 70.

[6] *Barrington Family Letters 1628–1632*, ed. Arthur Searle (Camden Society[4], 28, 1983), 183.

truth in the hints in the opening sermons to the Long Parliament that this was the last chance for a full godly reformation.[7]

However, it is equally necessary to say that a conjunction between these three causes of difficulty was always a serious possibility. Since the Scottish reformation was such a beacon to the hotter reformers in England, and the further reformation of England an ideal so dear to Scottish honour, as well as zeal, the chance that the issue of multiple kingdoms would merge with the issue of English religious division was always real. Indeed, attempts to merge the issues had been being made since the 1580s, and it was perhaps only necessary for one of these attempts to coincide with a vacuum of royal authority for it to succeed. The impoverishment of the monarchy was such a perennial problem, and so daily present, that it is hard to see how it could have failed to merge with any problem happening at any time.

It was particularly unfortunate for the monarchy that the major threat happened to come from Scotland. English military weakness was overwhelmingly a weakness in land warfare. From that weakness, they could normally retreat, and remain, as Sir Robert Phelips put it, 'like the tortoise, withdrawn . . . into their own shell, from whence they do not upon slight motives sally.'[8] Failing the appearance of another Owain Glyn Dŵr, there was only one frontier on which the English could not avoid trouble in this fashion, and that was the Scottish. The attempt which Charles made in 1637 to enforce English religion on Scotland, was thus by far the likeliest reason for a merging of these three long-term causes of instability. It is difficult to argue that Charles took this risk with his eyes open. It is equally difficult to see what action a king could have taken which would have been better designed to precipitate an English civil war.

It is possible to argue that this line of argument over-stresses the British dimension in the English Civil War. It could be argued that the English Civil War was fought between Englishmen on English soil, and therefore deserves English explanations. Such an argument would be an example of the philosophical proposition that the only true statements are tautologies, since the proposition that the English Civil War was fought by Englishmen on English soil can only be accurately translated as the statement that the English Civil

---

[7] Stephen Marshall, *Sermon* (1641), Epistle, pp. 19, 32; John Gauden, *Love of Truth and Peace* (1641), 31-2.

[8] Russell, *PEP*, pp. 83-4.

war is the name we give to that part of the British Civil Wars which was fought by Englishmen on English soil. That part is rather a small one. It is not even the first part of the British Civil Wars: Newburn held that honour, followed by the Irish Rebellion. At no time did the English Civil War hold the stage alone, since the war against the Irish rebels continued from 1641 to 1649. Moreover, the period during which the fighting in England was only done by Englishmen lasted only for sixteen months from August 1642 to December 1643. After that, the Solemn League and Covenant and the Irish cessation provided a British dimension on both sides. Nor was the end of the English Civil War the end of the British Civil Wars. After the King was defeated, Gardiner observed that the struggle between King and Parliament was rapidly broadening out into a struggle between England and the rest for supremacy over the British Isles.[9] That was the issue at stake at Preston, Dunbar, and Drogheda. It was the same issue which had been at stake at the very beginning of the troubles in 1637. It is symbolic that the final battle of the Civil Wars, at Worcester in 1651, was an attempt to repel the fourth Scottish invasion in thirteen years, as the first British battle, at Newburn in 1640, had been an attempt to repel the first. If we look at the British Civil Wars as a whole, it is clear that they began and ended as a struggle between England and the rest for supremacy over the British Isles.

Because England began this struggle under a highly unpopular regime, the struggle divided England itself. The Scots exploited these divisions with great political skill, and it was not until they had been resolved that England could get back to the original quarrel. The English Civil War, then, was something of a diversion: it was the fourth round in a ten-round battle. This statement perhaps convicts this book, along with much else, of the sin of Anglo-centricity. In the long run, it is not enough to explain the English Civil War as if it were an isolated event. We should be explaining, in the same framework, the Bishops' Wars, the Irish Rebellion, the Solemn League and Covenant, the Irish Cessation, the Second Civil War, and the Cromwellian conquest of Scotland and Ireland. However, when we consider the millions of words of documents which must be read before such a work can be written, it is perhaps fair to offer a book which stops at the interim finding that this is the

---

[9] S. R. Gardiner, *Commonwealth and Protectorate*, i (1903), 27.

context in which the English Civil War must be explained. Contemplating the magnitude of the task ahead, and remembering that it has taken twenty-eight years of research to get this far, I may perhaps conclude with the 'last words' of Constance Spry: 'someone else can arrange this'.

Appendix

THESE figures, and these classifications, do not pretend to any objective precision. In the first place, not all of us, when dividing our members, would make the same divisions. It is therefore fair to say what sort of division is attempted here. The category of supporters of further reformation has been construed strictly, and is designed to exclude those who merely wished to return to the pre-Laudian church. Calvinism, for example, has not been a sufficient criterion for inclusion in the list of supporters of further reformation, and Sir Robert Hatton, Archbishop Abbot's former steward, emphatically does not belong in it. Nor does mere anticlericalism qualify for inclusion. Support for Bishops' Exclusion, by Sir Henry Slingsby for example, does not qualify for inclusion, nor does condemnation on Erastian grounds of the Laudian canons. In the case of Sir Thomas Smyth, not even a passing support for Root and Branch, if it runs against the tenor of a member's career, has been a sufficient criterion for inclusion.

Two convictions, if they can be discovered, have automatically justified inclusion. One is D'Ewes's, that the Reformation of 1559 was insufficient, and must be improved upon. The other is Harbottle Grimston's, that Laud was attempting 'the alteration of the Protestant religion'. Sir Edward Dering's contrary belief that Laud was merely on the brink of popery excludes from the list. Anti-Arminianism does not qualify for inclusion, but the belief that Arminians could not be Protestants does qualify for inclusion. Where discoverable, support for the Commons order of 8 September qualifies for inclusion, and Harbottle Grimston is the only man included who is known to have opposed it. Belief that the Laudian church was guilty of idolatry, and corresponding support for iconoclasm, has justified inclusion.

Since people are individuals, criteria will often conflict. Support for the Book of Common Prayer, for example, has normally qualified for inclusion in the list of opponents of further reformation. Only in the case of Harbottle Grimston has it not done so, since he also held the belief that Laudian religion was popish. In cases such as his, it has been necessary, as it is in political debate in any period, to classify people on a turn of phrase and a degree of emphasis, as well as on formal, classifiable positions. Such things are signalling systems, and are well understood as such by contemporaries. Some attention must be paid to the context in which a member was speaking. Sir Roger Burgoyne's attacks on the churchwardens of St Giles Cripplegate, if made in another context, might not have qualified him for inclusion in the list of godly reformers, but he made them in a context which clearly committed him to supporting the campaign for the enforcement of the 8 September order, and it is this fact which aligns him with the supporters of further reformation.

It is, of course, unfortunate that evidence rarely comes to us in a form which answers such logically conceived questions: we must make do with what we have. This is why these classifications should be regarded as provisional, and subject to future revision, refinement, and refutation. Wherever possible, classification has been based on a member's participation in debate, but since, in any Parliament, the number of speakers is small, this has not always been possible. In a considerable number of cases, I have provisionally followed the classifications of Mrs Keeler, or of the relevant county historian, but since they are not always using the same method of classification as I am, this is a chancy procedure, and error is bound to have crept in. Members have not been classified by association, and, for example, Charles Pym and James Fiennes have not been classified among the supporters of further reformation. It is hard to imagine either feeling free to vote against it, but hypothesis, however strong, has not been used as a substitute for evidence. Evidence of service as teller has been used, but with caution, and only when it does not appear to conflict with what is known from other sources about the member concerned. Evidence from the presentation of a petition, on the other hand, has not been used unless it comes from a time when it required courage and initiative to present a petition in favour of that particular cause. We do not know how far members felt bound to present petitions with which they disagreed, and in the absence of knowledge, the evidence should be used with caution. However, when all is said and done, though many of these individual classifications are questionable, it is very hard to see how, even with the most determined partisanship, the evidence could be put together to provide any different overall picture.

This point holds only for the House of Commons. In the House of Lords, where true support for further reformation was not very common, the picture is strikingly different. Men like Pembroke and Northumberland were not godly reformers, but rather concerned with what they increasingly saw as the King's incapacity to govern. This was, by its nature, a view seen from close quarters, and therefore one less likely to be shared in the country at large than the more long-range view of the Commons. On this point, the list of areas which produced volunteers is a small straw suggesting that views in the country were in fact nearer to those of the Commons than to those of the Lords. This, however, is a subject on which research, and debate, will continue.

MEMBERS OF THE COMMONS IN FAVOUR OF FURTHER REFORMATION

Members on this list were Parliamentarian or neutral in August 1642 unless otherwise indicated.

R. = Royalist.

d. = died before August 1642.

William Allanson
John Alured
Sir Henry Anderson[1]
Sir William Armyne
John Ashe
Ralph Ashton the younger
Sir Edward Ayscough
John Bampfield
Sir Nathaniel Barnardiston
Sir Thomas Barrington
John Blakiston
Dennis Bond
Godfrey Bosvile
Sir William Brereton
John Browne
Richard Browne
Samuel Browne
Sir Richard Buller
Sir Roger Burgoyne[2]
William Cage

Sir Thomas Cheke
Sir John Clotworthy
Sir Robert Cooke
Miles Corbett
William Coryton R.
Matthew Cradock d.
John Crew[3]
Oliver Cromwell
Henry Darley[4]
Sir Symonds D'Ewes
Sir John Dryden
Sir Walter Earle
William Ellis[5]
Sir John Evelyn of Surrey[6]
Sir John Evelyn of Wilts
Sir Ferdinando Fairfax[7]
Nathaniel Fiennes
Sir Miles Flettwood d.[8]
Sir Gilbert Gerrard
John Glyn[9]

[1] This is a marginal case. I have tentatively followed the classification of J. T. Cliffe, *Yorkshire Gentry* (1969), p. 276.

[2] D'Ewes (C.), p. 98.

[3] I am grateful to Dr J. S. A. Adamson for discussion of Crew. On 19 April 1639 Robert Sibthorpe claimed that he had undergone a recent conversion: Huntingdon Library Stowe Temple MSS 1876–1896. I am grateful to Dr R. P. Cust for this reference. Cliffe, *Puritan Gentry*, 37, 41.

[4] This classification does not only rest on Darley's identification with the Providence Island Company. He referred to 'Michaeltide' instead of 'Michelmas'. J. S. A. Adamson, thesis cit., p. 32. Cliffe, *Yorkshire Gentry*, 292, 306.

[5] D'Ewes (N.), p. 58 might not be sufficient by itself, but in conjunction with Ellis's office as Recorder of Boston, it creates an overwhelming presumption.

[6] D'Ewes (C.), p. 223.   [7] Cliffe, *Yorkshire Gentry*, p. 306.

[8] Beds. RO St John MSS J 1361; D'Ewes (N.), p. 139; Bodl. MS Rawlinson C. 956, fo. 39ʳ.

[9] D'Ewes (BL Harl. MS 163, fo. 304ª) dismissed Glyn as 'a swearing profane fellow'. D'Ewes may be right about Glyn's personal morals, though August 1642 is not a month for which he is a particularly unbiased witness, but there is no doubt of Glyn's political record as one of the godly. See e.g. *PJ* i. 139, 411.

Arthur Goodwin[10]

John Goodwin

Robert Goodwin

Sir Harbottle Grimston

Mr Harbottle Grimston[11]

John Gurdon

John Hampden

Sir Robert Harley

Richard Harman

John Harris

William Hay[12]

Sir Arthur Hesilrige

Roger Hill

Cornelius Holland[13]

Denzil Holles

Thomas Hoyle[14]

Sir Edward Hungerford

Sir Thomas Hutchinson

Sir Arthur Ingram[15]

Sir Anthony Irby

Sir Thomas Jervoise

William Jesson

Sir Oliver Luke

Sir Samuel Luke

Sir Martin Lumley

Sir William Masham

John Maynard

Sir Henry Mildmay[16]

Gilbert Millington[17]

Edward Montagu the younger

George Montagu

Sir Sidney Montagu

John Moore

Richard More

Herbert Morley

Sir Edmund Moundeford[18]

Robert Nicholas

Anthony Nicoll

Sir Roger North[19]

Samuel Owfield[20]

Edward Owner

Edward Partridge[21]

George Perd

Sir Thomas Pelham

Mr Pelham (Henry or Peregrine)[22]

Isaac Penington

[10] D'Ewes (C.), p. 55; *PJ* ii. 155.

[11] Harbottle Grimston and Edward Bagshaw have been two of the hardest decisions in this list. Grimston was a supporter of episcopacy and the Prayer Book: D'Ewes (N.), p. 6; D'Ewes (C.), p. 150; BL Harl. MS 5047, fo. 58ʳ. He is included, tentatively, on the basis of his charge against Laud of trying to bring about 'the alteration of the Protestant religion'. Rushworth III. i. 122. Bagshaw, equally tentatively, has been excluded for deciding to defend Peter Smart on the ground that, had he preached the same sermon in Queen Elizabeth's time, he would have been made a bishop for it: D'Ewes (N.), p. 20. This is the defence of an Abbot man rather than of an advocate of 'further reformation'.

[12] Anthony Fletcher, *A County Community in Peace and War: Sussex 1625–1660* (1975), 282.

[13] *PJ* ii. 197, 241. [14] Cliffe, *Yorkshire Gentry*, p. 324.

[15] Bodl. MS Rawlinson C. 956, fo. 52ᵛ; *CJ* ii. 422; D'Ewes (C.) p. 334.

[16] *CJ* ii. 279; *PJ* i. 126. [17] D'Ewes (C.), p. 290.

[18] D'Ewes (N.), p. 63. [19] Ibid. 270.

[20] Owfield is included because he employed Christopher Feake as his household chaplain. Cliffe, *Puritan Gentry* (1969), 207. He is the only person in this list who is included because of his associates: a household chaplain is an appointment which must at least give a clue to the limits of a man's tolerance in matters of religion.

[21] D'Ewes (C.), p. 308; *PJ* i. 354. Partridge's hostility to the theatre is not by itself religious evidence, but it is suggestive.

[22] BL Harl. MS 164, fo. 903ᵃ. There is no way of telling which 'Mr. Pelham' is here referred to.

Sir Gilbert Pickering
Edmund Prideaux
William Purefoy
Thomas Pury
John Pym
John Pyne
Robert Reynolds
Alexander Rigby
James Rivers d.[23]
Sir Samuel Rolle
Francis Rous
Sir Benjamin Rudyerd
Oliver St John
George Serle
William Spurstow[24]
Sir Philip Stapleton
Anthony Stapley
Nathaniel Stephens
Sir William Strickland
William Strode
Zouch Tate

Thomas Toll[25]
John Upton
Sir Henry Vane the younger
Samuel Vassall
John Venn
John Waddon
Valentine Walton
Sir Peter Wentworth[26]
Laurence Whitaker
William Whitaker
John White, member for Southwark
Richard Whitehead
Sir Thomas Widdrington
John Wilde
Edward Wingate[27]
Sir Thomas Woodhouse
Sir Christopher Wray
Sir John Wray
Sir Christopher Yelverton[28]
Walter Yonge

Total: 127

MEMBERS OF THE COMMONS OPPOSED TO FURTHER REFORMATION

Members on this list were Royalist or neutral in August 1642 unless otherwise indicated.
P. = Parliamentarian.
d. = died before August 1642.

Richard Aldborough
John Arundell
John Ashburnham
Sir Edward Baynton P.
Henry Bellasis
John Bellasis

Sir Henry Berkeley
Sir Thomas Bowyer[29]
Orlando Bridgman
Sir John Brooke
Arthur Capel
Lucius Carey, Viscount of Falkland

[23] Fletcher, *Sussex*, p. 244, and other refs.   [24] *CJ* ii. 328.
[25] BL Add. MS 24,346, fo. 10. Toll in 1632 was one of a committee who tried to persuade the bishop to allow King's Lynn to have a preacher who would not be tied to read the Book of Common Prayer. I am grateful to Dr K. C. Fincham for this reference.
[26] *PJ* ii. 296.   [27] Ibid. i. 171.
[28] *CJ* ii. 693, but also Cliffe, *Puritan Gentry*, p. 229.
[29] *CJ* ii. 279.

Sir William Carnaby
Richard Chaworth
Sir Hugh Cholmeley P.
Henry Coke
Thomas Coke
Lord Compton
Fitzwilliam Coningsby[30]
Sir Frederick Cornwallis[31]
John Coventry[32]
Sir Nicholas Crispe
Sir John Culpepper
Sir Patrick Curwen
Sir Thomas Danby
George Digby
John Digby
William Drake P.[33]
John Dutton
Dr Eden
John Fettiplace
Francis Gamull
Sidney Godolphin[34]
George Goring
Giles Green P.
John Harris of Radford
Sir Robert Hatton[35]
Sir Henry Herbert
Robert Holborne
Sir John Holland P.[36]
Gervase Holles

Sir Ralph Hopton[37]
Charles Howard Viscount Andover
Sir Robert Howard
Edward Hyde
Robert Hyde
Joseph Jane
Sir Thomas Jermyn
Edward Kirton[38]
Thomas Lane P.
Sir Richard Lee
Thomas Leedes
Peter Legh d.
Sir William Lewis P.[39]
John Mallory
William Mallory
Henry Marten P.[40]
Thomas May
John Meux
Sir William Ogle
Geoffrey Palmer
George Parry
Henry Percy
Sir Thomas Peyton
William Pleydell
Hugh Pollard
Sir Neville Poole P.[41]
Endymion Porter
Charles Price
Sir Henry Rainsford d.

[30] Tyacke, p. 219. [31] D'Ewes (C.), p. 54, and other refs.
[32] BL Harl. MS 163, fo. 665ᵃ; D'Ewes (C.), p. 205.
[33] This judgement is based on a provisional examination of Drake's commonplace books in Ogden MSS in University College London Library. Drake was no Puritan, but he would be better classified as a Florentine than as an Anglican.
[34] D'Ewes (C.), p. 228, 228 n; *CJ* ii. 330. Whether this was Sidney or Francis Godolphin must in the end be a matter of conjecture.
[35] *CJ* ii. 438. Sir Robert Hatton is a good example of the fact that Calvinism alone was not enough to make a man a supporter of further reformation. He was Archbishop Abbot's former steward and ally.
[36] Ibid. 438. [37] *PJ* i. 134, 253, 503–4.
[38] D'Ewes (C.), p. 176.
[39] Lewis is a marginal case. He is included because he acted as a teller for leniency to priests (*CJ* ii. 339) but he also acted as a teller against Sir Edward Dering (Ibid. 411).
[40] BL Harl. MS 5047, fo. 57ʳ.
[41] *Notebook of Sir John Northcote*, ed. A. H. A. Hamilton (1877), 51.

John Russell
Richard Seaborne
John Selden P.
Sir Francis Seymour[42]
Sir Henry Slingsby
Sir John Stawell
Sir John Strangeways
Robert Strickland
Robert Sutton[43]
Edmund Waller
Thomas Webb

Sir George Wentworth of Wolley
Sir George Wentworth of
    Wentworth Woodhouse
Nicholas Weston
John Whistler[44]
John White, member for Rye
Sir William Widdrington
Sir Charles Williams d.
Henry Wilmot
Sir Francis Windebank

Total: 90

VOLUNTEERS

The following is a list of towns and villages which raised volunteers for the Parliament before the raising of the standard in August 1642. It omits volunteers raised on a county basis, whose local habitation cannot always be precisely determined. London has been treated as a county. Evidence in all cases from *LJ* and *CJ*.

Nottingham
Basingstoke
Watford
Ashford (Kent)
Gloucester
Cambridge
Dorchester (Dorset)
Shewsbury
Boston (Lincs.)
Poole
Bury St Edmunds
King's Lynn

St Albans
Canterbury
Colnbrook and the Chiltern
    Hundreds
Taunton
Rayleigh (Essex)
Cranbrook
Coventry
Bristol
Southwark
Bridport

[42] *Clar. SP* ii. 115; Laud, *Wks*, VI. ii. 430.
[43] D'Ewes (C.), p. 290 and BL Harl. MS 5047, fo. 72ʳ, taken together, seem to show him as that very common combination, a churchman and an anticlerical.
[44] BL Harl. MS 164, fo. 85ᵃ; D'Ewes (N.), p. 337; *CJ* ii. 436.

Index

Abbot, George, Archbishop of Canterbury 49, 84–5, 89, 95, 110, 174
Abbot, Robert, Bishop of Salisbury 80
Adamson, Patrick, Archbishop of St Andrews 36–7, 46, 48
Addled Parliament (1614) 179–80
Admonition to Parliament (1572) 33
Advertisements, The (1566) 33, 88–9
alchemy 75
Alford, Edward 170
Alford, Francis 92–3
allegiance 23–4, 40, 202–5
   see also King's Two Bodies
Allegiance, Oath of (in Scotland) 47
altar rails 22
altars 32, 78 and n., 84, 86, 99, 101, 125
ancient constitution 123
Andrewes, Agnes, *alias* Pym 170
Andrewes, Lancelot 3, 47 and n., 49, 99, '01 and n., 104, 116
Anglicanism, origins of 84, 92–3, 107–8, 197–8
Anglo-Saxon Chronicle 170
Antrim, Randal MacDonnell second Earl of 125
Apology of the Commons (1604) 41
Appleby (Westmorland) 68
Archcliff Fort, Dover 124
Argyll, Archibald Campbell eighth Earl of 125, 211
Arminianism 50, 80, 82, 85–6, 91–2, 99, 102–5 *passim*, 107–8, 109–11, 116, 122, 123, 165, 182
arms, shortage of 13 and n., 163
arms, union of 30 and n., 56, 204
Army Plot, First (1641) 121, 137, 209
Array, Commissions of (1642) 141
Arundel, Thomas Howard 21st Earl of 130
ascending theory of power 34, 35, 134, 145–6, 147
Ashburnham, Jack 163, 190, 197–8, 203, 206
Ashford (Kent) 21

assurance, doctrine of 79–80
Astley, Sir Jacob 163
atheism 58, 64

Bacon, Sir Francis 39, 169
Bagshaw, Edward 138, 150, 223 n.
Baillie, Robert 47 n., 115, 116, 117–18
Balcanquall, Walter 111 n.
Ball, Peter 143
Banbury (Oxon.) 78
Bancroft, Richard, Archbishop of Canterbury 15, 36, 38, 45, 48, 81, 85, 99, 100, 102–3, 140
Bankes, Sir John 5–6, 101–2, 114–15, 123, 143, 158
baptism 50, 70, 72, 90–1, 92–3, 95, 116
   Cross in 88
Baptists 58, 67, 125
Barclay, William 151–2
barns, unsuitable for worship 125
Baro, Peter 91–2
Barrell, Robert 83–4
Barrett, William 91–2
Barrington, Sir Thomas 20, 73–4, 124
   Barrington family 216
Barry, John 16, 19, 126
Basingstoke (Hants.) 21
Bastwick, John 83
Bate's Case 17, 156, 158, 174
Beale, Robert 36, 93
Beale, William 152, 180
Becket, Thomas, Archbishop of Canterbury 34, 35
Bedchamber, the 30–1
Bedford, Francis Russell fourth Earl of 4, 153, 167
Bell, Robert 176
Bentham, Thomas, Bishop of Coventry and Lichfield 88
Berkeley, Sir Robert 152
Berkshire, Thomas Howard first Earl of 5–6, 26
Berwick, Pacification of (1639) 12, 189, 195–6